> Now Jesus loved Martha and
> her sister and Lazarus.
>
> —John 11:5 (NIV)

Extraordinary Women of the Bible

HIGHLY FAVORED: MARY'S STORY
SINS AS SCARLET: RAHAB'S STORY
A HARVEST OF GRACE: RUTH AND NAOMI'S STORY
AT HIS FEET: MARY MAGDALENE'S STORY
TENDER MERCIES: ELIZABETH'S STORY
WOMAN OF REDEMPTION: BATHSHEBA'S STORY
JEWEL OF PERSIA: ESTHER'S STORY
A HEART RESTORED: MICHAL'S STORY
BEAUTY'S SURRENDER: SARAH'S STORY
THE WOMAN WARRIOR: DEBORAH'S STORY
THE GOD WHO SEES: HAGAR'S STORY
THE FIRST DAUGHTER: EVE'S STORY
THE ONES JESUS LOVED: MARY AND MARTHA'S STORY

Extraordinary Women OF THE BIBLE

THE ONES JESUS LOVED

MARY AND MARTHA'S STORY

Carole Towriss

Extraordinary Women of the Bible is a trademark of Guideposts.

Published by Guideposts
100 Reserve Road, Suite E200
Danbury, CT 06810
Guideposts.org

Copyright © 2023 by Guideposts. All rights reserved.

This book, or parts thereof, may not be reproduced, stored in a retrieval system, or transmitted in any form or by any means, electronic, mechanical, photocopying, recording, or otherwise, without the written permission of the publisher.

This is a work of fiction. While the characters and settings are drawn from scripture references and historical accounts, apart from the actual people, events, and locales that figure into the fiction narrative, all other names, characters, places, and events are the creation of the author's imagination or are used fictitiously.

Every attempt has been made to credit the sources of copyrighted material used in this book. If any such acknowledgment has been inadvertently omitted or miscredited, receipt of such information would be appreciated.

Scripture references are from the following sources: The Holy Bible, King James Version (KJV). New American Standard Bible (NASB). Copyright © 1960, 1962, 1963, 1968, 1971, 1972, 1973, 1975, 1977, 1995 by the Lockman Foundation. Used by permission. The Holy Bible, New International Version (NIV). Copyright © 1973, 1978, 1984, 2011 by Biblica, Inc. Used by permission of Zondervan. All rights reserved worldwide. www.zondervan.com. Holy Bible, New Living Translation (NLT). Copyright © 1996. Used by permission of Tyndale House Publishers, Inc., Wheaton, Illinois 60189. All rights reserved. Contemporary English Version (CEV). Copyright © 1991, 1992, 1995 by American Bible Society. Used by permission.

Cover and interior design by Müllerhaus
Cover illustration by Brian Call represented by Illustration Online LLC.
Typeset by Aptara, Inc.

ISBN 978-1-961125-97-1 (hardcover)
ISBN 978-1-961125-98-8 (epub)

Printed and bound in the United States of America
10 9 8 7 6 5 4 3 2 1

Extraordinary Women OF THE BIBLE

THE ONES JESUS LOVED

MARY AND MARTHA'S STORY

DEDICATION

To my Redeemer, who gave me the words.

ACKNOWLEDGMENTS

To my family, for time, space, understanding,
and encouragement.
To my beta readers for their time and opinions.
And special thanks to the Spring OBX writers' group,
who helped me to bring this story to life.

Cast of CHARACTERS

BIBLICAL

Yeshua

His talmidim • Simon (Peter), his brother Andrew, James and John (sons of Zebedee), Philip, Judas Iscariot, Matthew (Levi), Thomas; James (the son of Alpheus), Nathanael (Bartholomew), Thaddeus, and Simon (the Zealot).

The Family:
Martha • the older sister
Mary • the younger sister
Lazarus • their brother
Simon • their father

Annas • father-in-law of the high priest
Caiaphas • high priest
Herod Antipas • son of Herod the Great, ruler of Galilee, Perea
Jairus • synagogue leader in Capernaum
Nicodemus • a Pharisee
Pontius Pilate • procurator (governor) of Judea from AD 26/27 to 36/37
Tiberius • emperor of the Roman Empire

FICTIONAL

Adah • resident of Bethany
Asher • carpenter who moves to Bethany

Beulah • resident of Bethany
Daniel • Martha's betrothed
David • resident of Bethany
Elisheba • resident of Bethany
Enoch • Daniel's father
Gershom • the priest of Bethany
Hannah • resident of Bethany
Joel • Asher's brother-in-law
Kemuel • resident of Bethany
Leah • Asher's first wife
Levi • host in Jericho
Mishael • Gershom's student
Nekoda • Gershom's student
Neriah • Martha's daughter
Orpah • host in Jericho
Selah • resident of Bethany
Seth • Gershom's student
Tabitha • Asher's sister
Tobiah • Gershom's student
Yoash • resident of Bethany

Glossary of TERMS

abba • father

ach/achi • brother/my brother

achot/achoti • sister/my sister

adon • lord, master, sir

Adonai • Lord (God)

ahuvati • beloved, my love (to a female)

ahuvi • beloved, my love (to a male)

amphora (*pl.* amphorae) • a pottery container for liquids

bet cholim • house of the sick

Hallel • songs sung for certain Jewish festivals, consisting of Psalms 113–118

Hanukkah • Feast of Dedication, first celebrated in 164 BC

imma • mother

ketubah • a marriage contract

Levite • members of the tribe of Levi who were not priests but musicians, gatekeepers, guardians, temple officials, judges, and craftsmen

Mashiach • Messiah

mikveh • a bath used to perform ritual purification

mitzvah (*pl.* mitzvot) • commandment

mizmor (*pl.* mizmorim) • psalm

motek • sweetheart

Pesach • Passover

Pharisee • a teacher of the law

praetor • Roman ruler

praetorium • house of the praetor

quern • the upper stone of two used to grind grain; the upper hand stone is rubbed against a flat slab

Rosh Hashanah • the "head of the year" that begins the ten days before Yom Kippur

Sanhedrin • council of Jewish elders

sabba • grandfather

savta • grandmother

Shabbat • Sabbath

shalom • peace

Shavuot • Pentecost, Fest of Weeks

Shema • the first two words of Deuteronomy 6 and the title of a daily prayer

sukkah • a temporary shelter made of organic material

Sukkot • Festival of Tabernacles

talmidim • students (usually translated as disciples)

todah (rabah) • thank you (very much)

Torah • the first five books of the Bible

tsara'at • an unknown disfiguring skin disease; also mold in clothing or houses (mistranslated as leprosy); it is not the same as what we call leprosy or Hansen's disease

Yom Kippur • Day of Atonement

Hebrew Months of the Year

Nisan • March-April

Iyyar • April-May

Sivan • May-June

Tammuz • June-July

Av • July-August

Elul • August-September

Tishri • September-October
Cheshvan • October-November
Kislev • November-December
Tevet • December-January
Shevat • January-February
Adar • February-March

INTRODUCTION

Scripture doesn't tell us much about the Bethany siblings. We don't know their ages. Most assume Martha is the oldest since she is named first, but we don't know for sure. As for Simon, most scholars believe "Simon the Leper" is in some way connected to Mary, Martha, and Lazarus (as their father or Martha's husband, or even another name for Lazarus himself) since the house where Jesus stays is variously referred to as Martha's and Simon's.

Though all of the Gospels tell the story of Jesus the Messiah, each one emphasizes a different part of His ministry. They work together to provide a complete testimony. For the most part, I have followed the Gospel of John.

The cleansing of the temple is mentioned in all four gospels. The Synoptics (Matthew, Mark, and Luke) place it at the end of Jesus's ministry. John places it at the beginning. Scholars differ on whether there were two incidents or one. I have no problem believing the same issues that caused Him to clean it at the start of His public life existed once again three years later.

The story of Jesus's anointing by a woman is also mentioned in all four Gospels. Luke tells us of an unknown sinful woman, but his story takes place in the northern region at the house of

"Simon the Pharisee." (Many have equated this woman with Mary Magdalene, but there is no Scriptural evidence for this.) Matthew, Mark, and John all place the incident at Bethany. Matthew and Mark also tell us it takes place at the house of "Simon the Leper." In John, the woman is identified as Mary of Bethany, the sister of Martha and Lazarus. Again, scholars differ as to whether these are separate incidents or the same one described differently by the gospel writers. I believe they are two separate events.

I hope you come to love Martha and Mary as much as I do.

CHAPTER ONE

In the fifteenth year of the reign of Tiberius Caesar—when Pontius Pilate was governor of Judea, [and] Herod tetrarch of Galilee...
—Luke 3:1 (NIV)

Jerusalem, province of Judea
Nisan 10
Four days before Pesach

Martha's blood ran cold at the distant sound of pounding hoofbeats. Every muscle in her body struggled to flee, to hide from what was coming, but her legs were as cedar.

"Martha!" A sharp voice cut through her fear as a strong hand grabbed her by the arm, pulling her backward toward the western wall of the temple.

Thank Yahweh for Daniel.

She crept backward, closer to the massive stones of the wall towering behind them, trying to leave a safe distance between the broad, stone-paved street and herself. She perched on her toes and searched north along the Roman-built road that ran beside the temple from Herod's Gate in the north to the Water Gate in the south. The deafening, rhythmic noise of trotting horses, banging drums, and armored men swelled.

He must be close.

Sight abruptly caught up with sound. At the head of the procession was Pontius Pilate. Astride a magnificent white warhorse, Judea's newest Roman governor stared ahead, ignoring the people either cheering for him or cowering below him. The sun caromed off the gleaming silver armor covering both man and beast.

Marching behind him, a line of leather-clad soldiers strutted as one into the City of God. Enormous banners emblazoned with SPQR—*Senatus Populusque Romanus*—the Senate and People of Rome—swayed on silver poles.

Martha moved closer to Daniel as three cohorts filed past, their shields, helmets, and swords boasting of Rome's absolute power over Judea.

Drums thumped. Bridles clinked. Leather creaked. Hooves pounded. Every sight and sound was intentionally, strategically designed to instill awe and terror.

The ranks of soldiers seemed endless, but finally the last row passed under the bridge that connected the temple courts to the Upper City. Just past Martha and Daniel, they turned right, marching through a gate in the wall that cocooned the wealthy upper city from the rest of Jerusalem and her struggling inhabitants. That gate was normally shut and locked. No need to allow the poorer residents to gape and gawk at the villa-sized homes of the elite.

Their final destination was the *praetorium*, the once glorious palace of the wicked king Herod. At his death, his territory had been divided among his sons. Archelaus had received the lion's share but had done such a monstrously bad job that Emperor Augustus deposed him and replaced him with a

Roman ruler. His brother Antipas governed Galilee, and Philip ruled even farther north, leaving the palace empty most of the year, since the Roman governors preferred to control Judea from the luxurious seaside city of Caesarea Maritima.

Martha flinched as the gate slammed closed. The procession was over.

Until next year.

Only moments ago, she'd been laughing in the city's market south of the temple, chatting with vendors she'd known and bargained with for most of her life, obtaining those last few items needed for the Pesach meal.

Now she sucked in deep breaths until her heart calmed. "Thank you, Daniel."

"Let's go home." He offered a warm smile, erasing any fear that he thought her foolish.

She stepped away from the wall, squared her shoulders, and shook her head. "He's a day late. He was supposed to arrive yesterday. That's why I came on the second day of the week." She grunted. "I'd really hoped to avoid him this year."

Daniel shrugged. "It's his first year to be in Jerusalem for Pesach. Maybe he took longer in Caesarea to make plans."

"They've had the same plans for almost a hundred years." She swallowed the bitterness that soured her tongue. "At least he left his eagles at home this time."

Daniel chuckled. "I don't think even he would be foolish enough to try that again."

Martha had been among the crowd in Jerusalem last summer, the day Pilate had arrived to succeed Valerius Gratus as *praetor* of

Judea. Under cover of night, Pilate had arrived at the praetorium and promptly installed imperial banners all around the city, each one bearing the golden eagle and worse, the image of Tiberius Caesar. The Israelites immediately decried the blatant idolatry.

She scoffed. "I still can't believe he did that. And in such a cowardly way. I thought Romans were fearless."

"Fearless, maybe, but not necessarily the smartest ones around. Most are here as either some sort of reward or punishment. Either way, they think it's an easy assignment. They don't plan to stay long and don't bother to learn about the people they intend to rule."

No one was a better example of that than Pilate. An angry mob had sent him scurrying back to Caesarea last summer, without his banners. The priests promptly sent a delegation demanding he remove the pagan images from the holy city. Instead, Pilate threatened them with death. Negotiations lasted six days, until the Jews showed they were willing to die for the holiness of their God and their city.

The images disappeared within days. Whether it was because he feared further violence or was impressed with their sincerity of belief was uncertain.

"Did you get everything?" Daniel gestured to the wide basket on her arm.

"Let's see." She rummaged through her purchases. "I have horseradish, radishes, and chicory for the bitter herbs. Cinnamon. Oh, I haven't bought oil yet. I wanted to get some olive oil flavored with garlic. I don't have time to get the flavor strong enough. It's on our way back to the gate."

They continued on their way up the road next to the temple. It hadn't taken long for the vendors to return to hawking their wares. Strident voices boasted the choicest olive oil, the finest cloth, the tastiest spices. Martha quickly bought the infused oil, along with an *amphora* of honey. Daniel tucked one pottery container in the crook of each arm.

"Do you need this much for Pesach?"

"We never know when guests may arrive in need of food and shelter." She caught his gaze. "Will you and Enoch be joining us?"

He shook his head. "I think *Abba* is planning to join our relatives in Jerusalem again."

"Oh." She tried to hide her disappointment. Since he and his abba had arrived two years ago, they'd not shared one feast meal with anyone in Bethany. They hadn't yet found their place in the village, hadn't helped with much of anything. That would all change next year, surely. Daniel would be her husband by then.

Daniel led them back under the arched gate north of the temple, leaving the paved streets of the city for the wide, well-traveled dirt path that led to Bethphage and Bethany. Tension melted away from her shoulders, her neck. The air was sweeter, and away from the crowds, even cooler.

A slight breeze stirred the flowers that emblazoned the hillside, making the climb up the Mount of Olives more enjoyable. Red chamomile and blue alkanet peeked from among fig and olive trees. Olives just beginning to bud emitted a slight musky scent. A crested hoopoe called for its mate. *Oop-oop-oop.*

Jerusalem fell away behind them. Isaiah had called Jerusalem Mount Zion, the place of the Name of the Lord Almighty. But he'd also prophesied Jerusalem would be utterly destroyed because of her faithlessness. Today, knowing both Herod Antipas and Caiaphas, the high priest, would be at the prefect's house tonight currying favor, she believed it wouldn't be long.

Bethany
Eastern slope of the Mount of Olives

Mary cringed. A knife-edged rock pierced the sole of her bare foot as she crouched against the stone wall that surrounded the courtyard of Gershom's home. She ignored the pain and held her breath, trying to remain silent.

Though she couldn't see over the wall, Mary knew precisely what was happening at this moment. Gershom was the rabbi of this house of the book, where children studied and memorized the scriptures. He would be sitting on a low stool under the ancient olive tree that dominated the open space, one of the sacred scrolls held gently and reverently in his hands. Nine boys—unless one was ill—would be in a semicircle at the feet of the old man, each with a wax tablet and stylus in his lap, waiting to hear the holy words like a nest of hungry baby birds with their mouths open.

At least that's what they would do if they realized the unfathomable treasure that could be theirs should they but listen. Every walled city in Judea had a teacher, but very few villages the size of Bethany had one. Yet half the boys seemed irritated that they were required to attend school from age five to thirteen.

While she, who would give anything for the privilege, was forbidden. The priest before Gershom had allowed her to study, as did many others teachers in Judea. But Gershom had expelled her, though she could have studied another year.

She reached above her head to grip the edge of the low wall, her fingers just over the top, then pulled herself up slowly, hoping to catch a mere glimpse of the scrolls.

"Today we begin our study of Hallel."

A low groan reached her ears. Probably from Tobiah. He was nearly thirteen, and if it were up to her he would have been banished long ago. He cared nothing for the words of Adonai, and his constant complaints ate at her patience.

"Tobiah, can you tell me what *Hallel* is?" Gershom's voice revealed no irritation with the boy at all. How could he not be frustrated with a student who clearly didn't want to learn?

"I don't know. A *mizmor* of David?"

Mary scoffed. Hallel was *six* psalms, not one, and none of them were written by David.

"Perhaps you should use your voice only when you know the answer," Gershom said.

She suppressed a giggle at the gentle, yet surprising, rebuke.

"Nekoda, can you tell us?"

"Hallel is a prayer. It is made of six *mizmorim*." The boy answered confidently. He was a good student, though one of the youngest.

"And when do we say this prayer?" asked the teacher.

"It is sung for Pesach, Shavuot, and Sukkot," said Nekoda.

"And Rosh Hashanah," added Tobiah.

"No," Gershom corrected Tobiah. "Hallel is not sung at Rosh Hashanah nor at Yom Kippur. Who knows why?"

Silence.

For once, Mary did not know the answer either, though she'd often wondered why the songs of praise were not sung on the Day of Atonement.

"We do not sing it at those times because Adonai is then sitting on His throne with the Books of Life and Death open before Him. It is a time for repentance and forgiveness, not a time for joy."

Ah. That made sense.

"But we do sing it at the Feast of Hanukkah!" The voice was so soft Mary almost couldn't hear him. Mishael was the youngest, and he loved the holy texts as much as she did.

"Yes. *Toda*, Nekoda and Mishael. Now, who can tell me the first words of each of these mizmorim?"

Mary longed to shout out the answer: *Hallelu Yah*. A holy command to praise the Lord. She ached to be part of this group openly studying and rejoicing over the holy words of Adonai instead of hiding behind rough stone and straining to hear.

"Hallelu Yah." Mary didn't recognize the voice. Gershom must have a new student. Who could it be? She quickly ran through each family in the village, trying to remember their sons.

"Yes, *todah*, Seth."

Ah yes. Seth, Tobiah's younger brother. Hopefully he wouldn't catch Tobiah's terrible attitude.

"Everyone, repeat after me." Gershom's voice was clear and strong. "Hallelu Yah! Servants of Adonai, give praise! Blessed be the name of Adonai from this moment on and forever!"

The boys mumbled the first sentences of the first mizmor of Hallel, words tumbling from their mouths like pebbles.

The prayer threatened to burst from her chest. If she were sitting with the boys, they would hear her in Jerusalem.

"This is not how you praise the Creator of the universe!" Gershom scolded his students. "If you cannot give Him the praise He deserves, He will cause rocks to do it for you! Now, give Him praise! Together!"

The boys recited loudly, though not quite in unison.

"Give praise to the name of Adonai!" Not waiting for the boys, Mary recited the verse silently along with the teacher. "From sunrise until sunset Adonai's name is to be praised. Adonai is high above all nations, His glory above the heavens."

If she could not shout the words aloud along with the boys of Bethany, she would have to settle for allowing her heart to speak.

"Who is like Adonai our God, seated in the heights, humbling Himself to look on heaven and on earth?"

Mary tried to envision Adonai seated on an enormous throne, resplendent in gold and jewels and incomprehensible light, even more magnificent than the temple on the other side of the mount. But such a holy God was beyond her ability to imagine.

"Seth, return to the lesson, please." Gershom's voice was sharp. "We do not wander as we study the holy words."

A short, skinny arm jutted out above her head, followed by a head covered with curly hair. "But Rabbi! There's a girl here!" The newest student peered down at her, a mischievous grin on his dirty face.

Why was he worrying about her instead of studying the sacred scroll held by the rabbi? He was wasting a precious opportunity.

But there was no time to think about that now. Rustling tunics, legs unfolding, and the sound of footsteps on dirt heading her way told her she had been caught.

Mary jumped to her feet and raced down Bethany's only road. The house of the rabbi perched at the northern edge of the village, and her home was at the other end. Still, it was a tiny village, and she'd learned to run—fast.

CHAPTER TWO

Your word is a lamp for my feet,
a light to my path.
—Psalm 119:105 (NIV)

Bare feet pounded after her. Mary knew Gershom could no longer keep up with her—he was too old, and it was at any rate undignified for a grown man to run. But the boys—they'd turned it into a game, looking for her, chasing her every day she dared to creep near enough to listen to the holy words.

And they'd learned to run faster as well.

Her lungs were on fire, but the courtyard wall to the home she shared with Abba, her brother, and her sister was in sight. She strained, demanding every ounce of energy from her body and sending it to her legs. She looked over her shoulder. She would beat them by only a cubit or two.

Maybe.

Not looking where she was going, she slammed into her abba. His arms wrapped around her, holding her close. He smelled of earth and grape leaves, and she breathed in his scent. Sweet safety.

Boys poured into her courtyard, surrounding her as if they were lions after prey, and she squeezed her eyes tight.

Abba held out his hand. "Back away!"

Footsteps abruptly halted then retreated.

"She did it again!" The same voice that had called attention to her moments ago accused her. She twisted her head slightly, trying to peer under Abba's arm to see the boy.

The new student, scrawny and skinny, pointed his bony finger at her back. He'd seen, what? Five summers? Yet he stood with his hands on his hips, as if he had total charge over her.

If only she'd been born a boy. Then she'd be in class with him, showing him how much more she knew than any of them.

The rabbi approached. "Shalom, Simon."

"Gershom." Abba's voice was polite but strained.

"She was in my home again."

"I was not! I remained outside!" A small difference, but still, truth was truth. She would not be accused of what she hadn't done, when what she had done was enough to bring the entire school to her home.

"Hush, Mary," Abba whispered as he patted her back. "She only wants to hear the words of Adonai, as the boys do." His voice was louder as he spoke over the snickers of the boys.

"More than they do!" Why couldn't she control her outbursts?

"Mary, *please*." Abba held her a bit tighter.

"*She* is a female." Gershom spat the word as if he spoke of rats. Or snakes. "Her mind is too weak. Anything she does learn she will only use to hide her sins."

Mary wrenched away from Abba's grasp, her hands in fists at her side. "I already know more of the sacred texts than any of these boys!"

"No, you don't!" The boys dissolved into laughter. "You couldn't possibly!"

She squared her shoulders and jutted out her chin. "Adonai is high above all nations, His glory above the heavens." Her voice rang out as she calmly but confidently recited the rest of the psalm the boys had been studying before they decided it was more important to chase her down.

"Who is like Adonai our God, seated in the heights, humbling Himself to look on heaven and on earth? He raises the poor from the dust, lifts the needy from the rubbish heap, in order to give Him a place among princes, among the princes—"

"Enough!" Gershom's screech caused the sparrows peering down from the roof to flee. "I will not hear a female profane the sacred words." He smoothed his cloak as he drew in a slow breath through his long nose. "Keep her away from my home."

"With joy." Abba placed his hand on her back and steered her inside.

As soon as she crossed into the main room, she whirled around, her hands clasped at her chest. "*Todah rabah*, Abba! I don't know why—"

"Mary." He shook his head, a frown on his sun-browned face.

She froze. Was he unhappy with her?

"Mary, how many times have I told you to stay away from the rabbi's house?"

Her heart broke. Stay away? "But Abba, how else will I learn more of the words of Adonai?"

His frown melted. "Come here," he whispered. He located a stool then lowered himself to it.

She neared him, and he grasped her hands in his. "We'll figure something out. But this is not the way. It leads only to anger, and that cannot be what Adonai desires. Do you agree?"

She nodded, a tear tracing a path down her cheek.

Lazarus burst breathlessly into the room. "I saw the boys here again. What happened?"

Mary sniffled.

"You got caught again?"

She nodded.

"We'll think of something," Abba said. He tilted his head. "Maybe Zar could help you."

Lazarus's brows rose and he let out a slow breath of air. "I can try. I struggled to learn it myself, but I'm happy to help however I can, *achot*."

"Why don't you talk about it? I'm going to talk to Gershom. No matter what, he cannot encourage his students to chase you."

Lazarus took Abba's place on the stool and pulled her close. "I'm so sorry, Mary. I wish there was more I could do."

She twisted her head so her ear was over his heart. The strong, rhythmic beating calmed her, as it always had, ever since *Imma* died so many years ago.

Abba meant well, and Lazarus would do whatever he could to help her. But what could they do? They had none of the sacred texts, but even if they had, she couldn't read. And she couldn't learn what she couldn't hear.

Martha chuckled as she pulled on the rope, its heavy, wet cargo sloshing against the stone walls of Bethany's only well, in the very center of the village. "Of course. Why wouldn't I have a wedding feast?"

"But who will do the cooking?" The group of young women laughed along with her.

"You, of course!" Martha squinted against the setting sun as she fixed Elisheba with a gleeful stare.

Elisheba's jaw dropped. "I can't cook for an entire village!"

Martha grinned. "There are barely one hundred of us. And maybe someone will help you." She dumped the contents of the leather bucket into her water jar before lowering it once more into the well.

Only recently married, Elisheba glanced nervously at the others, silently begging for assurance.

Adah patted Elisheba's arm. "Of course we'll help." With her other hand, she pointed at Martha. "You will do no cooking for your own meal."

Martha released an exaggerated gasp as she passed the bucket. "Not even my raisin cakes?"

"Maybe your raisin cakes," said Beulah. "I think they're the main reason Daniel is marrying you, anyway."

The group laughed again, and then Adah turned to the youngest. "Beulah, do you know any more about the arrangements your abba is making?"

Beulah emptied the bag into her water jar, her face clouded. "They're close to an agreement, he said. But—" Her voice quavered. "I'll have to move to Jerusalem."

An empty silence hovered over the women like a dark wet cloud.

It wasn't entirely unexpected. The village was too small for every woman to find a husband. At least one woman left each year, while others were brought to Bethany by village men. The only response was to bravely exchange childhood friends for new ones.

"I, um, I should get home. I left Benjamin with the baby." Adah flashed a pained smile and hurried away.

"I should go as well." Elisheba hoisted her jar onto her shoulder, and she and Beulah headed for the northern end of the village.

Martha inspected her water jar. Not quite full. She dropped the bucket once more and topped up the jar. She set the leather bag on the side and looked up to face a man waiting a few paces away.

Strangers were not uncommon in Bethany, but he just stood there. It was unnerving. "Do you need a drink?"

He smiled. "That would be lovely, but I have neither bucket nor cup."

"Come here." Martha set her jar on the ledge and dropped the water bag into the well yet again, bringing it up half full. "Hold out your hands."

He cupped his palms together, and she poured out a thin stream of clear water into them as he sipped until he was satisfied.

His hands and sun-browned skin spoke of hard labor, but his eyes were kind. He was tall and thin, with thinning hair. "Thank you. I've had quite a walk."

"Are you going to the city for Pesach? You'll be lucky to find lodging at this late date. Many have been there for days already."

The village regularly offered shelter to those fulfilling the *mitzvah* requiring all males to return to Jerusalem for Pesach, Shavuot, and Sukkot. Abba's house was the largest in Bethany, and was usually saved for large groups, but none had asked so far this year. Might as well start filling it up with whoever asked.

"Yes, I'm very much in need, but my Rabbi and the other *talmidim* will be joining me tomorrow. We can sleep on the mount under the trees and stars if you have no room left."

Rabbis and their students often stayed with them, usually groups of six or seven. "How many?"

"Five, including the Rabbi."

Perfect. "We have plenty of room. Would you like to see?"

He nodded and flashed a smile. "I'd be most grateful."

"Come." She led him east toward her house.

He fell in step beside her. "Is your abba home?"

"Yes." She frowned. "Why?"

"Shouldn't I ask him if we can stay in his home?"

She laughed. "There's no need. This is what we do in Bethany. We care for the travelers, the sick, the poor. It's the way we serve Adonai." She stepped through an ungated opening in a low stone wall and led him into the courtyard. To the right of the house, under a sprawling pomegranate tree, sat the large flour mill used by all the women of the village every morning. She pointed to the roof. "There is the roof, of course, but we also have seven bedchambers."

He shook his head. "That isn't necessary. We're quite used to sleeping on the ground."

"We're very happy to share our home." She led him through an open doorway into a large room, the left two-thirds open to the sky. A wide table stood to the right, with bowls of nuts and jars of spices shoved against the wall. To their left, shelves held still more jars, and *amphorae* lined the ground on both sides.

She set her water jar on the table and led him through a narrow door next to the shelves. A hall jutted to the right containing seven small rooms with fabric for doors—four on the back wall side and three on the other. A storage room occupied the area next to the door. "These are the rooms for our guests. There are seven." She retraced her steps to the common room and pointed to the far wall to the left of the table. "My abba and *ach* sleep in that room, but we've used that as well when needed. My sister and I will remain in our chamber there." She gestured to a door to the right of the table.

"This is such a large house!" He spun in a slow circle, taking it all in.

"It's been my family's home for generations. My *sabba*'s sabba had many sons. Each added to it as he married. Eventually they moved to the cities, or back to Galilee. But my own sabba had one child only, my abba. Now we use the house to shelter guests like you. Will you be staying here tonight while you wait?"

He shook his head. "I'll be going back to meet them and then return with them. Can we meet you here the morning after we visit the temple?" He dug in the folds of his sash. "We carry some money for our needs. May I give you some coins for our food?"

"Of course not."

His hand, still holding several silver coins, paused in mid-air. "Five men for seven nights. That's a lot of food."

She shook her head. "We're not permitted to accept payment from those keeping the mandates. Adonai provides all we need."

"Todah then. We'll see you in three days." He turned to go.

"Excuse me." She called after him. "What is your name?"

"I'm James ben Zebedee."

"Goodbye, James."

He headed back up the road that led to Bethphage and then to Jericho.

She had plenty of food. The women had been grinding extra grain for days to prepare for visitors. She'd need to pick more greens, but she had jars full of nuts and olives in the storeroom. She would need one of the village boys to wash feet. It was entirely inappropriate for a woman to wash the feet of a man not her husband.

Thank Yahweh she'd bought extra oil and honey.

CHAPTER THREE

The Jews then responded to him, "What sign can you show us to prove your authority to do all this?"
—John 2:18 (NIV)

Nisan 14
Day of Preparation

Martha knelt in the courtyard before the yearling, his woolly head nuzzling her face.

It was no longer her job to care for the lamb in the days leading to Pesach. That belonged to the youngest girl, and so Mary had done it for years. But each year, Martha still bade him farewell.

She drew one hand over the soft wool of his head while he nibbled the grass she clutched in the other. "Oh, *motek*, I'm so sorry for what will happen to you this afternoon." Even as a small child she'd given up naming the lambs. It was too hard to say goodbye. Now she just called all of them *sweetheart*.

She wasn't sure how much it eased the farewell, though.

"Let me look at you once more." She checked his ears, his legs, his belly, searching for any hint of a mark or blemish that would render him unfit to be the required sacrifice.

Satisfied he was perfect, she moved a few steps away and sat on a brightly colored woven mat under the pomegranate tree, a bowl of dough in her lap. She patted out a round of flatbread and slapped it on the side of the hive-shaped oven in front of her. A warm, gentle breeze set the leaves dancing, and splotches of midday sun chased each other across the ground. The cackling *chuk-chuk-chuk* of a male partridge calling for a mate was interspersed with the chatter of a golden squirrel in the treetop above her.

Flatbread was not her favorite. No honey or wine to add flavor, no olives or nuts for texture, just water and a bit of salt added to barley flour. She much preferred the fluffy, tasty loaves she made the rest of the year.

Mary approached and sat across from her. "I can help you until we leave."

Martha scooted over, leaving more room on the mat, then placed the bowl of dough between them.

They sat silently for a while, patting out small, flat circles of dough.

Martha eyed her sister with a sideways glance. "Are you sure you want to go to the temple? You know Lazarus can do it." Due to the number of worshipers crowding the temple, it was customary for only two from each family to go.

"Of course. Why not?"

"Because every time, you come home crying because the lamb was slain."

Mary sat up straighter and lifted her chin. "I won't cry this time."

"Are you sure?"

"I am."

"Why? What's different this time?"

"Well, I was thinking about how unfair it is that this perfect little lamb should die."

Oh, Mary… Just as Martha had feared.

"Then I thought it was even more unfair that we should have to care for it for four days before we take it to be killed."

Martha studied Mary's face, looking for any sign she might burst into tears. She saw none—yet.

"Then I felt guilty about questioning Adonai's plan."

It was a wonder Mary could have a conversation at all with anyone. Her mind jumped from one idea to the next and to the next and back again without any semblance of order. Yet somehow, it always made sense to her.

Mary's hands stilled and fell to her lap, a small blob of dough between them. "Then I thought about the story of how Adonai led us all from Egypt."

"As you should."

"And I remembered that the lamb had to die so the first-born son wouldn't have to."

Martha pulled one round of bread off the oven's wall and replaced it with another round. "That's true. But you've always known that. What's different this time?"

Mary was quiet for a long moment. "I think it's supposed to hurt."

"What do you mean?"

"I think we have to care for him for four days so we come to love him. He comes to be a part of us, and when we have to sacrifice him, it hurts. And then we remember it could be our blood that was spilled, and we see how much our sin costs. Except we don't suffer, he does."

And there it was. The profound thought that somehow always—eventually—clawed its way to the top through the murky chaos of Mary's disorganized mind.

"I wonder if that's what Abba is thinking when he makes the sacrifice."

It would be, because in some strange way, Mary's thoughts very often reflected his, although his were generally much more ordered. "I'm sure it is. But that still doesn't explain why you won't cry."

"I can't cry."

"Why not?"

Mary shrugged her shoulders as if the thought was so obvious she shouldn't have to explain. "I'll be too busy being thankful."

"Mary?"

They looked up to see Abba standing before them. "Are you ready?"

"Yes, Abba." She grabbed the plate of bread stacked precipitously high. "I'll take these in." She flounced away.

"I'll get the lamb and wait for you at the gate," Abba said.

Martha had raised Mary since their imma had died five years ago. Most of the time she was more a mother than a sister.

Yet at other times, like now, Mary was older and wiser than them all.

Mary wavered between joy and sadness as she trudged along the dirt path that would take them to Jerusalem. Abba walked before her, the blissfully unaware lamb over his shoulders. Each large hand folded gently around a pair of knobby legs resting against his chest.

At the top of the ridge, this narrow path connected with the wider road that led from much larger Bethphage. A village of just over a hundred people meant only ten to twenty would need to make the trip this afternoon to sacrifice their lambs, but once those from the larger town joined them, the crowd instantly tripled.

Although Bethphage was outside the walls of Jerusalem, it was considered by the Sanhedrin to be an official part of the city. For certain decisions, such as those involving measurements of the city, the seventy-one members of the Sanhedrin convened at Bethphage instead of their normal meeting place in the temple courts.

The priests of Bethphage looked down on little Bethany, whose residents spent a great deal of their time ritually unclean because of their work with the sick. Although that meant only that they could not worship at the temple, and usually could become pure again simply by immersing at sunset, the priests, like the Pharisees, took inordinate pride in their righteousness.

Once a year, however, the two groups came together. The Torah commanded that the Pesach meal be eaten in Jerusalem, and for one evening Bethphage welcomed Bethany within its walls.

Abba stepped onto the path, now wider and smoother, and Mary struggled to keep up with him as they were swept along with the crowd on their journey to Jerusalem.

A moment later, they paused at the crest of the ridge, the highest point of the road from Jericho to Jerusalem. Before them lay Jerusalem, the Holy City of God, her walls encircling the hill like a crown. On the eastern edge of the city, the temple gleamed like a jewel. Sunlight struck the white marble walls and the gold capitals topping the four columns on the wall of the Holy Place, then bounced back, causing her to shield her eyes. Even from here, it was clear that every square cubit of the temple's courts was jammed with bodies, both human and animal.

Her eyes dropped below the walls and landed on the eastern gate. On most of their trips, they veered to the north and entered through the gate by the pool of Bethesda. But today, they would enter the eastern gate, climb the underground staircase, and step straight onto the Court of the Gentiles.

She had no trouble keeping up with Abba on the last leg of their journey, down through the Kidron Valley and back up to the gate's double doors.

Her heart beat faster as they stepped under the wide brick archway that loomed over her head. They climbed the stairs and finally stepped into the midday sun shining on the holy ground of the temple.

The body heat and sweat of thousands assaulted her. She reached up and slipped her fingers through the cloth sash around Abba's waist. He let go of the lamb for only a moment to reach down to pat her hand.

The tiny sheep's head moved from side to side, seemingly as perplexed and disturbed by the noise and jostling as she was.

Every priest and every Levite was on duty this week, called in from every village in Judea. Levites lined up in rows, a priest at the head of each line. Faithful Judeans faced the priest one or two at a time to offer their sacrifice.

Abba ambled to the end of the line, with Mary close behind. The line moved quickly, and sooner than she expected, they were next in line. She leaned to the right and peered around Abba, the lamb's hooves dangling over her head.

A man straddled his lamb, left hand under its jaw, right hand clasping a knife. His right hand disappeared behind the animal's head, and then his elbow jerked back. A crimson stream poured out, captured in a silver bowl held by the priest. He handed the bowl to the young Levite behind him, who handed it to another. Her eyes followed the bowl from hand to hand until it disappeared behind the Nicanor Gate, where it would be thrown against the altar.

Followed by the man, a Levite carried the slain animal to the wall and hung it on a hook. He drew a long knife from his waistband.

Mary looked away.

Abba stepped forward and set their lamb on its feet. The priest handed him a long knife, its blade dripping in crimson.

Each worshiper had to draw the knife across the neck of his own sacrifice, offering it in place of the lives of his family, as Moses had instructed.

Mary's heart clenched, and for all her audacious promises to Martha, she couldn't bear to watch. She hurried back to the eastern end of the court, to Solomon's Porch. To safety.

It happened every spring. At least Abba would know where to find her.

Would she ever be strong enough? Adonai had made a way for His people to draw near, to be redeemed, and she couldn't even watch it happen.

She stepped onto the covered walkway and turned north. The columns on either side of her soared high above her head, taller than eight men, and walls of brilliant marble were topped with panels of fragrant cedar. She hugged the outer edge, touching and counting each column as she passed, trying to ignore the bleats of lambs and the overwhelming iron scent of blood.

At the end of the portico, she turned south. She repeated the ritual, touching, counting. As she drew closer to the Royal Stoa that stretched across the southern wall, human voices began to rise above those of animals. They grew louder, more strident. She counted aloud, but the clamor continued to grow. Voices overlapped, making it impossible for her to distinguish any words.

A crowd gathered near the southeastern end of the Royal Stoa. She quickened her step. What could be happening to draw so many spectators? She rose on her toes, trying to find a line of sight between shoulders, but she was too short to see anything. Weaving among those gathered with their lambs, making slow but steady progress, she moved forward until she was stopped by a wall of men, then skirted the edge until she found a break.

At last she learned what had commanded everyone's attention.

A man followed a herd of sheep and a few oxen, smacking a soft whip made of cords against the rear of an ox to hurry it along. The traders scurried out behind the animals, leaving their stalls unattended.

Money changers leaned over their tables, scrambling to scoop money into boxes.

The man strode toward them. Mary studied His face, calm and yet deeply unhappy. What had upset him so?

The men backed away as he rounded one end of the long row of tables. Standing behind the first one, he tucked his fingers under its edge, pulled up, and tipped it over.

Mary's jaw dropped as coins scattered. Children raced to collect them while adults gasped and shouted, hands in the air, fists waving.

One by one, the man upended the tables. Coins of all sizes, shapes, and metals, from all nations, bounced and rolled along the marble floor.

Sandaled feet pounded behind her, and she turned to see a group of the Jewish leaders running. She swallowed a chuckle. Such learned, respected men never ran. Until money was involved.

The man turned to the dove sellers that lined the back wall of the portico. This offering for the poorest was the most common of all sacrifices, so crates made of branches or willows housed two, three, or four doves each, stacked on the floor as high as a man could reach.

"Get these out of here!" The man opened the lids of those on the top row, and birds fluttered in all directions, causing men to duck and children to jump, reaching for them, laughing.

One of the chief priests marched toward the man, finger wagging. "What do you think you're doing?"

The man turned, one hand still grasping the top of an empty basket. He stared at the religious ruler as if he'd asked a ridiculous question. "You have made My Abba's house a market!"

Was that a Galilean accent? She'd heard enough of them to know. Galileans always stayed in Bethany when visiting Jerusalem.

"Your *abba*?" The priest chuckled. "This is the house of Adonai, not your abba."

The man ignored their retort and continued releasing doves.

"Under whose authority do you teach? Which rabbis laid hands on you?"

The man remained silent.

The priests and scribes talked among themselves a moment, apparently deciding what to do about this madman who had released all the animals that had been set aside as sacrifices and offerings, earning the temple cartloads of money.

A Pharisee stood apart from the others, one arm across his chest, the other elbow resting on it, his hand stroking his beard. A deep furrow etched his brow. He stood back a while, watching the crowd, then made his way to a group of young men who seemed to be waiting for the one causing all the trouble. He pulled one aside and talked to him.

The other teachers resumed questioning the stranger. "If you have authority to do this, show us a miraculous sign to prove it."

Finally the man stopped and walked toward them, arms at his sides, his face soft. "Destroy this temple, and I will raise it again in three days."

The crowd burst into laughter. Men slapped their thighs as they guffawed. "Three days? They've been working on it for forty-six years, and it's still not finished! You couldn't do it in three *decades*, let alone three years."

The priests began to move toward him, their anger palpable.

But the man simply walked past them, disappearing into the crowd like mist.

CHAPTER FOUR

*Now there was a Pharisee, a man named Nicodemus
who was a member of the Jewish ruling council.*
—John 3:1 (NIV)

The sun had begun its downward journey when Martha stepped into the courtyard and glanced up the road just in time to see Mary hurry past the well. She stepped back into the open room and began filling small bowls with nuts, olives, dried grapes, and figs. Their visitors would be here soon as well, and they would be hungry after such a long journey.

Mary bounced into the room. "Martha, you won't believe what happened at the temple!"

"Mary, I need you to fill some small jars with olive oil, vinegar, and honey to take to Bethphage."

"But Martha, I need to tell you about the man at the temple. He let all the doves out of their cages, and He chased away the sheep!" Mary looked as if she would explode—and probably believed she would—if she wasn't allowed to talk, but there was simply no time.

Martha gently steered her toward the bowls and oil. "Mary, tell me later. We must gather everything for the meal, and our guests will be here soon. Oh, first, I need you to take some bread and vinegar to the roof for them."

"But Martha!"

"Later, Mary." She shoved a stack of small bowls at her sister. Mary was always so excitable. Whatever she'd seen couldn't be that unusual and could certainly wait until the hours they'd be waiting while the lamb roasted.

Mary tromped up the steps.

"Time to get to work."

Martha looked up at Lazarus, who leaned back against the table, grinning.

"Get to work?" She lightly punched his arm. "What do you think I've been doing *all day*?"

He laughed, a deep, joy-filled sound much like Abba's. Their laugh had always made her smile and calmed her nerves. At the moment, though, it was simply annoying.

"Where's Abba? Is he already in Bethphage?"

Lazarus nodded. "He is. But there were some travelers right behind me. Are they ours?"

Martha peered back outside as the group entered the courtyard and silently counted as she approached them. *Four, five.* "Welcome. James, right?"

James nodded as he approached. "Let me introduce you to the Rabbi. He is called Yeshua."

The Rabbi had to be at least thirty years old to be recognized as a teacher and have His own talmidim, but His calm face and bright eyes made Him look much younger. "Shalom on this house. Todah for sheltering us, Martha."

James must have told Him her name. But had she told James? She didn't remember doing that, but she must have.

"You are most welcome. And shalom to You as well. We're honored to host You and celebrate the feasts."

Lazarus gestured to the table in the courtyard. "Come. We'll get your feet washed, and you can rest a bit until it's time to go to Bethphage."

"Mary just took bread and vinegar to the roof for you."

"First let me introduce you to Simon and his brother Andrew," Yeshua said. "James you know, and this is his brother John. We call them the Sons of Thunder." He grinned, and the men chuckled.

"Come, join me." Lazarus led the pairs of brothers to the steps.

Yeshua lingered a moment. "Todah again, Martha. You must have been cooking all day." He pointed to the platters filled with bread, bowls of olives and almonds, and plates of bread.

His hands seemed to be covered with tiny scratches, a few of them deep enough to draw blood, but just barely.

"May I get you some honey?" She pointed to His hands.

He lifted His hands and turned them over and back a few times. "I hadn't noticed, but that would be very kind of you."

She led Him to her worktable in the common room and then poured fresh water into a bowl. "Let me wash them first." She dunked a clean cloth in water and reached for His hands then gently rinsed the dust and wood debris away. "May I ask how You got these cuts?"

A crash caused Martha to jump. "That's Him!"

Martha jumped at Mary's shrill voice behind her, then looked over her shoulder at Mary's pale face and outstretched arm. She stood in a puddle of oil and shattered terra-cotta. "What are you talking about?"

"That's what I've been trying to tell you! He's the one who turned over the money tables and let all the doves go free."

Martha turned her gaze to the visitor, who was focused on her little sister.

"Hello, Mary." He flashed her a warm smile. He knew her name too? Martha had certainly not told Him that.

"Is that true? What she said?" asked Martha.

He turned His complete attention from Mary to Martha. "They had turned the temple into a market. I stopped it. For now, at least."

She looked back to Mary. "I'm sorry, Mary. I thought you were exaggerating."

"The tale invites such a judgment. I think Mary will understand." He offered Mary a quick glance and a smile.

"It's all right, achot. I know it sounded silly."

"The temple is the house of Adonai. It is holy, to be revered, not used for such commercial purposes," the Rabbi said.

He was right, of course. But who would go to such lengths—and take such risks—to correct it?

Nisan 16

Third day of the Feast of Unleavened Bread

Sitting on the wall of their courtyard, Mary gazed at the full moon over the Mount of Olives, showering her tiny village with radiant light. That same moon also now shone on Jerusalem and all of Judea.

"Good evening, Mary."

Mary was snapped from her thoughts by a deep voice, and turned to see a Pharisee standing three or four strides away. His striped robes and tasseled cloak could only belong to a member of his sect. His gray beard told his age, but wrinkles around his eyes softened his look.

She stiffened. Was he actually talking to her? Most Pharisees stayed far away from women, fearing they might be made unclean or simply subject to the inferiority of females. But to speak to her when they were alone? It was close to scandalous. And how did he know her name? Was she in trouble?

His eyes widened in horror. "I apologize. I never meant to frighten you. I've known your abba and your ach, and I've heard of you and your achot for so long, I feel as if I know you. But I don't really, and I forgot you don't know who I am."

She shook her head, afraid to speak for fear she might break one of the many rules she wasn't even aware of.

"I am Nicodemus. Your abba and ach come to temple each month to report the sighting of the new moon."

Ah yes. She relaxed. Now it made sense. Lazarus had often spoken of the Pharisee who didn't seem like all the others.

"And you are his younger achot."

She nodded. "Yes, I'm Mary." She groaned silently. He knew her name. Now she'd appear even more a child.

"May I ask what you are thinking when you observe the moon?"

Should she tell him? Or simply make an excuse and leave? She couldn't look any worse. "I was thinking how gracious it is that Adonai causes the same moon to shine on Bethany that shines on Jerusalem."

He nodded slowly, his mouth pursed. "Hmm. That's very interesting. I haven't thought about anything such as this in a long time."

Shame heated her cheeks. She should have held her tongue. What made her think such a learned man would be interested in her childish thoughts? "I apologize for my foolishness, *adon*."

He shook his head. "You misunderstand me. I don't consider your words foolish. Far from it. I meant it's been too long since I simply contemplated the goodness of Adonai."

How did she respond to such a statement?

"May I serve you in some way?" she asked.

"I wish to speak to your guest, if He is not yet asleep."

"Our guest?"

His brow furrowed for a moment, and he gently shook a long finger at her. "You were there the other day, weren't you?"

Oh no. But she was allowed, so what could cause his disapproval?

His smile brightened. "Yes, yes, you were there. So was I! I asked one of His talmidim where they were staying. They said they'd be here, at Simon's house."

Should she allow him to disturb them? But then, how could she refuse a Pharisee? "I think they're all on the roof, enjoying the night air. Would you like to join them? I can show you the way."

He winced. "I would much rather you bring the Rabbi to me, if that's possible."

"All right." Did he consider himself above the Rabbi, so that the man must be brought to him? If that were true, she would have expected him to summon the Rabbi to his residence in the Holy City.

"And I would prefer no one else knows I have come to see Him, please."

Ah, that explained his odd request.

"I'll let Him know. Would you like to wait in the courtyard? I can bring you something to drink."

"I'll just wait over there by that olive tree." He jerked a thumb over his shoulder toward the enormous tree off the southeast corner of the house. "We can talk there."

"As you wish."

"And Mary?"

"Yes, adon?"

"The tree is wide enough to allow someone to remain unseen and yet hear."

Did he just give her permission to listen to his conversation with the Rabbi? Did he know she would have tried anyway? What had Lazarus told him?

Mary hurried to the house and climbed the stairs to the roof. Yeshua and His students sat in a misshapen circle, Yeshua at one end and the talmidim in a messy row facing Him. She crept toward the group, afraid to interrupt.

"Yes, Mary?" prompted Yeshua.

"I— The Rabbi has a visitor."

"Who is it?" Abba asked.

"I think he wishes to speak to the Rabbi alone."

Abba shook his head. "Tell him to return tomorrow."

"It's all right, Simon. I'll speak with him." Yeshua rose and faced the group. "I think you should all get some sleep now."

Mary led Him down the stairs and out of the courtyard to the Pharisee. She stopped several strides away and pointed to the tree. "He waits for You there."

"Todah rabah, Mary." Yeshua smiled at her before heading for the Pharisee, who led Him to the other side of the tree.

Mary waited a moment before creeping closer, careful to keep the wide, gnarled trunk between her and the pair.

"Nicodemus, shalom. What brings you here in the darkness?"

"Rabbi, You must know You have been the subject of discussion in every home in Jerusalem for the last three days. The Pharisees have not stopped talking about You and Your actions in the temple courts."

"If you say."

"We've all heard about the miracles You have performed both here and in Galilee. Yet there is a group of us who agree, who believe, that You are a Rabbi who is sent by Adonai. No one could do what You are doing if Adonai was not with Him."

"I'm going to tell you something that will upend everything you think you know. You believe that because you are a Jew, and you are a Pharisee, and know and follow the whole of the law, that you will without fail be part of His kingdom. But the truth is, no one can enter the kingdom of Adonai unless he is born from above."

"How can someone be born when he is old?" Nicodemus scoffed. "Surely no one can enter a second time into his imma's womb to be born!"

"I'm telling you, *no one* can be part of the kingdom of God unless he is born of water and the Spirit. That which is born from flesh is flesh, and only that which is born from the Spirit is spirit. So you shouldn't be surprised when I say you must be born again."

There was a long silence.

"How do you know there is wind?" asked Yeshua. "You hear it, but you can't see it. You can't tell where it comes from or where it's going. So it is with all who are born of the Spirit. The Spirit is unseen and beyond the control of man."

"How can this be?" Nicodemus's voice was so soft that Mary had to strain to hear him. Was he speaking to himself?

"You are Israel's most learned teacher. How can you not understand these things? My talmidim and I come here, and we speak of what we know and what we've seen. And still, you and your friends will not accept our testimony. If you don't believe Me when I've spoken to you of earthly things, how will you believe if I speak to you of heavenly things?"

Yeshua paused, but Nicodemus again remained silent.

"No one has ever gone *into* heaven except the One who *came* from heaven—the Son of Man. Just as Moses lifted up the snake in the wilderness, so the Son of Man must be lifted up, that everyone who believes may have eternal life in Him."

"I'm not trying to be difficult. I *am* trying to understand, Rabbi."

"Then let me say it this way. Adonai loved this world so much that He gave His one and only Son. Whoever believes in the Son will not die but will instead have eternal life, because Adonai did not send His Son into the world to *condemn* it, but to *save* it."

"Mary!" Martha's harsh whisper drew Mary's attention from the conversation on the other side of the tree. "What are you doing out here? Come inside. It's time to go to sleep. We have a lot of work to do tomorrow. You need rest."

Mary suppressed a groan. Yeshua's words were far more interesting—and necessary—than rest. But even if she tried to explain it to Martha, she would never understand.

CHAPTER FIVE

On the seventh day the priest is to examine them.
—Leviticus 13:5 (NIV)

Nisan 22
One day after Pesach

Martha rolled her shoulders and tipped her head from side to side. The holy feast had been wonderful, and she'd thoroughly enjoyed having a full house, but she was exhausted. Today's meals, and probably tomorrow's as well, would be quite simple.

She reached for a knife and chopped up some carrots and added salt. Next she chopped an onion, a bulb of garlic, and some leeks. All of it was tossed into a frying pan with olive oil and salt.

Within moments, the house smelled of pungent garlic and savory onions. She breathed in deeply. She'd missed taking her time with a meal, deciding which spices to add, sometimes trying new ones. Last week she'd concentrated on quantity. She would never serve less than her best, but she'd simply moved too fast to enjoy the process.

Four handfuls of lentils went into the large stewpot—she had to remember to stop at four. It would take a day to get used to cooking for four again instead of nine. She added barley and then enough water to cover everything.

Abba sauntered in from the vineyard, his tunic dusty but dry. "I love this time of year. The air is warm enough to make the hard work quite pleasurable without ending up drenched in sweat."

"How are the grapes looking this year?"

"Lovely. The vines are bursting with flowers. We should have a particularly large crop."

"Adonai is good." She gave the stew a stir and carried the pot to the outside stove, setting it on the open top.

Abba followed her. "Can you mend this for me?" He held his right arm up, bent at the elbow. "The hem is frayed."

"Of course, Abba. Can you take it off for me? I'll do it right now."

"It doesn't have to be now."

"I'll be glad for the chance to sit a while. Let me see it." She fingered the edge of his sleeve. "This won't take long at all."

"Todah, motek."

She laughed. "You don't think I'm a little old to be called *that*? I'm not a little girl."

"You'll always be my little girl. Even when you're married and an imma yourself. Even when you are a *savta*, you'll still be my little girl." He bent to kiss her on the cheek.

"I love you too, Abba."

He ran his hands though his hair.

"Abba, what's this?" She pointed to a white spot on his lower arm near his elbow.

He twisted his arm to inspect the spot. "I don't know. I haven't noticed it until now. Perhaps I should go see Gershom."

A chill clutched at her heart. "No, Abba. You know what he'll say anyway. You know the texts better than I do. He'll just tell you to isolate for seven days and return to him. Can't you just isolate, and go a week from now if it's still there?"

"Motek, the law is the law. We cannot pick and choose which parts we will obey and which parts we won't because we think we know better. That would lead only to chaos."

"I know," she whispered.

He placed his hand on her cheek. "I would never have expected you, my orderly, practical child, to say this."

She sniffed back tears. "I'm sorry, Abba. I'm just afraid. I cannot lose you too."

"Why do you think you'll lose me?"

"If the priest says... You won't be able to live with us anymore. You'll have to go to the *bet cholim*."

"But that hasn't happened yet." His voice was soft, gentle. "Even if he isolates me, I can stay here, in my chamber, as long as I stay away from you, yes?"

"Yes, Abba."

"And what does the prophet Isaiah say?"

"He said many things." She hoped he couldn't hear her bitterness.

"He said, 'So do not fear, for I am with you; do not be dismayed, for I am your God.' You must remember these words."

"I know."

"As soon as you finish my cloak, I'll go see Gershom."

She blinked away tears, resisting the thought to go as slowly as possible. "I'll get you some bread and wine first."

She fingered the loaves left from last night, searching for the softest ones. She'd planned to bake leavened bread this morning, full of olives and salt. She'd have some ready for him when he returned, whatever the priest's answer.

She placed two rounds of flatbread on a pottery dish, then poured him a cup of well-honeyed wine before ducking into her chamber for a needle and thread.

Her hands shaking, she searched through a wooden box and selected some thread and a bone needle. She tried to thread the needle, but her vision was blurry. She sank to her bed and clapped hand over her mouth, stifling her sobs.

Adonai, no, please. Not Abba. I've already lost my imma. I cannot lose him as well.

Silent words spoke to her heart.

Do not fear, for I am with you.

She whispered the words over and over until her breathing calmed and her tears ceased. She swiped her cheeks, threaded the needle, and began stitching the tear in Abba's sleeve. Down, up, down, up. Each stitch perfectly straight and all exactly the same length. She reached the end of the frayed section, tied a knot, and bit off the remainder of the thread.

She held it up and inspected her work. It was all she had to offer him right now. That, and a calm face.

She stepped back into the inner courtyard, where Abba sat on the low wall drinking the last of his wine, as calm as if he were going only to the market for more oil and not to the priest for a judgment on the rest of his life.

"Todah, Martha. Delicious as always, even the day after." He rose. "I need you to do something for me."

"Anything, Abba." It stung a bit that he even asked.

"Let's not tell Mary and Lazarus, all right? No need for them to know yet. I hate to ask you to carry the burden all by yourself, but…"

"I understand, Abba. And it won't be all by myself, because—"

"Because I'll be carrying it too."

She shook her head. "Because Adonai through Isaiah said, 'I have made you and I will carry you.' We'll be carrying this burden, and He will be carrying us."

He beamed. "I knew I was right when I taught you the scriptures along with Lazarus."

She nodded. "May…" Her voice cracked. "May I have a hug before you go?"

"You know you'll be unclean."

She nodded. "I know. I'm usually unclean." She chuckled. "It's part of living in Bethany."

"That it is." He neared her and held her close with his left hand, his right arm held safely away from her. Not that that made any difference. She'd still need to immerse.

Abba pulled away and walked, just a little faster than usual, through the courtyard and down the road to Gershom's house.

Martha closed her eyes, trying to feel the arms of Adonai, around her, under her, carrying her.

And if she concentrated, she could. But would it last?

Iyyar 6

Mary walked beside Abba, her arm slipped through his, for his fourth visit to a priest in two weeks. He'd refused to show any of his children his arm before he left this morning, which only made all of them suspicious. He'd tried to come alone, but Mary had demanded she accompany him, and he finally relented.

"Martha's bread was especially good this morning, don't you think?" Abba's voice was weak. It was clear the bread meant nothing to either of them, but the silence had become unbearable.

"I liked the olives in it," she said.

"Yes, yes, it was very good."

When Martha had first discovered the sore on Abba's arm, he went quite happily by himself to see Gershom. The priest had told him to go home, isolate himself for seven days, and return.

The plan to keep Mary and Lazarus unaware of his plight had lasted exactly half a day, and they both knew by nightfall why Abba was hiding away in his chamber. Martha was a terrible liar. Her explanation of a toothache was simply not to be believed, and the truth quickly came tumbling out. Abba wasn't very happy about it, but together, the four of them managed to make the time go by quickly. Abba kept telling them that at his next visit, he would be pronounced clean and life would once again be as it was.

A week later, the sore on his arm had not worsened, and it appeared Abba was right. He saw Gershom again, alone, confident the whole ordeal would soon be over.

But the priest must have seen something he didn't like, as he repeated his instructions. For the second week, a fragile hope filled the house. They were the longest seven days they'd ever known.

This morning, Gershom told Abba he'd have to see the temple priests for a final decision.

They crested the mount and began the descent to the Holy City. As they had almost exactly a month earlier, they entered through the eastern gate, the excitement and joy of the last visit achingly absent.

Just before they reached the gate, Abba grabbed her hand. "You can just go back home now if you want, you know. There's no need for you to wait. It might take longer than we think."

"But why, Abba?"

"There's just no need for you to go with me. I've done this three times now. And Martha might need your help."

Martha never needed her help. Why was he so anxious to get rid of her?

"But you haven't done it *here*, Abba. Anyway, you can't enter the temple grounds. You need someone to bring a priest to you. I came with you, and I'll stay with you."

He offered a sad smile and leaned in to kiss her cheek. "I'll wait here then."

She ducked under the arched doorway and climbed the underground stairway until she reached sunlight. She crossed the Court of the Gentiles to the barrier that warned those of other nations to keep out of the sacred area on pain of death, climbed the stairs, and stepped onto the Court of the Women. Priests hurried in all directions, all of them looking past her as if she were invisible.

She needed someone, though. How to get their attention?

A younger priest passed her, heading back toward the entrance to the Women's Court, then entered a storeroom just to the right of the entrance.

She followed, pausing before an acacia wood door, hand raised. Could a woman even knock on this door? If not, why place it here? Why not in the Court of the Israelites?

She took a deep breath and tapped her knuckles on the wood, twice.

Nothing.

She repeated the summons.

Finally the door opened, and a priest peered out. "Yes?" His voice showed his irritation at being interrupted from doing whatever it was he did behind the closed door.

"I need a priest to inspect my Abba."

"Inspect him? For what?"

"For *tsara'at*." The words caught in her throat, and the revulsion on his blanched face wasn't helping.

"Wait here." He slammed the door in her face.

Mary leaned against the wall and waited, tapping her foot. She glanced toward home. The sun still hovered above the tower on the eastern wall, only a sliver of sky between orb and stone.

She waited. And waited.

At length the door handle rattled, and she jumped away. A priest not much older than Martha pushed it open and stepped out. He smiled weakly. "Where is your abba?"

"Outside the gate."

"Todah." He strode to the stairway and gestured for Mary to precede him.

Outside, he neared Abba. "Shalom. I am Obed. May I see the…the…"

Abba lifted his arm, and the priest examined it.

One look at their faces gave Mary the answer she'd been dreading.

"I'm so sorry." He shook his head and backed away, his eyes misting as if it were his own abba he had just pronounced unclean. "This is the first time I've ever had to do this. I even checked with one of the older priests to be sure I had the law straight, but…"

"We understand. You are following the law. And without the law…" Abba shrugged.

The priest began to recite the laws Abba must now follow.

Mary's mind shut him out. She should thank him, as he was only doing as Adonai had instructed. But she couldn't. She simply took Abba by his good elbow and led him up the wide path and back toward home.

They needed to avoid nearing anyone else, at least until they reached the point the path veered away from Bethphage and toward Bethany.

The voices reached her before she could see them. A large group, headed this way. She pulled Abba off the road and into the maze of dark gray olive trees, their enormous knotted trunks full of bumps and fissures. They ducked behind a tree, hoping the group passed by without noticing the odd pair. But another traveler followed, so Mary picked a trail between and around trees until they once again reached the narrow road to Bethany.

They hurried east toward home, ignoring the stares of their friends, then hurried inside.

Martha stepped back from the cooking that had no doubt failed to distract her, knife still in hand. Lazarus rose from a low stool, tossing a handful of raisins on Martha's table.

No one spoke for a long moment.

"Oh, Abba!" Martha raced to his arms and sobbed into his shoulder.

"Don't cry, motek." He patted her back then set her away from him. "We'll need to tell the community. Lazarus, you can do that. You'll need help with the vineyard. Martha and Mary, you'll need to scrub my chamber, and then you all need to immerse at dusk."

His instructions were unnecessary. They'd dealt with tsara'at their entire lives. They knew the laws regarding ritual purity inside and out.

"I'll pack some clothing then head for the bet."

Mary wiped away tears at the thought of not seeing Abba every morning, every day, for every meal.

Abba ducked into his chamber for a moment and came right back out, a tunic clenched in his fist.

"That's all you're taking?" asked Mary.

He shrugged. "What else do I need? You can bring me anything else I need. I assume you'll visit?"

The question was appalling. Why would he even ask such a thing? Either Mary or Martha visited nearly every day, along with others from Bethany. Bread and cheese each morning, lentil stew at night, clean clothes. Men came to help with bathing. People were there several times a day. If anything, they would be there more often now.

And he should know that.

He surely did. Perhaps it was just his way of telling them he'd miss them.

Not nearly as much as they'd miss him.

CHAPTER SIX

The Lord is close to the brokenhearted
and saves those who are crushed in spirit.
—Psalm 34:18 (NIV)

Iyyar 7

Martha rose from her bed still exhausted. She'd lain awake most of the night trying to figure out why Adonai would allow a man such as her abba to contract tsara'at. No one was irreplaceable, but he played such a critical role in Bethany. He encouraged the sick, assisted the poor, grew the grapes, and helped plow the field that grew the grain that fed that entire village along with those they cared for.

And now he was gone. Who would take over? Lazarus could care for the grapes and help with the plowing, but he was a bit young to command the respect Abba had.

Martha rose silently and dressed. She'd heard Mary next to her trying to cry quietly until deep into the night, so best to let her get some sleep. No need for both of them to be tired.

She grabbed the water jar and trudged to the well. She'd not wanted to face the women last night. After filling the jar, she turned to head back to the house when Daniel approached. Her heart lightened. "Daniel! Why aren't you in the vineyard?"

"I stopped at the house, but Mary said you'd come for water."

"She's awake?" *Obviously.* "I didn't come last night."

He offered a sad smile. "I understand."

"I'm glad you're here though." She reached to touch his hand, but he pulled away.

"I need to tell you something."

"Of course." She turned to set her jar on the well.

"This is not my decision, Martha."

"What's not?" She glanced over his shoulder at Enoch, his abba, hovering several strides behind him, his hands behind his back.

"It's about the wedding."

Her legs trembled, and her stomach felt like stone. *No, no, please.* "What about it?"

"My abba says…" He paused, the words trapped in his mouth. "He says…" He took a deep breath. "He says we cannot marry." He blurted out the sentence like a child finally admitting to his misdeed.

"Why?" She knew very well why, but she wanted to hear him say it, wanted to hear him admit he was succumbing to unreasonable fear and unnecessary distance.

"Because of your abba, because of the tsara'at."

Anger flared up, obscuring her pain, her grief, her indignance. "But *I* don't have it!"

"I know, but—"

Her arm shot toward their home. "He's not even in the house with us now! He's in the bet cholim. Isn't that enough?"

"It should be. I know. I'm telling you it's not my decision!"

"Then you are a coward, Daniel ben Enoch!"

He stared at the dirt, unable to answer her.

"Why did you move to Bethany, anyway? You don't want to serve. You don't want to be part of us. You don't approve of half the things we do. Did you even know Bethany's purpose before you came?"

Enoch hurried toward her. "You may not speak to my son in such a manner." He shook a chubby finger in her face.

She longed to grab it and snap it backward, but she was already in enough trouble. "Then *you* answer me. Why did you come?"

"I was told Bethany had women who needed to marry, who made good brides. Obviously I was misinformed."

"Then maybe you should go back to Jerusalem."

"We are. We're leaving today." He handed a small cloth-wrapped bundle to his son.

Daniel's face reddened, but he held it out to her. "I need to return this."

"And what do you think I'll do with that?" The back of her throat burned. The last thing she wanted to do was cry in front of Daniel and Enoch and look even more pitiful than she did now. She swallowed hard. "No one will marry me now. I'm a divorced woman. And I did *nothing* to deserve that! I was not unfaithful. I haven't displeased you in any way that I am aware of. Yet you cast me aside and ruin the rest of my life because you cannot face the truth."

Enoch stepped even closer. "I will not allow my grandchildren to be raised in a house of tsara'at."

His grandchildren would be blessed to grow up in her house. "It is not a house of tsara'at! It is clean. Ask Gershom. You have nothing to fear from my home or my family."

"This entire village is contaminated! We should never have come." Enoch stomped away.

"I'm so sorry." Daniel set the bundle on the edge of the well and followed his abba.

The cloth slipped away, revealing the alabaster flask of priceless perfume their imma had given her before she died. She left one to each of the sisters to be used to start their married life. By law, it had to be under the husband's control once married but was to be her protection in case of his death.

Martha picked it up and studied it. A soft, translucent white, it was beyond beautiful, and a tangible reminder of their imma's love. It was filled with nard, an unbelievably expensive oil.

It would serve no purpose now.

Feeling as if she'd been kicked by a donkey, Martha stumbled home. Nothing made sense. First Abba, now this. And she wasn't totally sure which was the greater disaster.

She was now a divorced woman, having never even truly been married. What had she done that was so wrong as to deserve this? Hadn't she dedicated her life to caring for others? Was that to be the sum total of her existence? Did she have no right to even a small amount of personal happiness? To have someone who loved her, who would be there for her on the hardest days, the days when they'd lost someone in the bet cholim? Or to celebrate with when someone was pronounced clean, restored to the community and able to worship in the temple? Not that that had ever happened, but it was the dream of all in Bethany.

And what about children? She would never hold her own baby, sing over her or nourish him from her own body, teach her the mizmorim or hear him recite the Shema.

The loss was too great to bear.

Mary waited on the roof, watching Martha and Daniel at the well.

Daniel coming to the house the morning after Abba left could not be a good sign. He should have rushed to Martha's side yesterday, the moment he heard the news. He should have held her, comforted her. Prayed with her. But he stayed away.

Grief consumed Martha's face. But was her sorrow due to Abba's condition or something her betrothed had said?

Daniel set something on the ground and left.

Mary's heart shattered. There was only one thing he could have given her.

Mary raced down the steps and to the vineyard. Lazarus had to know about this.

"Zar!" She raced along the rows, looking for her ach. "Zar!"

"Why are you shouting?" He answered without pausing the pruning. "It's too early for that, and my head aches already."

She delivered the news. His face was a battleground between rage and sorrow. The pair raced back home.

Martha stood at her table, staring at the wall.

"I never liked him," declared Lazarus. He leaned a hip against her worktable.

"What?" Martha whipped her head around to face her younger brother. "Who are you talking about?"

"That snake, Daniel." Mary spat out the words.

She groaned. "So you heard."

Lazarus reached for a fig and peeled it as he talked. "Martha, the whole village will know before I finish this fig. Did you expect to keep it a secret for any length of time?"

"Of course not. I'd just hoped to avoid talking about it for at least a day." Her eyes, already red, brimmed with unshed tears.

Mary folded her arms across her chest. "He wasn't good enough for you."

"She's right," said Zar. "Neither he nor his abba really wanted to be part of our work. Or the village. How many times did you ask him to help? Did he help even once?" He took a huge bite of the fruit and gave the rest to Mary.

Her brother was right. He hadn't. They'd asked him to visit the men in the bet, to help serve when they had guests, to bring in wood to cook the lambs. His abba refused not only to help but to attend even a single feast.

Lazarus finished his fig and wiped his hands. "What would it have been like after you married? Would he have made you stop your work at the bet? They didn't like it here. My guess is they would have moved you to Jerusalem before the first rain."

Mary hadn't thought of that, and Martha likely hadn't either. And that would have destroyed Martha. She was made for this life.

"I think that's why Enoch demanded to know what you would bring to the marriage," Lazarus continued. "He never intended for you to live here."

"I don't want to talk about it now." Martha pointed to the jar, still hidden in the cloth Daniel had wrapped it in. "Mary, would you put this back in our chamber next to yours?"

"Of course." She flashed Martha a huge grin.

"Why are you so happy?"

Her cheeks heated. "I didn't want you to marry him. He was mean."

"Mean?"

"He never spoke to me. Not once."

Martha's face softened, and tears lined her eyes again. "I'm sorry. I didn't know that."

It wasn't as if Martha had spent much time with him, let alone Mary. But the few times the families had gathered, he could have talked to Mary. Now that she thought about it, his abba rarely spoke to any of them at all.

Mary reached to grab the vessel but instead bumped it. It toppled on its round base, tipping one way and then the other. Her stomach roiled. She reached to grab it, save it, but her arms refused to obey.

Martha lunged to catch it but wasn't quick enough. The long neck hung over the edge of the table, pointing to the floor, the weight of the oil pulling the bottle behind it. It crashed against the tile floor, shattering into a hundred pieces.

The musky, earthy scent of nard rose, saturating the air.

Mary looked up to see Martha, mouth open, eyes as wide as figs, staring at the remains of Imma's precious gift.

One hand on her stomach, the other over her mouth, Mary searched for words that could communicate her regret. "Oh, achot… I can't believe I did that." She choked on her sobs. "I'm so sorry."

Martha reached for her and pulled her into a hug. "It's all right. It was an accident. I know you didn't mean to do it."

"But after everything else…" Mary squeezed her arms tighter around her sister. "You can have mine."

"It's not like I'll ever need it."

Mary pulled away. "Why not?"

"I'm a divorced woman now."

Mary laid her head on Martha's shoulder and sobbed, and Martha joined her. Lazarus wrapped his arms around both, and all the sorrow that had piled up for the last two weeks rushed out like a flash flood running off the Mount of Olives.

CHAPTER SEVEN

The day is yours, and yours also the night;
you established the sun and moon.
—Psalm 74:16 (NIV)

Nisan 1
Fourteen days before Pesach

The early-morning sun warmed Martha's shoulders as she stepped through the double wooden doors of the bet on the eastern edge of town. Three sides of the mud-brick building were halls with small rooms on either side, and curtains for doors.

The center courtyard was shared by all. An enormous acacia tree, wide enough to cover most of the open space, offered shade. Already, those too weak to move had been helped to a comfortable spot to spend the day.

Martha searched the area for Abba. Her eyes scanned the courtyard, under the tree, in the corners…there. As usual, he was comforting one of the new residents. Though it had only been eleven new moons since that horrible day he became one of them, he was regarded as the leader of the small group of ten or so. He must spend all days listening to them, crying with them, praying with and for them.

He glanced her way and caught her eye. He nodded, letting her know he'd join her as soon as he finished. Then he bowed his head, took the young man's hand. His lips moved in hushed prayer. When he finished, both men swiped away tears.

"Martha, motek." Abba approached, a wide smile on his face. His hair hung below his shoulders, and his beard ended in the middle of his chest. "I didn't expect to see you today. You were just here yesterday."

He'd always been so clean, so neat. Even after long, hot hours tending the vines, he made sure to wash his face and comb his hair before the evening meal. Her heart broke anew every time she saw his torn clothes and the dust caked on his face, but she smiled through the pain. "Yesterday was for everyone else. Today I'm here just for you."

"And the others?"

"Adah will be here later. Let's sit. I brought you some fresh bread and cheese." She turned toward the tree, blinking rapidly to banish threatening tears. She spread the woven mat under the tree and sat, leaning against the rough bark. From a covered basket, she pulled out the simple morning meal. "How is that young man? He's new, yes?"

Abba nodded. "He's been here only a few weeks. He's so young. At least I had lived most of my life before this. I married, had children. He had just begun talking to his abba about marriage."

"Did he have someone in mind?"

"He did. He assumes she'll be given to another now."

"That's terrible." A too-familiar pain stabbed her. "I'm so sorry. You told him we pray for all of you, every day?"

"I did. It's not helping him much. Yet." Abba flashed her a sad smile.

"I imagine not. But I know you'll do whatever you can to help him."

"Pesach is almost here again." Abba broke off a small piece of bread and placed it on his tongue.

"Yes, it is." Neither of them mentioned the fact that this would be the first time in his life Abba would not be at the temple to sacrifice the lamb. Even when her abba was a babe in arms, his abba made sure he was there every spring.

"The vines are in bloom. They're beautiful this year. We should have another bountiful harvest," Martha said.

"I'm sure Lazarus has been taking very good care of them. Did he find anyone to help him?"

She chuckled. "Mary."

"Oh, that must be quite a sight to see. I would love to watch them." He laughed.

Oh, how she missed his laugh at home! "They do bicker a bit, but they manage to get it all accomplished."

He reached for a piece of cheese, a bony arm extending from his cloak.

She grabbed his arm, and even through the cloak, she could feel his bones. "Abba, you've grown so thin!"

He nodded and ripped off a sliver of cheese before placing it in his mouth.

"Are you eating?"

"As much as I can."

"What does that mean?"

He breathed in a long, slow breath. "It hurts too much."

"It hurts to eat?" Her heart rate sped up. "How do you mean? Your stomach hurts? Your teeth?" Perhaps she could bring him something else, something softer, or easier to digest.

"My mouth." He pointed to a sore at the corner of his mouth. "I can't open it wide enough to enjoy your stew."

"Oh, Abba!"

"Motek, I'll be fine. I eat plenty of bread."

"That's not enough, obviously. You'll waste away to nothing. Why didn't you say something before now? I'll ask Adah for a salve, and we'll bring you something else—"

He laid his hand on her arm. "You are so busy, I didn't want to bother you with something so simple. You have so much to do, so many to care for already. I don't wish to add to your burden. I told you, I'll be fine."

"You are never a burden! Abba, how could you even say that?" The tears she had repelled earlier came bursting forth, leaving hot, wet trails down her face. "I love you, Abba. I would do anything for you, as I know you would for me."

"I know, but motek—"

She sat up straighter. "Then if you won't accept that as a reason, hear this: You are causing me to disobey the law of Adonai."

His eyes widened. "How am I doing that?"

"Adonai commands us to honor abba and imma. If you don't let me care for you, how can I properly honor you?" She fixed him with a cold stare. He couldn't possibly argue with her on this.

His face slowly softened, and a sly smile appeared. "You've learned well, motek."

She matched his smile with one of her own. "I had a good teacher."

CHAPTER EIGHT

People will dwell again in his shade;
they will flourish like the grain,
they will blossom like the vine—
Israel's fame will be like the wine of Lebanon.
—Hosea 14:7 (NIV)

Nisan 5

Nine days before Pesach

Mary leaned forward, all her weight on the wooden pole grasped in her hands. Round and round, again and again. Barley kernels, caught between the wide round wheel above and the flat quern underneath, crunched and dragged as they were ground into flour.

At least it was better than grinding the flour by hand. Thank Yahweh for the generous traveler who had gifted the mill to the village when Mary was only a child. She'd never had to grind barley like that, but she'd heard stories of the women grinding for days at a time before a feast to have enough flour ready to feed the visitors.

She'd become a woman in the last year, and had been assigned to help with the flour-making. Even with the mill, at least one in four women made flour and bread each day to feed the village and the residents of both the bet cholim and the house of the poor. Most of the village women started here, although occasionally a young woman wanted to be with her imma, or showed a particular skill at weaving or making tunics. The oldest in the village gathered in old Avigail's courtyard and spun wool into yarn, a skill that required neither strength nor especially good eyesight.

Mary pulled one hand back from the handle and flexed her fingers, then switched hands.

She might consider marriage if it meant she'd never have to grind grain again. However, that would mean someone else would be doing it for her, and that wouldn't be fair. Unless she married a wealthy man, with servants…

But that was not the way of Bethany. The Essenes didn't approve of servants, and though most of Bethany's residents weren't Essenes, their beliefs still dictated the way things were done. Most of the time those ways had been proved best. They didn't believe in marriage, either, but that was more a command for themselves. Most of Bethany married and had families.

"Mary!"

She jumped at the harsh sound of her own name. "What?"

"What are you daydreaming about this time?" Martha asked.

"The man she'll marry, of course." Hannah laughed. She'd only recently moved to Bethany from Jerusalem, after her wedding to Yoash, a village man. She was only a year older than Mary but already pregnant. Mary couldn't imagine life as a married woman.

The others laughed, but Mary remained silent.

"I can send Kemuel to help again for Pesach if you like. I'm sure you'll have a great number of guests, and without..." Adah's voice trailed to a whisper. "I'm so sorry, Martha." She turned to Mary and grasped her hand. "I'm sorry."

"It's been a year. It's all right." Martha smiled, and Adah relaxed. Martha excused herself and disappeared into the house.

The others may have believed Martha's smile, and her lie, but Mary knew it wasn't genuine. No matter what she said in the courtyard, at night Martha agreed it was most certainly not all right. Everything was different, worse. Empty.

They'd muddled through Shavuot, Sukkot, and Hanukkah, and now prepared for Pesach, but they weren't the same.

Mary pushed against the pole, shoving it forward, constantly moving but never going anywhere.

The scent of warm raisins and honey tickled her nose. She whipped her head around to see Martha approaching, a wide woven platter in her hands, overflowing with fresh treats. Mary abandoned her job and hurried to her sister.

"Mary, you can't just stop. It takes half a day as it is."

Mary looked over her shoulder. "Hannah took over."

"That's not the point, Mary. You have to help, do your part."

"I did! I've been pushing that pole all morning." She stopped herself from sticking out her lower lip. She was no longer a child, as Martha kept reminding her.

Adah neared them and reached for a raisin cake. "She was working, Martha, right up until she smelled your raisin cakes.

Besides, we're almost done." She laughed and bit off half of the small cake. "These make it all worth it."

"Todah, Adah." She handed the basket to Mary. "Want to pass these around?"

Mary swallowed what was in her mouth, nodding.

"Don't eat them all. Make sure everyone gets some."

She groaned. "I *know*, Martha. You say that nearly every day." She took the basket and moved among the women hovering around the mill, whether pouring the barley kernels into the hole in the top stone, moving the bar that turned it, or gathering the flour as it slid from between the stones and scooping it into baskets.

The basket of cakes now almost empty, Mary moved to those who sat together mixing dough, patting it into rounds, and pasting them onto the sides of the open-topped ovens. Rounds of dough piled ever higher. Later, others would collect them and take them to the bet, along with steaming, thick lentil stew.

Adah sat beside her. "You'll make a good wife soon."

"I'm not getting married, you know that."

"I don't know that."

Adah was always so encouraging, even when she wasn't quite telling the truth. Had anyone approached Lazarus about marrying her, the entire village would have known. But no one had, and no one would. Mary worried for Martha, but for herself, she didn't particularly care. She was happy as she was now. From what she'd seen of marriage, it rarely ended well. Women died giving birth, babies died, husbands died. Somehow women always ended up alone anyway. As long as she lived in Bethany, married or not, she'd be taken care of as long as she contributed.

And that was enough for her.

Mary studied the vines that had changed from drab brown to a vibrant green in a matter of days. Up and down the length of the vines, delicate leaves burst from fuzzy pointed lumps in a flurry of energy.

"These will turn to clusters of grapes?" she asked.

"Not really. If they all became grapes, they wouldn't all survive. Or at least they wouldn't all be big, fat, juicy grapes. Most, if not all of them, would be scrawny and sour. There's not enough water, sunlight.... That's why we prune them so often. If there's too much foliage, the sun can't reach all the berries." Lazarus knelt and pulled a weed from near the roots. "Each shoot can really only support one good cluster."

"What about all these? What happens to them?"

"We prune them. Cut them away."

"No! If you cut them all off, there won't be enough grapes!"

He rose. "Have we ever not had enough grapes?"

She thought of the platters overflowing with fat purple grapes, of the amphorae in the broad room full of sweet wine. "Well, no..."

"Because Abba is—was—out here all the time pruning."

"I guess so."

He continued inspecting the vines. "Grapes are one of Adonai's most wonderful gifts to us."

"How can you talk of gifts when we face Pesach with Abba in the bet?"

"Do you know what the prophet Habakkuk said about grapes?"

"No! Because no one will teach me!" Her entire body stiffened, her hands clenched at her sides.

He seemed unconcerned with her anger. "He said, 'Though the fig tree does not bud and there are no grapes on the vines, though the olive crop fails and the fields produce no food, though there are no sheep in the pen and no cattle in the stalls, yet I will rejoice in Adonai, I will be joyful in God my Savior.'"

She scoffed. "What does that even mean?"

"It means that no matter what happens, even if we have no grapes, no grain, no olives, no sheep—even then, we should rejoice just because Adonai is our salvation."

She knew he was right. Abba had somehow remained joyful ever since that horrible day. Mary put on a smile every time she went to visit him, but it was only to keep him from worrying. What would he say if he knew how often she cried herself to sleep? How often she prayed for Martha, that somehow her life wouldn't be as lonely as it promised to be?

He wouldn't be happy. But she didn't know what to do to change it.

CHAPTER NINE

*She watches over the affairs of her household
and does not eat the bread of idleness.*
—Proverbs 31:27 (NIV)

Nisan 7
Seven days before Pesach

Martha looked up as Adah poked her head into the open room. "I need to get started baking."

Martha followed her out.

Adah gathered her things while Elisheba reached for a basket of hot bread.

"Me too. I've got the washing," added Elisheba. "I'll walk with you."

Hannah, a newcomer, crept near her, head down.

"Martha, may I ask you something?"

It had been nearly a year, and still people, meaning only the best, were asking her if she was all right. Martha stiffened but forced a smile. "I'm doing well. But thank you for asking."

"No—I mean, I'm glad, but I wanted to ask something else."

"Oh." She shouldn't have been so assuming. "Of course. What do you need?"

"Would you teach me how to make your stew?"

That wasn't what she expected. "What?"

"My husband hates my stew." She winced. "He hates everything I make, actually. He's never said that exactly. He's very kind. But I can tell."

"Did you not pay attention when your imma taught you?"

"She didn't." Sadness came over her face. "Imma died when I was about seven."

A familiar pain stabbed Martha's heart, and she placed her hand on Hannah's shoulder. "I'm so sorry. I didn't know."

"You couldn't have. It's all right."

But still… "No sisters or aunts who could help?"

"My sister tried, but she was so busy caring for all of us. She was the oldest. Everything fell to her, and there were three others besides me. I was the youngest, so I never had to learn. Until now."

"Yes, of course. I'd be delighted to help you." She pointed inside. "I'm making some now. Would you like to help?"

Relief lit up a wide smile. "Yes! Let me take this home first. Shall I bring anything?"

"Bring your stewpot and lentils, and whatever else you use. Whatever you don't have, I will."

"I'll be right back." She grabbed her bread and hurried off.

Martha's conscience pricked her. She'd done the same thing to Mary that Hannah's sister had done to her. If Mary found a husband tomorrow, she wouldn't be able to cook for him either.

It didn't take long before the bottom of Hannah's pot was covered with onions, carrots, and garlic softened in sizzling olive oil. "Take this home and add water and a handful of lentils for each person, then let it cook slowly until evening."

Martha handed her the warm pottery. "And I have an idea. Would you like to go with me the next time I go to the market in the city?" Martha asked. "I can show you which spices you'll need most and where to buy them."

"Oh yes, todah!" Hannah threw her arms around Martha's neck. "Todah rabah, Martha! Yoash will be so happy!"

"Anytime you want to learn more, let me know."

As the woman hurried home, a rush of satisfaction and joy flooded Martha's chest. She hadn't felt anything like it since… since Abba left. She'd forgotten how much helping was a part of her. Even what she did for the bet had soured since Abba was now part of it. But the look of hope and gratitude on Hannah's face was new, something Martha didn't usually see on the faces of the men in the bet. And it came with such little effort—doing just what she did every day.

She laughed softly. She'd hadn't realized how much she'd needed this reminder from Adonai, this nudge that what she did was important, was appreciated, was good, even when she couldn't see it or feel it.

Todah rabah, Adonai.

Her heart lighter than it had been in months, she picked up this morning's bread for the bet and headed to the edge of town.

Mary sat on the flat roof on their house, hunched over, her chin and hands on the low wall built around the edge to keep people from tumbling off.

Someone was moving into Daniel's house.

The house across the road had remained empty since Daniel and his abba moved shortly after they dissolved his betrothal to Martha. They weren't much missed, not only because of what they had done to Martha, but also because they'd never truly made themselves a part of the community. They'd kept to themselves, gave nothing, received nothing. They'd stayed with relatives in Jerusalem for every feast and yet refused to let visitors sleep even on the ground in their courtyard.

They hadn't been here long when Enoch came one night to talk to Abba. Mary had been sent to their chamber with Martha, and the next morning Abba asked Martha if she wanted to marry Daniel.

There was such rejoicing! Abba had always said Adonai had a husband for Martha, someone special, but they'd doubted. It wasn't as if Martha was undesirable. Even before Imma had died, Martha had turned down anyone who wanted to leave Bethany. And after, even though Abba had insisted he could care for Mary if she left, she still refused anyone who would not settle in Bethany. One man even came from Jerusalem searching for brides for his sons, but again, Martha had refused.

Finally, it was assumed she was too old to marry. Martha had accepted it with such grace.

Then came Daniel, and for a year it appeared that not only would Martha be a bride, but Bethany would gain a new family. After they left, it became clear they'd only come to find a wife.

Mary's attention returned to the present. So who was this, planning to live in the house? Some relative, apparently. Houses and land stayed in families.

Would he be doing as Daniel had done?

This man was older than Daniel, old enough to have a wife and children, but he appeared to be alone. Were they coming later?

Was he staying or was he too only seeking a bride?

Mary hated questions, especially those with no answers. Maybe she should just go ask him.

She jumped up and ran down the stairs on the side of the house, bolted across the courtyard and across Bethany's lone street.

At the entrance to Daniel's courtyard, she paused.

This might have been a bad idea, but for Martha's sake, she needed to know.

She crept inside, toward the inner courtyard. The doors to all the other rooms, save one, were shut tight. Was he in there? She tiptoed inside, peered around the door.

Empty.

Where had he gone?

"Shalom."

Mary gasped and spun around to face the new owner.

He was tall, and older than she'd first thought. Dark short hair and a trimmed beard framed his face. One eyebrow was raised, but a crooked smile pulled up one corner of his mouth. "Are you looking for someone?"

Part of her wanted to run home, but she was here now, and may as well get some answers. "Who are you?"

"I'm Asher."

"Oh." That didn't tell her much. She should have chosen a better question. "Why are you here?"

The skin around his eyes crinkled as his smile turned to a grin. "No, no. It's my turn. Who are *you*?"

"I'm Mary."

"Shalom, Mary. Are you looking for someone?"

She shook her head. "My turn. Why are you here? In Bethany? In this house?"

"I think that's at least two questions, maybe three."

"One question. Two parts."

He laughed. "All right, let's just get this over with. I'm Asher. Daniel is my imma's cousin. I used to live in Gennesaret. My wife died about three years ago, and I didn't want to stay there anymore. I heard they need carpenters to work on the temple, and Enoch offered to sell me the house for a very good price, so I moved."

"Do you have children? Any other family?"

He shook his head. "No." His face clouded. There was more to the story, but it was clear she shouldn't press him on this.

"Are you going to stay here, or are you just here to find a wife?"

His brows furrowed. "I'm sorry?"

"Like Daniel. He came to find a wife, but he'd planned to leave all along. Then he left my sister when my abba got tsara'at."

"Oh, I didn't know that." He closed the distance between them. "I'm very sorry to hear that."

"He shouldn't have done that." She crossed her arms and pouted.

"No, he probably shouldn't have." Asher knelt and looked up at her, waiting until she caught his gaze before he spoke again. "Mary, I am not like my cousin or my uncle. I don't know why they came or why they left, but I didn't come to cause trouble. I came to find peace. I know what you do in Bethany, and I plan to be part of it."

"You do?"

"I do. I don't know how yet, but I will be."

She brightened. "Do you want to help with the grapes? I've been helping since my abba... Anyway, Lazarus does most of it. I'm supposed to be helping, but I'm afraid I do more harm than good. You can also help us at Pesach. We usually have guests, and we need men to serve them."

"I can't do that. I'm going to be working on the temple. I hope."

That didn't make sense. "Why do that when you can help us?"

He grinned again. "Because if I don't work, I won't get paid, and I won't be able to eat."

She scoffed. "Then you *don't* understand how things work in Bethany."

"What do you mean? Everyone has to eat." He stood and grabbed a broom that stood in the corner and began to sweep a year's worth of dust and leaves from the packed earth floor on his common room.

She grabbed a cushion from the low table and stepped into the courtyard to bang it against the wall, releasing a cloud of dust. "We share everything here. We all work, and we share whatever is produced, with each other and with the bet cholim." She exchanged the cushion for another. "Some of us bake the bread, some cook stew, some make or wash or mend clothes for the residents there. We have a barley field and a vineyard, sheep and goats.... It takes a lot of work to produce enough for ourselves and those in the poorhouse and the bet."

"Most villages can barely manage to support themselves. How can you feed yourselves and more besides?" He moved the low table aside for her.

"The women of the poorhouse help. Most of them are capable women who've been abandoned or widowed or were somehow unable to feed themselves and their children. And those in the bet cholim…" She shook her head to banish the images of the frail, weak men. "They don't often eat much, and there's only ten or twelve of them. It's not much different from caring for an aging parent."

He stopped sweeping. "All right. I won't go to the temple, at least tomorrow. I'll join you and your ach in the vineyard."

"You don't have to wait until tomorrow." She flashed him a smile of triumph and headed toward the opening in the wall. She turned to find him standing still in the common room, brows furrowed.

"What are you waiting for?" She beckoned to him. "Come. Work is waiting."

She headed for the vineyard southeast of the village. She didn't look back. Either he came or he didn't. Either way, she had work to do.

CHAPTER TEN

I desire to do your will, my God;
your law is within my heart.
—Psalm 40:8 (NIV)

Nisan 10
Four days before Pesach

Mary blinked against the midmorning sun as she, Lazarus, and Asher left the vineyard to return home for the day's first meal. Martha had gone to the bet to feed and visit the residents, but she would have left some bread and cheese for their morning meal.

Soft voices singing reached her ears as they passed the bet. "What's that?" asked Asher.

"That's my achot, Martha. She's singing with them," Mary said. Martha always somehow managed to get those in the bet to sing with her.

"Is that her voice I hear, louder than the rest?" Asher asked.

Mary nodded. "Pretty, isn't it?"

Asher looked over his shoulder as they passed, his gaze fixed on the building as if he could see inside. "No, it's beautiful."

Mary smiled to herself. Asher said he didn't want to marry again. Martha said she'd never marry due to her age and

Abba's tsara'at. But maybe Adonai had saved them for each other.

Down the road, Gershom strode toward them, likely on his way to the bet to share the day's reading from the scriptures. As his eyes met theirs, he quickened his stride. Just past their house, he stopped short, blocking their way.

Her blood boiled.

"Ignore him, Mary," said Lazarus.

They continued walking, veering toward their courtyard. But before they reached it, he sidled right, again keeping them from moving.

"Gershom, why do you confront us whenever we are near?"

Lazarus approached her, taking her upper arm. "Leave him, Mary. Don't start trouble."

The teacher lifted his chin, looking down his nose at the siblings. "You come from an unclean house."

"My abba no longer lives here, as you well know," said Lazarus. "We are not unclean."

The teacher's jaw tightened. "You come from a house of sin. It's the same thing."

Mary's heart hurt. Why would he pile abuse and scorn upon unrelenting sorrow? "It is *not* the same thing! There is no sin in our house."

"Your abba became impure because of his sin in letting *you* learn the words of Torah." The old man spoke to her as if she were a small child, unable to comprehend the enormity of his words. He shrugged and shook his head, exaggerated sorrow covering his face. "I warned him about this, but his pride would not allow him to hear my words. And look what happened."

Her jaw dropped. "You cannot possibly think the God of everlasting kindness afflicted my abba because I learned Hallel."

"'But your iniquities have made a separation between you and your God, and your sins have hidden His face from you so that He does not hear.' So says the prophet Isaiah."

"And King David said, 'But you, O Lord, are a God merciful and gracious, slow to anger and abounding in steadfast love and faithfulness.'"

She barely suppressed a smirk as Gershom's face turned a delightful shade of crimson.

"Adonai is, of course, forgiving and good, but He is above *all* holy. He cannot make mistakes, and He cannot dwell amid the sin of His people. His judgments are not only absolutely true but must be evident to all, as a warning to those who might follow the path of the wicked."

Mary closed her hands into fists. "My abba is not wicked! How dare you say such a thing?" Her voice was much louder than she had intended. No matter what the priest was saying, she had no right to yell at him.

"I think your behavior at this moment is sufficient cause for me to say that." Condescension dripped from his words. "You should be married, tending to the needs of your husband and a child by now. And your sister… Well, nothing more needs to be said on that topic." Gershom returned to the road, steering as far from them as possible.

She turned to see Asher staring, his mouth open. Humiliation displaced her anger and indignation. She dropped to her knees and sobbed. Months of pretending all was fine, of hosting travelers and continually smiling, of telling them that Abba was not feeling well, had taken their toll and she could no longer hold it in. People far worse than her abba, with sins more heinous and more evident, had lived long and prosperous lives since time began, and had never been afflicted with so much as a spot. And others, like Abba, who were righteous and caring and spent their lives caring for others lived with pain. She knew of several in the bet right now. How could Gershom say only sinners were judged with tsara'at and only the righteous enjoyed a happy life?

"That was unforgivable." Asher shook his head. "I don't know what to say."

"I'm sorry. I shouldn't have done that."

Asher's face paled. "Oh Mary, I didn't mean you." He pointed down the road. "I meant *him*. His behavior was appalling."

Zar knelt beside her and held her head to his chest as she cried. The sound of his heartbeat calmed her, reminding her that life is a precious gift from Adonai. He alone knew why their abba was in the bet and not home with them. He and He alone commanded life and death and health.

Not Gershom.

So why did his comments skewer her like a Roman blade?

In the year since Abba had moved to the bet cholim, Martha had tried to develop new ways to keep her mind from thinking about him.

Or Daniel.

Or the fact that as a divorced woman, she was now almost certain to spend her life alone.

The first months were abysmal.

But each day, each month, each feast was a little easier.

Martha and her siblings had celebrated Shavuot, Sukkot, and Hanukkah without Abba, and the Day of Preparation was looming. Why was this one feast turning out to be so much harder than the others?

Maybe because this was the one they'd last spent with Abba—laughing, celebrating, whole, healthy, joyous. Carrying the lamb on his shoulders, Mary following him.

A tug on her sleeve pulled her back to the task at hand.

"Martha, can I eat one yet?" A young girl stood next to her, a platter of still-steaming raisin cakes in her hands.

In all the ways Martha had tried to dull the pain, this one—teaching young women and girls how to cook—was the only one that had worked. Pity she had not found it earlier.

Selah selected one of the first cakes and touched it to her tongue. She nibbled off a tiny portion, swallowed it, then took a bite. "Mmmm." She closed her eyes and savored the flavors, tasting her own hard work.

Martha glanced at the road. "Your imma is coming."

Selah gobbled down the cake and reached for another, catching Martha's eye for approval.

Martha nodded. She had promised, after all.

Adah approached and knelt beside them. "Selah, did you make these?"

Selah head bobbed like a baby bird's.

"They look wonderful. May I have a taste?"

"Take several. She made them. You might as well enjoy them." She pushed the pottery platter nearer.

"How about just one each?" She gathered five and left the others.

Lazarus would be grateful.

"Thank you for teaching her. I finally got her baby brother to sleep."

"How is your son?"

"Much better, thank you. His fever is gone."

"He should be running around again soon then."

"I didn't think I'd ever miss that." She blinked back a tear. "So thank you again, very much."

"We both had a delightful time, didn't we, Selah?"

The girl nodded. "Yes, Imma." She turned to Martha. "Can I come again?"

"Any time you like. Truly."

"That's very sweet of you to say." Adah placed her hand on Selah's back. "Come, let's go home."

Adah thought Martha was helping her out by taking the girl for the afternoon, but she had no idea how much Martha loved it. Needed it. Looked forward to it happening again.

Because a spark had taken hold that had long been dead.

CHAPTER ELEVEN

*Now while he was in Jerusalem at the Passover Festival,
many people saw the signs he was performing
and believed in his name.*
—John 2:23 (NIV)

Nisan 14

Day of Preparation

It should be easier this time, but the heaviness that engulfed Martha every time she tried to imagine another festival without Abba had not lessened at all.

The sound of men laughing alerted Martha to their guests' arrival but also pricked her heart. How long had it been since Abba's laugh had cheered her?

And how would she explain his absence to the Rabbi and His talmidim?

She stepped outside to see even more men than had come six months ago for Sukkot. She quickly counted—ten, eleven, twelve, thirteen men.

When He'd left last year, He'd mentioned there would likely be a few more when He returned. But this was twice as many, and she'd have nowhere near enough food.

Her stomach clenched. What to do?

She could pick more greens. She could easily make more bread while the men were at the temple. Should they buy another lamb?

Mary stood at the wide doorway to the cooking area, the lamb in tow.

"Mary, get that animal out of here!"

"I am, don't worry!"

Mary was a woman now, but sometimes…

"I just came to see if I could go to the temple with Zar."

Martha pointed beyond Mary to the group nearing the wall. "Do you see them out there?"

Mary grimaced. "Let me guess. You need my help?"

"Desperately. Please?" Martha clasped her hands in front of her chest.

Mary grinned. "Of course, achot."

"Todah rabah. I know you're disappointed."

"I am, but I couldn't leave you here to do all this. Let me tie up the lamb." She disappeared for a moment and returned. "What can I do?"

"Make some dough?"

"Sure." Mary moved to the storage room for flour as Lazarus entered.

He neared the table he'd built for her. It was wide and long enough for her to make enough bread to feed all of Bethany. "Anything I can do to help? Make bread? Mend clothes?" He grinned.

"Hush." She drew her fingers over the curling grain of the dark, smooth acacia wood. "Have I ever thanked you for this table?"

He chuckled. "Many times."

"You could maybe gather some more wild lettuce?"

He glanced at the bowl of washed greens. "You don't have enough?"

"Did you see how many are coming?" She pointed to the courtyard where the group gathered, shoving down fear. "Mary is making dough, and we can make more bread quickly since I won't be using leaven."

"Don't worry," Lazarus said. "You'll have enough. And your bread could feed an entire village. Stop fussing."

"I'm sorry. I just don't want anyone going hungry."

"Don't be sorry. It's endearing."

She raised a brow. "How's that?"

"It shows how much you care." He kissed her cheek.

"If you say so."

"I do."

"You know, I'll get the greens," Martha said. "Could you greet our guests, settle them in the courtyard, and find Kemuel to wash their feet? Mary and I will take care of the food." She glanced at the sun, just past its apex. Shabbat did not begin until sundown, giving her plenty of time to prepare enough food and get it to Bethphage. "When will you go to the temple?"

He shrugged. "I thought I would let them decide. If they wish to rest, we'll go last." He turned to go.

"Wait." She grasped his bicep. "I think we'll need another lamb. We didn't plan for this many. We'll be well over ten people."

He studied the group outside for a moment. "I think you're right. I'll buy another when we get there." He stepped outside and approached the visitors, then led them to the long table in the courtyard.

"Mary, I'll be right back," she called. She left to go outside to the town's garden to gather greens.

Yeshua stepped into her path. "Martha, todah for hosting us once again." Yeshua smiled, His eyes lighting up His face.

"You're very welcome. It's what we do in Bethany."

"I hope the extra guests won't cause you too much trouble."

She shook her head. "Of course not. It's no problem at all."

"I'm sure it's at least a bit of an inconvenience." He fixed her with a stare. "Where is Simon? I want to thank him as well."

"He's...around somewhere."

Yeshua said nothing but continued to hold her gaze gently.

"All right. We'll return later." He smiled and returned to the group.

Nisan 21
Last day of the Feast of Unleavened Bread

Martha jumped as Lazarus burst into the house.

"Martha, you should have seen it!" Zar bounced around the room, hands in the air, his face radiating joy. "It was... amazing! Astonishing! It...it..." His mouth moved, but no sounds came out, as if he were searching for words that didn't exist. "It was the most incredible thing I've ever seen. That *anyone* has ever seen!" He laughed as he continued hopping around like a sparrow searching for seeds.

"Zar!" She grabbed his arm and tugged him closer. "Be still. Now, what are you talking about? And where are the others?"

"They're on the way. I couldn't wait to tell, so I ran ahead."

Mary came in, her face a mirror of Zar's. "You won't believe it!"

Martha's frustration was growing, and if they continued like this, she would no longer be able to hide it.

"You know that man at the pool of Bethesda?" Lazarus pointed west toward Jerusalem. "The one who can't walk?"

"He's been there for years, yes?" said Martha.

"Yeshua healed him!" He laughed again. "Do you understand me?" He grasped Martha's upper arms and brought his face nearer. "He...healed...him."

"Who healed him?"

"The Rabbi! Yeshua," he said.

"Completely?" asked Martha. That was hard—impossible—to believe.

"Yes! The man stood up, picked up the mat he'd been lying on for who knows how many years—"

"Thirty-eight years!" Mary bounced on her heels.

"—for thirty-eight years and *walked away*," Lazarus said.

Martha raised a brow. "Just like that?"

"Just like that. The Pharisees were not happy about it, let me tell you."

"Why not?"

"It's Shabbat." He laughed.

"And..." What did that have to do with it?

"They told the man he couldn't carry his mat!" Zar chuckled like a child who had played a great joke. "His mat!"

"They looked for Yeshua, but He'd already gone." Mary shrugged then sucked in a sharp breath, as if an idea had just come to her. She grabbed his arm. "If He healed that man, why couldn't He heal *Abba*?"

"Oh, Mary, don't be silly!" Martha turned back to her table.

Mary rushed to her and spun her around. "Think about it. The man hasn't walked or even stood in almost forty years. Abba just has problems with his skin. It has to be easier than what He did today!"

Maybe, but still… "We can't just ask Him to do that!"

"Why not?" asked Mary.

Martha sputtered. "He's our guest, for one thing."

"He's a *healer*. This isn't the first time He's done this," Lazarus added.

"Says who?" Martha wanted proof before embarrassing them all by asking Yeshua to do what couldn't be done.

"His talmidim," Lazarus said. "He's healed at least two more who couldn't walk. And John said He healed Simon's wife's imma. She was so ill she was unable to get out of bed. But He told her to rise, and she did!"

"And then she fed them—all thirteen!" Mary said. "And He's given blind men back their sight, and made wine from water—"

"Are you sure about all this?" It was hard—too hard—to believe there was a chance Abba could once again celebrate Pesach with them. To be filled with breathtaking hope, only to lose it again? If Abba was left as he was before, she would be crushed beyond repair.

"We have to ask Him, achot," Mary said.

"I don't know." She pondered the idea, but the risk was too great. "I can't. I just can't, Mary."

Mary turned to her brother. "What do you say, Zar?"

"All right, let's be logical about it," he said. "If you ask Him and He can't or won't, what happens?"

"Other than being humiliated? Nothing, I guess," Martha said.

"Right. We're no worse off. But if you *don't* ask Him, and you find out later *He could have healed him*, what will you think?"

Her head spun. "I'm sorry. I still don't know."

Mary folded her hands into fists at her chest, an angry frown dominating her face. "Oh, Martha!" Her face softened, and her hands opened. "Then I'll do it." She turned and marched toward the door.

Martha reached for her knife once again but saw Mary return out of the corner of her vision. She smirked. "Change your mind?"

Mary stepped aside, and Yeshua entered. "I want you to tell me where your abba is. We started a conversation last year that I'd like to finish."

Did He know? The sly smile on His face seemed to indicate He desired more than a conversation. But maybe it was just her guilt at having lied to her guest.

"He's in the bet cholim." Mary's eyes widened, and she slapped her hand over her mouth, as if the words had escaped of their own accord.

Oh, Mary… Martha squeezed her eyes shut and groaned. Did she have to blurt out every single thought?

His smile brightened. "We should go to him then. Night isn't far away." Yeshua turned and strode out of the house.

Martha looked at her sister. "Where's He going?"

Mary beamed. "The bet, I guess." She giggled and hurried after Him.

Martha wavered. Did she stay here, safe, and miss what could very likely be the most amazing day of her life? Or did she follow and risk utter devastation? And what did night have to do with anything?

She paced to the other end of the room and back, then hurried out the door.

Yeshua and His talmidim, along with Zar, were halfway to the bet by the time she reached the courtyard gate. She raced to catch up, part of her regretting it already, the other part desperately grasping at any chance to have Abba home and whole.

When she reached the bet, the talmidim crowded the entrance, but she did not come this far to stare at the backs of men. She stretched to see over their shoulders and between their heads.

Zar tapped one on the shoulder. "Excuse me."

James turned then gently pushed aside the others, creating a pathway for them to reach the front.

Zar led the way, and Martha crept forward. Her chest felt like stone. Hope struggled to rise within her heart, but fear weighed it down.

Yeshua waited patiently by the door.

"What's going on?" she asked James.

"John went in to get your abba. And anyone else who wants to be healed."

The door opened. John held it as Abba exited, the narrow path widening as he walked past the talmidim, his face etched with pain and shame.

"No one else?" asked Yeshua.

John shrugged. "They just laughed."

"Shalom, Simon. I've missed you." Yeshua placed His hand over Abba's, but he pulled it back, his shoulders hunched as if trying to hide his face.

"Simon, would you like to be made whole?"

Abba's shoulders shook gently, and he allowed an almost imperceptible nod.

"Remove your cloak."

Abba frowned as if he'd rather do almost anything else, but slowly extended his arm. Tears snaked down his cheeks, and blisters and red spots dotted his skin like rotted olives on the ground after harvest. He pulled his arm back and through the sleeve, and when he removed it, his skin was as clear as a baby's.

Beside her, Mary squealed. Martha wrapped her arms around Mary's waist. Was she really seeing what she didn't dare to hope for?

Mary's hand grasped her arm and squeezed, her nails digging into Martha's skin, but the pain only served to remind her this wasn't a dream.

Abba let his cloak slip from the other arm and onto the floor.

The talmidim chuckled and whispered among themselves. He lifted one foot, a perfect leg showing. Then the other.

Zar rushed forward, laughing. "Abba!"

Abba raised his other leg. "Look!" His face wavered between laughter and tears. "Have you ever seen such a thing?"

Beside her, James chuckled. "Several times."

She turned to him. "Seriously?"

He nodded. "Yes."

"He's done this before?"

"Yes," he repeated and gestured to Abba. "Go to him."

"Will he stay this way?"

"Yes. He's completely cleansed."

She could no longer hold back the tears. She rushed to embrace him. "Abba!" Tears choked her words.

He wrapped his arms around her. "I'm here, motek. I'm here. And I'm not leaving again."

She sobbed into his tunic. "I'm so sorry. I didn't believe." She turned to Yeshua. "I'm sorry."

He laughed. "Take your abba to the river to wash, then take him to the priest to be pronounced clean. And hurry. Night is near."

So that's what He meant by night is near. He'd known what would happen from the moment Mary told Him where Abba was.

Maybe even before that.

CHAPTER TWELVE

The person to be cleansed must wash their clothes, shave off all their hair and bathe with water; then they will be ceremonially clean. After this they may come into the camp, but they must stay outside their tent for seven days.
—Leviticus 14:8 (NIV)

"I'll find Gershom. You bring Abba."

Mary bolted from the bet, past the house, past the well, chuckling at the absurdity of her racing toward Gershom instead of away from him.

She jumped the wall, ran to the door of his small home, and pounded her fist against the wood.

"Gershom!"

No answer. She banged again, with more force. "Gershom!"

Inside, shuffling footsteps made their way to the door. The handle jigged. The door opened. He glanced up and down at her.

What a mess she must be! Her headscarf hung off her elbows, the hem of her tunic was covered in dust, and her sash rested low on her hips. She covered her hair and tightened her sash.

"Yes?" He sneered.

"You have to see. Abba is healed!"

He scoffed. "No one since Naaman the Assyrian has ever been cleansed of tsara'at."

"My abba has. And we need *you* to pronounce him clean."

He glanced at the sun hovering over the mount. "Perhaps tomorrow. It is Shabbat."

She recoiled at his scowl. "No!"

His eyes widened. "Do not raise your voice to me. Ever."

She dropped to her knees. "I'm sorry, adon. But please, whatever you think of me, of my abba, please have mercy and do what only you can do." Her throat burned with unshed tears as she contemplated the damage her anger may have done. Then, another thought. She rose, smoothed her tunic, adjusted her scarf.

"No matter. We'll go to the temple then. Find a priest there." She turned to go.

It took only a few steps before Gershom realized the consequences of such an action. He would surely be called to account for his refusal to attend to his priestly duties.

"All right. But bring him *here*."

She turned and smiled as sweetly as she could. "Todah. He is already on his way." She peered down the road and saw Lazarus and Abba near the well. "In fact, he is almost here."

Tears formed again—of joy, not sorrow—as she watched Abba stroll down the road, next to Zar. Zar was Abba's perfect match. They shared the same build, the same height, they even walked in perfect harmony. Abba seemed even younger than he had been the day he left for the bet.

They entered the courtyard, but before they came within ten paces, Gershom extended his hand, palm out. "No closer!"

Mary bit her tongue. It would do no good to remind him that Abba was clean.

Then again, he wasn't legally clean until Gershom said he was.

"Please remove your cloak."

Abba complied.

Gershom instructed him to push up his sleeves, lift the hem of his tunic, and finally remove the garment. Abba obeyed every command without hesitation, each move revealing more and more perfect skin. Gershom's voice softened as he continued. "Please come inside and we'll finish the inspection."

Mary wanted to jump and shout. Abba was moments away from being restored to the community, from returning to his family's arms.

Lazarus moved to stand next to her. "I'm still not sure I believe it. I mean, I saw what He did at the pool, but when it's someone you know, someone you love…"

"I know. I keep thinking I'll wake up from a dream and none of it will be true."

He laughed softly. "If Gershom pronounces him clean, you'll know it's true. You'd never dream that, because you'd never imagine it."

Abba stepped outside, wearing a clean linen tunic.

Gershom nodded. "A clean man should have clean clothes."

Did Gershom just give away an expensive tunic? To Abba?

"T-todah. Todah rabah." Mary stammered.

"That's it? He can go home with us?" asked Zar.

"Not quite."

Her heart dropped to her sandals. What did that mean? What now? Was he not truly clean?

"He is clean, but there is a ritual we must first perform. After that he must wash himself, his clothes, and shave all his hair. Then he must wait seven days before he can enter the temple—or even Jerusalem—and during this seven days he must not enter his house. On the eighth day, he must go shave and wash again, go to the temple, be inspected once again, and make an offering. Only after that may he be completely restored to his family, this village, and be able to worship in the temple of the Most High God."

"We will do all that is required." Lazarus said.

Gershom pursed his lips. "You should know I'm not happy about this. This doesn't happen. I'm not at all sure there isn't some sort of witchcraft involved here, and you can be sure I will do all in my power to find out. Adonai cannot be mocked."

He waited for Abba to precede him inside, and closed the door.

Zar huffed. "Let him search all he wants. This isn't witchcraft. And I think he knows that."

Mary fought the disappointment that threatened to strangle her joy. Gershom had tried to spoil their happiness, as always. What did he have against them?

But it was only seven days. A small price to pay to have her abba back.

Nisan 28

If they had wings, they could fly to the temple.

"Come on, Abba!" Mary grabbed his hand and pulled him up the rough path to the top of the mount. "The light will be gone if you do not hurry!"

"I may be cleansed, but I am still an old man, motek. The light will last. And if it doesn't, we'll return tomorrow. It's been a year. Waiting one more day to be declared clean, to go to temple and hear the words of Adonai sung by the choir, will be a small price."

Mary slowed to match his pace. "You really missed that, didn't you?"

A smile spread slowly across his face. "I did. Gershom came the first day of each week to read the words to us, as long as we huddled in one corner of the courtyard and he in the opposite, and as long as the wind wasn't blowing to him. But it's not the same as hearing the Levites lift their voices to God. And on Pesach, when there are a hundred voices, oh, the glory!" His eyes misted over. "Yes, motek, I missed it."

A thought struck her, one that was so obvious but had been swept aside in the chaos and excitement. "Abba, you will be clean for Shavuot! You will be able to hear the Hallel and take the offering yourself to the priests!"

"I know, my daughter. I'm not sure my heart can hold any more joy!"

The way down was much easier on Abba's legs, and they reached the temple gate quickly. Mary left Abba at the arch and ran up the steps. She entered the Court of the Gentiles and ran to the Court of Women and to the first priest she saw. "I need a priest! My abba has been cleansed of tsara'at, and he needs to be inspected."

The man looked down his nose at her. "Has he been to his local priest?"

"We're from Bethany, and yes, we've seen the priest. He said to come to the temple on the eighth day. But we can't come in yet, as he hasn't been inspected. So I need someone to come out to the gate with me."

"I'm sorry. I can't do that. Let me see who I can find." He wandered away, seemingly not in any hurry to help her.

Another talk with another priest yielded the same result. How much longer would this take? Abba might be fine with waiting, but she wasn't. One more day for no reason other than a priest couldn't be bothered? She stood with her arms crossed, toe tapping.

A Pharisee exited the chamber of the Sanhedrin. He looked familiar, but where had she seen him?

She scanned the court. Would either of them return?

"Mary?" A gentle voice drew her attention.

"Yes?"

"It's Nicodemus. I celebrated Pesach with you last year. Do you remember?"

Ah, yes. "You came back later."

"I did." He chuckled lightly. "You look troubled."

She eyed him. How much did she tell him? "My abba was healed of tsara'at. We need a priest to come to the gate to check him, but no one seems interested."

"Healed of tsara'at? How did that happen?"

"The Rabbi. Yeshua."

"Let me find someone for you." He hurried off.

Another holy man not interested in helping anyone.

She resumed her search.

Nicodemus returned in only a moment, a young priest behind him. "This man will go with you. I'm not a priest, or I would do it myself."

Ah. That explained it. Nicodemus had done what he said, which was more than the other two.

The young man's face radiated anticipation. "He's at the gate?"

She nodded. "Yes, just outside the arch."

Nicodemus touched the priest's forearm and then pointed to a room built into the wall next to the entrance to the women's court. "Bring him back here when you're done, I'll have someone ready the chamber of lepers."

The chamber of lepers? What was that?

He nodded and raced to the entrance to the underground stairs.

Nicodemus turned to her. "Mary, he has to thoroughly inspect him, so this might take a while. May I offer you a cup of wine?"

"Yes, todah." Why was he being so nice to her?

"Come with me." He led her to the door he'd pointed out to the priest and opened it.

She hesitated. "Am I allowed in here?"

He grinned. "There hasn't been a leper cleansed in Israel in what? Nine centuries? I think I'll be excused for allowing his daughter to wait in here." He crossed to the other side of the room and whispered to a Levite, who nodded and hurried away.

She followed him into the room and suppressed a gasp. Richly dyed fabric panels hung from ceiling to floor, breaking up the long walls of limestone polished to a marble-like shine. A bank of windows looked east toward the Mount of Olives. Mosaic tiles of various colors decorated the floors. A row of about twenty high-backed chairs sat in a semicircle, facing another which sat at the head. Behind that chair, a long marble table spanned the width of the room. "What is this place?"

He took a seat and patted the one beside him, then gestured to another Levite, who poured two glasses of wine. "This is one of the lower Sanhedrin chambers. There is another on the eastern wall. These are only about one-third the size of the great Sanhedrin. Cases are sent here from the cities, and if they can't be settled or decided here, they go to the great Sanhedrin in the priests' court."

She accepted the gold cup and sat.

"Are you hungry? There's always something here to eat."

She placed her hand on her somersaulting belly and shook her head.

She studied his weathered face. He seemed perfectly at peace, without a shred of concern that Abba might not be declared cleansed. True, Abba was only a friend and not family, but still, his confidence almost seemed out of place. "You speak as though he has already been healed."

"Has he not? If he had not remained clean for seven days, you wouldn't be here. You only need a pronouncement. The deed is done, yes?"

True, but…

The door slammed open, revealing the young priest and Abba, huge smiles on both faces.

Mary jumped up, but Nicodemus grabbed her hand, pulling her back to her seat. "Not yet," he said gently. "Let him see the priest first and immerse."

"Almost, motek. I need only to be seen by another, and I will be clean."

The joy on his face made her heart leap and her eyes fill with tears. "I'm so happy, Abba."

Nicodemus rose. "Uriel is in the chamber." He pointed to the room on the northeast side of the temple reserved for those cleansed of tsara'at, where a *mikveh* awaited.

"Todah. We'll be back." The priest led Abba away.

Nicodemus sat beside her again.

"Now what are they doing?"

"There is a ritual, and then he will immerse once again. Then he goes home with you." He smiled.

To hear those words spoken with such authority—she'd not realized how much she'd been afraid it might never happen.

"Have you touched him?"

"Of course." What a ridiculous question. How could they not, after such a wonder occurred before their eyes?

"You'll have to immerse as well then."

"That's life in Bethany."

He grinned. "I suppose that's true."

"I never realized how much he missed coming to the temple."

"Yes. Every time I see someone made whole, restored to the community, I see anew how much it means."

She would never take it for granted again.

CHAPTER THIRTEEN

Praise the LORD, my soul;
all my inmost being, praise his holy name.
Praise the LORD, my soul,
and forget not all his benefits —
who forgives all your sins
and heals all your diseases,
who redeems your life from the pit
and crowns you with love and compassion.
—Psalm 103:1–4 (NIV)

"Did you get enough?" Martha reached for the dried fish Lazarus had gone to the city to purchase. The seven-day waiting period had passed, and Abba had left to see the priest for a final pronouncement.

"Twelve." He plopped a net bag full of dried fish on her table. "That's all they had."

"I don't think food will be lacking." She chuckled.

"How long ago did he leave?"

"Not long." She opened the bag and dumped the fish out, then grabbed a knife. "I'd have thought he'd be more excited about it, but he didn't seem to be in any hurry." She sliced one into chunks and dropped them into a bowl of fresh water.

"Could just be he has no worry about what will happen."

"I suppose. Now, we need all the cushions and stools you can find moved into the courtyard. There are tables out there already from some of the other families. We're all going to feast together at this end of the village."

Martha sliced the carrots into perfect coins, then scooped them into a wide, low-rimmed pan with a layer of sizzling olive oil. After several minutes, she sprinkled generous doses of ground cumin and salt over the discs, then dipped a large spoon into a wide-mouthed jar of date honey and drizzled the deep walnut-colored liquid in zigzags onto the carrots. She carried it to one of the three ovens at the edge of the courtyard.

A covered round pot sat on the next oven, and she lifted the lid. A sweet steam escaped, smelling of watered wine and onions. She waved away the mist and dropped half of the pieces of sea bream into the fragrant liquid. The rest went into another pot on the third oven. The savory fish wouldn't take long.

She surveyed the area. Tables, surrounded by colorful cushions, had been set up in and around their courtyard, and more cushions and mats dotted whatever empty space of ground remained. Although it had been only six days since a full week of hosting, every family had spent the day cooking and delivering food and furniture to Martha's house, awaiting the feast of joy that would begin as soon as Abba returned.

But where was he? She couldn't wait any longer.

She trudged up the road to the top of the mount to the Jericho road. From here she could see the length of the path down the mountain all the way to almost the eastern gate, which was hidden by trees. She sat on a low rock, her sash in her hands, bunching it into a ball, then smoothing it against her thigh, then bunching it again. Where was he? How long could this take?

Finally she saw them, strolling along as if there were no hurry.

Then again, he had no idea a village-wide celebration awaited, and Mary had been instructed not to let him find out. As they neared the ridge, she jumped up, searching his face. Was he happy?

Mary had her arm around his waist, and they laughed and talked as they sauntered up the path.

She hurried headlong down the path, her feet tumbling faster than was safe. But nothing else mattered other than reaching him. "Abba!"

He threw his arms around her, and she wrapped hers around his neck. Holding him so closely was like breathing in air after holding her breath. She grabbed his tunic and held on, her tears wetting the fabric. "I missed you so."

"I missed you too, motek. All of you." His voice broke. "Glory to Adonai!"

She pulled back and stroked his freshly shaved face. A spot of blood from the cleansing ceremony remained on his left ear. "He has given you back to us. Completely back." As hard as the last seven days were, with him whole and healed but still not home, it was now all worth it.

"He has indeed."

She slipped her arm through his and they descended to the village. As it came into view, he stopped and stared. Blankets, cushions, low tables, and stools filled the entire eastern half of the village from the well to their home. Martha's acacia table occupied the very center, piled high with pottery plates, amphorae, and bowls.

"What is happening?"

"We're celebrating! The entire village has suffered with us for the last year, and now they want to thank Adonai with us. Come on!"

She pulled him with her toward the feast.

Abba took a deep breath and marched toward the house. His jaw dropped. "You killed a sheep?"

"Of course we did. It was Yoash's idea, actually. It was his sheep, and he insisted."

"But, really, this isn't necessary."

"Abba, we have you back! As if from the dead!" Mary laughed. "We have every reason to celebrate, and that is exactly what we are going to do. The women have been cooking since you left. Martha made your favorite bread, and we have a table full of raisins and figs. The entire village is praising Adonai, and they haven't stopped bringing food."

"But so much fuss…"

"It's not just for you. Yeshua and His men are here as well. It's to thank Him, to honor Him. Don't you think He is worthy of it?"

Relief covered his face. "Of course I do. I believe He has been sent by Adonai. Of that, there can be no question. In fact, He may be the promised Redeemer, the *Mashiach* we have all been waiting for."

Mary neared Kemuel with a pitcher of water, a wide bowl, and a clean cloth. "Here you go. Start with the Rabbi, and go around the table."

"No." Abba neared them and held out his hands for the water. "I'll do it."

Mary shoved the bowl toward Kemuel. "But Abba! You can't! You are the host. Kemuel always does this for us."

"I had nothing. I was less than a servant." His voice soft, Abba pointed toward Yeshua at the end of the table. "This Man has made me clean. He has restored me to my family, to this village, and made it possible for me to worship once again in the temple. He has given me *my life back*. I owe Him everything."

Abba gently took the bowl from the confused boy. "There is little I have to give Him, but I can provide Him this simple comfort." He held the bowl up. "*This* I can do. Allow me, please, to serve Him in this way."

Mary nodded and stepped back.

"Todah, motek. You might fill another. We have many guests." He moved to the head of the table, where Yeshua reclined on a cushion, His feet extending beyond Him on a woven rug.

Abba knelt at His feet and removed His sandals.

Most people ignored the one who washed their feet. It was something even a half-decent host did for any guest, and it was so common as to be not worthy of mention.

But Yeshua stopped His conversation with those near Him, and focused all His attention on Abba, a soft smile gracing His face.

Abba slipped the bowl under Yeshua's bare foot and poured a little water over it, rubbing his hand along the top, then the sole. Dust fell away, leaving clean skin. He pulled the towel from his shoulder and dried the foot before doing the same to the other one.

Yeshua laid His hand gently on Abba's head. "Todah, Simon."

Abba looked up, his eyes moist. "Todah rabah." His voice cracked, "It's not enough. I—I don't know what to say."

"It *is* enough."

Abba grasped His wrist and kissed Yeshua's palm, and then silently moved on to Simon bar Jonah.

Mary had spent her life in Bethany serving others. It had become second nature. Yet in all that time, her service had never really cost her anything. She considered it a privilege, and it was her choice as to what to do and when to do it. Abba and her siblings had spoiled her in that way. She'd never had to humble herself as Abba had just done.

How selfish she'd been! Was it even an act of service if it didn't cost anything?

Nisan 29

Martha blinked her eyes in the dusky rose light of dawn. She looked at Mary, peacefully asleep beside her. How could she still be sleeping? Martha had tossed and turned all night, trying to comprehend exactly what had happened.

She didn't understand, but still, she felt that joy had so filled her body it threatened to explode. The last eight days had been beyond unbelievable. But now, Abba was whole! He was part of their family again, part of the village. Not since Naaman, hundreds of years ago, had anyone been cleansed of leprosy, and yet Yeshua chose to make Abba clean.

And the celebration! Everyone—except Gershom—had taken part, contributed, praised Adonai. Even Nicodemus had come from the city.

But the Rabbi and His students would be eager to leave, having spent an extra two days here to celebrate with them. She sat up, her feet on the floor. "I offer thanks to You, living and eternal King, for You have mercifully restored my soul within me. Great is Your faithfulness."

She slipped into her sandals and placed her scarf over her hair. She pulled the door open quietly and stepped into the common room. Pale pink light flooded the room, and Martha grabbed the water jar. She headed out of the house only to see Abba up, dressed and in the courtyard.

"Abba! What are you doing up so early? You should rest a while longer."

He laughed. "I've been *resting* for a year. It is so good to be dressed in clean, untorn clothes again. I can't wait to get back to work." He pointed to the jug she carried. "Going to the well?"

She nodded. "I'll be right back."

"Wait. I'll go with you." He strode past her to the table and grabbed two empty jars. "May as well top off the cistern."

"You're going to the well?"

"I know. Not a man's job. But that's never really stopped us in Bethany, yes?" He grinned, walking beside her with a jar under each arm. "Tell me about the young man at dinner. I didn't have a chance to speak with him much."

"He's from Gennesaret. Daniel's cousin, though he's much nicer than Daniel. Or Enoch. Actually, it's hard to believe they're related at all."

"And why did he come?"

"He lost his wife a few years ago. He moved down here because the memories of her were too great. I guess he bought the house from Daniel."

"And you know all this how?"

She laughed. "Mary kind of ambushed him the day he moved in. He'd intended to work as a carpenter at the temple, but she convinced him to help in the vineyard. He's been a great deal of help. I think he might be a good husband for Mary."

"For Mary? Why not you?"

"No." The word came out harsher than she intended. "I won't do that again. My happiness will come from helping others."

"But surely—"

Gershom strode toward them. "I cannot believe you and your family had the audacity to show off your 'healing' with such a public display yesterday. And to involve the whole village? That was disgraceful."

Abba stepped back as Gershom neared even closer.

"Why shouldn't I thank Adonai for His goodness?"

"Did it have to be done here?"

"This is my home. As it was my abba's, and his abba's before that."

"I doubt they were giving shelter to a false prophet." Gershom stopped his advance, folding his arms over his chest.

"A false prophet? To whom are you referring?"

"That Nazarene, Yeshua."

"He is no false prophet, I assure you." Abba stepped to the well and lowered the water bag.

"This cannot continue. You will be stopped, one way or another." Gershom spun on his heel and headed back toward his house.

Martha shivered. "What do you think he'll do?"

"What can he do?" Abba poured the water from the bag into the jar.

"Tell the Sanhedrin?"

Abba chuckled. "And what can they do?" He lowered the bag once again and turned to face her. "Do you believe He is sent by Adonai?"

She nodded. "I do."

"Then what can they do to Him?" He returned to filling the jars.

Martha took the one filled jar and turned for home. He had a point. What could any man do to God's anointed?

But it wasn't what they could do to Yeshua that worried her.

It was what they could do her. To her family. If Abba worried Gershom that much, would the Sanhedrin respond any better?

CHAPTER FOURTEEN

Count off fifty days up to the day after the seventh Sabbath, and then present an offering of new grain to the LORD.
—Leviticus 23:16 (NIV)

Sivan 5
Morning before Shavuot, the Feast of Weeks

Midday sun wended its way through the bright red-orange flowers of the pomegranate tree that dominated the courtyard. The hottest part of the year had not yet come to Judea, but Sivan was hot enough. The absence of both wind and rain did not help.

Mary wove the pliable willow branch in and around the ribs of the basket. Each row she crafted a little wider than the one before, fashioning a low, wide container.

She held it away from her, at eye level, and studied her work. It had to be perfect. When she finished, she and Martha would fill it with the family's harvest offering—two loaves of the finest wheat bread. Tomorrow morning Lazarus and Abba would carry it to the temple. They would hand it to the priests, but it was an offering to Adonai, and she refused to send a basket with a single imperfection.

This was the first year she'd made the Shavuot basket. She'd practiced since last year's feast, and already this time she'd ripped apart her work and started again at least six times. Martha had teased her, consoled her, and helped her, reminding her perfection wasn't necessary, only a willing heart. But that was easy for her to say, since her part in the offering would be two perfect loaves made from fine wheat. Martha never did anything that wasn't flawless.

She continued weaving the stripped branches, making sure each row was straight.

Her stomach rumbled, and she glanced up at the sun. No wonder. It was halfway to the crest of the Mount of Olives. She'd begun working on the basket as soon as she arose, not stopping for the morning meal.

Sitting hunched over had tightened her muscles, so she stood and stretched her arms over her head, clasping them together and arching her back. She tipped her head from one side to the other before she wandered toward the house.

Martha stopped in midstir and remained silent. Why?

Then Mary remembered how she'd barked at her achot for trying to help after the last time Mary had pulled apart her work. She neared her, wincing. "I'm sorry. Forgive me?"

Martha pulled her close. "Nothing to forgive, motek." She released Mary and reached for a raisin cake. "Hungry? I have a few left from this morning."

Mary grinned and accepted the treat. She bit off half of it. "I'm almost done, I think." She talked around a mouthful of food. "Want to check it?"

"I don't need to check it. I'm sure it's wonderful. It's been wonderful every time you've thought it wasn't and began again." She chuckled.

"All right then, would you like to *see* it?"

"Of course."

Mary stuffed the other half of the cake into her mouth as she returned to the tree. Wrapping her hand around the loose end of the basket to keep it from unraveling, she took it back inside and showed it to Martha. "It should take only a few more rows to finish."

Martha ran her fingers up and down the sides, peeked at the bottom, and nodded. "It's perfect. Todah for making it. Let me know when you're done, and I'll fill it."

"I can do that. I'd like to finish it."

"Making the bread too?" Martha raised a brow, but there was no scorn, no derision, only curiosity.

Mary laughed. "No, that offering's still yours. I don't think Adonai would be happy with my bread."

"Of course He would, Mary. I keep telling you, it's your heart that matters."

Mary grabbed another cake and returned to the tree. The midday sun now shone in her eyes, and she moved the mat to the other side to escape its glare before she finished the basket and inspected it once again. The basket was without a single flaw.

But the offering felt hollow.

Why?

She searched her mind. What was missing?

Only your heart matters to Adonai.

Martha was right.

Mary had made sure the tangible expression of her thankfulness was the best she could make it.

But she'd ignored her heart.

Then celebrate the Festival of Weeks to the Lord your God by giving a freewill offering in proportion to the blessings the Lord your God has given you. And rejoice before the Lord your God.

Celebrate. Blessings. Rejoice.

Had there been even a hint of rejoicing in her heart?

She had to admit there hadn't. Only striving, earning, comparing.

Adonai, forgive me. Take this offering as a sign of my gratitude for the harvest You have given us, have given me. And keep my heart full of thanks.

Once again, Martha was right. Except this time, that thought brought Mary joy instead of jealousy and resentment. Joy that in the loss of their imma, Adonai had given her such a wise and loving achot, who had never once complained about giving up her chance at marriage so she could take care of Mary, who worked hard to make Mary's life as enjoyable as possible.

A sister who could teach Mary so much more, if only she would slow down for a moment and learn. Martha didn't know the Scriptures by heart the way Mary did, but maybe she practiced what she did know much more.

Mary had a lot to learn.

Martha looked up from her table as Asher knocked on the doorframe. He'd been helping in the vineyard since he'd moved to Bethany and had also helped with the Pesach meal as well the Abba's celebration. But what did he want with her?

"Mary sent me to see if you need anything done for tonight." One side of his mouth rose in a crooked grin.

"Oh, um, let me see." She scanned the common room. "You can bring all the cushions from the dining area to the outside table."

"All right." He disappeared then reappeared with a stack of cushions under each arm.

Martha returned to cutting up carrots and onions for the meal as he continued bringing out the pillows.

When he had brought them all from the house, he arranged them around the long, low table before he returned to Martha. "How many are you expecting?"

She shrugged. "It's hard to tell. Not as many as Pesach, but we'll have no problem getting rid of all this food."

"Anything else?"

"Those amphorae of olives and wine can go under the tree." He grabbed the pottery containers from their spots near the shelves and lugged them outside, setting the pointed ends of the pottery containers in the holes dug under the tree for them.

"Done. Next?"

"That's all I can think of for now."

He leaned a hip against the table. "Your sister certainly speaks her mind, doesn't she?"

"She does." She set aside the bowl of carrots and reached for a bulb of garlic. "She'll have to learn to stop that."

"She will? Why?" He reached for a carrot disk and popped it in his mouth.

She narrowed her eyes at his familiarity but said nothing. "Men generally don't like it."

He grinned. "I find it amusing."

She threw him a sideways glance. "You'd be the only one."

"It can't be all that bad."

Martha paused her slicing. "I adore my sister, but she's... she's always been babied. Mostly by me."

"It's not wrong to spoil your little sister a bit."

"She was so young when our imma died. It was a rough illness and a prolonged death. Then suddenly, Imma was gone. She didn't really understand what had happened."

"You raised her?"

"I tried. I'm not sure I did a very good job."

"It looks to me as though you did."

"I tried to make everything as easy as possible for her. I never made her learn to cook. She just refused. We both used to cook with Imma, and when she was gone, Mary could hardly stand to eat, let alone cook. Me, on the other hand, I loved it. It was like a part of her was still with me."

"You must have learned well. Your food is delicious."

Heat flooded her face, and she began chopping again. He should be complimenting Mary, not her.

"Anyway, I promise she will learn to cook before she marries." No need scaring him off.

He laughed. "If you say so."

"She doesn't mean to be, but she can be difficult."

"How so?" He snagged another piece of carrot.

"Mary wants nothing more than to study the Torah."

"Ah. And the rabbi won't let her."

"And it kills her." Unbidden memories fought their way to the front of her thoughts. "She didn't want to be here—none of us did, at the end—so she spent a lot of time at the house of the book, and I think that's when she found her love of study. She was allowed to go to until she was ten years old. She was the only girl, of course."

"That's not surprising. And she went later than many schools will allow."

"Yes, and then that priest moved away. The new teacher, Gershom, won't let her join them. She's been caught more than once listening at the wall."

He raised a brow. "Really? She wants to learn that badly?"

Did he disapprove? Perhaps she shouldn't have mentioned it. But he'd find out eventually, so it was probably best he knew sooner. "She does. Lazarus has been trying to help her, but she already knows more than he can remember. He was never very good at memorizing anything."

"I can help her, if you'll let me."

She jerked her head up to face him. Was he serious, or teasing her? Was this just a way to spend time with Mary? "Are you a teacher?"

"No, but my abba was. He practiced on me. At any rate, I have a good memory, and I'd be happy to share whatever I know with her. If it's all right with you, and your abba."

His offer seemed genuine. "I'll ask him, if you like."

"Let me know. We can start after Shavuot." He strolled out of the house.

He would be perfect for Mary.

CHAPTER FIFTEEN

The L<small>ORD</small> is my strength and my shield;
my heart trusts in him, and he helps me.
My heart leaps for joy,
and with my song I praise him.
—Psalm 28:7 (NIV)

Martha moved to the ovens under the pomegranate tree and checked on the newest pot of stew. It had to be almost completely cooked before sundown, as Shavuot was a Shabbat no matter which day of the week it fell on. She smashed a lentil against the side—nice and soft. She gave it a good stir and breathed in the comforting scent of garlic, onion, and cumin, the scent of home and family.

All day, travelers had stopped just long enough to refill wineskins and perhaps enjoy a bite to eat before making their way to Jerusalem. As the sun slipped toward the west, weary travelers poured into Bethany from all over eastern Judea and Galilee, uncomfortably aware that if they didn't make it at least to Bethany by sundown, they'd at best be required to spend the night on the road, and the highway from Jericho was always a risky proposition, especially after dark. At worst they'd be too far to reach the temple tomorrow in a Shabbat's day journey and miss Shavuot altogether.

As soft lavender light replaced bright sunshine, travelers grabbed rounds of hot bread and cups of stew. The moment one finished, another took his place, and if the table was full, they ate standing. Every house in Bethany had prepared as many large pots of lentil stew as they had ovens. Men—and boys—had claimed every cubit of courtyard and open space in Bethany, and sleeping mats began to dot the mount like spring flowers.

"Smells delicious." Martha turned to see Asher standing behind her, peering over her shoulder.

She moved three steps away from him. "The sun is nearly down, and everyone will find a place to sleep. Then we'll eat."

"I can't wait." He flashed his by-now familiar crooked grin. "Should we continue to keep the roof spaces for the Rabbi, or should I begin directing guests there?"

Martha glanced down the road. Yeshua had said He'd return for the Feast of Weeks, but perhaps He'd been detained in Galilee.

"Wait a bit longer. If He doesn't arrive soon, we'll send others up there. People will be showing up for a while, so it won't go to waste."

"All right. Let me gather these cups for you."

"You don't have to. You can go home if you want."

"My house is full. I thought I'd sleep"—he shrugged—"wherever and let others have the space."

"You what? You gave up your house?"

He grinned. "Isn't that what you do here in Bethany? I know Simon and Lazarus have given up their room."

"Yes, but..." She couldn't find any reason he shouldn't have don't the same. Married men kept their rooms, of course, but like Abba and Lazarus, Asher wasn't married.

Yet.

He strode to the nearly empty table and gathered empty cups. He gathered the remaining bread into one basket then stacked the empty ones.

She wasn't quite sure what to make of Asher. Mary said he'd promised to become part of the village, and he had, more than Daniel and Enoch ever even thought about.

She just wasn't sure why. It was rare that a man moved into the village and became one of them. Usually, the woman joined the young man's family. But Asher had assimilated faster than any bride had.

But as long as he was good to Mary, it didn't matter.

Yeshua and His talmidim strode into the yard with the last fading rays of light. Martha hurried to meet them. "Rabbi!"

He reached to hug her. "Shalom, Martha. It would take quite a lot for Me to miss the Feast—and your cooking."

Her cheeks flamed, and she brushed aside the compliment. "We weren't sure You'd make it. You nearly ran out of daylight."

"But we didn't. And we are here."

She gestured toward the table. "Find some seats. I'll bring You some stew."

"Todah rabah." He strolled to the table, followed by His students.

Martha brought a full pot of stew and set it at the end of the table, then dished out bowls and handed them around.

Asher appeared at her side, a heaping platter of bread in one hand, a bowl of water in the other and a towel over his arm.

"Where's Kemuel?" she whispered.

"He went home. I thought we were done, and he was exhausted. I can do it." He moved to the end and knelt at the Rabbi's feet.

What a strange man. He didn't mind girls learning Torah, and he didn't mind serving meals.

He didn't even mind washing the feet of weary travelers.

Sivan 8

As soon as the sun set, Mary bolted for Asher's house. With her fists on her hips and her chin out, she strode to where he relaxed with a cup of honeyed wine in his courtyard. "Martha said you agreed to teach me Torah. Is that true?"

"As well as I can, yes."

"Shavuot is over, and our guests are gone. Will you teach me now?"

He frowned. "Now? Do we have time?"

"We have a while before the evening meal is ready. Martha's making fresh bread."

He glanced toward her house. "She is? That's unusual. Most women would serve whatever is left from last night."

"Martha *is* unusual." Mary laughed. "And she loves to cook and hates cold bread."

He chuckled. "I'll get some cushions."

Mary tapped her foot, waiting until he returned. It was only a moment, but she'd waited so long already.

"So how much do you know of the mizmorim of Hallel?" he asked as he handed her a cushion.

"I know all of the first one. And the second one."

"Truly?" He raised a brow. "How did you learn all that?"

"I heard the boys reciting them at Gershom's house."

"I didn't think you'd gone there that often."

"I went four…no, five times."

"And you learned two mizmorim?"

"Only two of the Hallel. I know lots of others. I only need to hear something a few times to learn it."

Asher let out a low whistle. "It takes me hearing something ten or twelve times before I can remember it correctly."

"Well, we also hear them at the temple. At Pesach, Shavuot, and Sukkot."

"All right, recite for me the second one." He closed his eyes.

Mary cleared her throat and sat up a little straighter.

> "'When Israel came out of Egypt, Jacob from a people of foreign tongue,
> Judah became God's sanctuary, Israel his dominion.

The sea looked and fled, the Jordan turned back;
the mountains leaped like rams, the hills like lambs.
Why was it, sea, that you fled? Why, Jordan, did you turn
   back?
Why, mountains, did you leap like rams, you hills, like lambs?
Tremble, earth, at the presence of the Lord, at the presence of the
   God of Jacob,
who turned the rock into a pool, the hard rock into springs of
   water.'"

He opened his eyes. "That's—that's perfect, Mary."

She flashed a huge grin. Gershom had never once complimented her.

"Can you tell me what it means?"

She shrugged. "It's about Israel's deliverance from bondage in the land of Egypt."

"What about the sea? And the Jordan?"

She quickly ran through the words in her mind. "The sea fled, and the Jordan turned back."

"You're just repeating the words, Mary. What do they *mean*?"

"I—I guess I don't know."

He tilted his head. "Can water be afraid?"

"I guess not."

"So why does the mizmor say the sea fled? Think about the story."

"The people came to the Sea of Reeds, and Moses struck the water with his staff, and it parted, and the people crossed on dry land."

"Good. So why did the sea part? Because it was afraid of Moses? Or his staff?"

She giggled. "No, of course not."

"Then what? Who?"

"I don't know." Frustration was beginning to steal the joy from this moment.

"Close your eyes. Take a deep breath."

She did as he asked.

"Now imagine it. Were the people alone at the sea?"

She called up the picture the words painted. The people huddling where land meets sea. Angry Egyptians racing toward them, hooves pounding, whips cracking. Chariot wheels spinning and archers taking aim. And over all, Adonai waited, a holy, fiery cloud of protection hovering over His people. "No, Adonai was with them in a pillar of fire. And He stood between them and the army of the Egyptians."

"Good, good. If you were there, how would you feel?"

"I–I'd be in awe of the power of Adonai." She popped open her eyes. "Are you saying the sea was in awe as well?"

"Yes. Well, it's poetry. I don't think water can be afraid or in awe, but it's a way of describing the power and might of Adonai. The sea fled at His presence, the mountains quaked—"

"Like at the end! 'Tremble, earth, at the presence of the Lord, at the presence of the God of Jacob.'"

"Yes!" He slapped his hands together and laughed. "But you must remember, you can't just repeat the words. I'm sure any Roman soldier could learn to say them. But they're meant to teach us about Adonai, about His character, His power, His everlasting love for us. Take the words into your heart."

"Like King David said? 'Your word have I hid in my heart, that I might not sin against You.'"

"Exactly. The sacred texts mean almost nothing if they do not change us."

Asher continued guiding her though each line of the psalm, helping her dig deep for meaning and truth. In one evening, she learned more than she had in all the years since she'd first sat in the priest's courtyard.

Martha climbed the stairs to the roof, a broom in hand. Only Yahweh knew what mess awaited after countless visitors slept there.

She began by rolling up sleeping mats. She knelt near the first one, marveling at the exquisite weaving. The women in the poorhouse wove them as their contribution. Willow leaves placed next to each other in perfect order, held together with the pliable stems.

She rolled them all then gathered them into a box near the stairs, then surveyed the roof.

Sweeping from back to front, moving from one side to the other, she smoothed out the footprints and drag marks from the mats.

At the far end, she looked out over the village.

Mary sat facing Asher in his yard. They laughed, and both faces bore bright smiles.

She shoved down a pang of jealousy. He would be good for her. He accepted her as she was, and she would blossom because of it.

She smiled as she contemplated Mary's future—and her own.

Adonai had given Mary a beautiful thing. Only He knew why He had not chosen to give the same to her.

CHAPTER SIXTEEN

For the Lord God is a sun and shield;
the Lord bestows favor and honor;
no good thing does he withhold
from those whose walk is blameless.
—Psalm 84:11 (NIV)

Sivan 10

Mary grasped a vine and removed the giant leaves covering the cluster of tiny grape berries. She stepped back and inspected her work. One sneaky little leaf still blocked the early-morning sun, which would prevent these berries from maturing into juicy, fat orbs of fruit. She snatched it away.

Ahead of her, Asher silently tied unruly vines to a stake. Odd. His brow was furrowed, and his mouth was twisted into a frown, even though this wasn't a task that required that much concentration. Asher usually flashed a bright smile, and unless his hands were occupied, he punctuated his sentences with rapidly moving fingers pointing and curling.

She cleared the foliage from another cluster and stepped to her right to prune the branches he had just secured.

Asher suddenly stopped, turning to face her. "Do you know where your abba is?"

She pointed to a spot several rows behind them. "Over there, I think."

"Todah."

Mary watched as Asher marched to the end of their row, then turned left, then moved down the row she'd indicated. What did he want? This wasn't like the times he'd needed further instruction as to what to do with the vines. He usually asked whoever was closest.

Was something wrong? Was he ill? Was he planning to leave Bethany?

She had to find out.

She slipped between the stakes, drawing closer to Abba. She bent her knees, creeping closer until she was on the other side of the row Abba worked. Asher neared and halted in front of Abba. Afraid to be caught listening, Mary sat on her heels. She couldn't see their faces, only their bodies from the waist down. But she could hear, and that was enough.

"Simon." Asher shifted his weight from foot to foot, cracking his knuckles as he waited for Abba's response.

"Shalom, Asher. It is a glorious day, is it not?"

Asher paused, as if he needed to think about his answer. "It is."

Asher remained silent, until finally, Abba spoke. "Do you need help?"

"No, I—I just need to talk to you."

The rustling of the vines ceased, so Abba's hands must have stilled. His feet turned to face Asher. "All right. Is something wrong? You look…stunned."

"I am, I guess." Asher chuckled lightly. "I never expected to do this again."

"Do what again?"

He sucked in a deep breath. "I want to marry your daughter."

Abba laughed. "Is that all?" The leaves moved again, and Abba's feet faced the row again.

"You know I lost my wife and our baby three years ago."

The vines again went silent, and Abba faced Asher once more. "I knew about your wife. I hadn't heard about your child. I'm so sorry." Abba's voice was gentle and soft.

"I came here to avoid being reminded of them with every step I took."

"It's hard, I know. I still think of my wife every single day." Pain laced Abba's voice. He often spoke of Imma but always in a way that celebrated her life and what she had given them. Mary had had no idea how much it still hurt him—perhaps even more than it hurt her.

"Anyway, I had no intention of marrying again, but I love your daughter."

Abba laughed. "You're not the first to ask for Mary."

Mary's breath caught. She had no interest in marrying anyone, let alone Asher. It was clear to her he loved Martha. Hadn't Abba realized that?

Asher stumbled back a step or two. "Mary? No—I'm not asking for Mary!"

"You're not?"

"No. I love Martha."

"Ah." Abba let out a low whistle. "That's an entirely different story."

"Why? Is she promised to someone else already?"

"No. But Martha was deeply hurt by your cousin. She feels humiliated, even though everyone in the village believes Daniel had no good reason to do what he did."

"So, she *is* free to marry another?" Hope colored his voice.

"She is free to marry anyone who wishes to marry a divorced woman, who is already older than most brides. So far, no one has expressed any interest."

"Well, I am."

"I can ask her, but I doubt she'll say yes. She's so afraid of being rejected again, she'd rather remain alone. I've not been able to convince her otherwise."

"Oh." Asher's voice was so soft Mary could barely hear it. "Don't bother her with this then. I don't want to cause her more pain." He turned and trudged away.

It was all Mary could do to not jump up and follow him. Instead, she crept back through the vines and pruned. And thought. And pruned.

Somehow, she had to fix this. But what could she do?

———

Martha laughed as Mary fluttered into the common room. "Having a good day?"

"A very good day. You won't believe what just happened!" Mary twirled in a circle, arms out, laughing.

With Mary, that could mean anything from seeing the first spring flower to the Romans returning Judea to the Jews. "You found a bird's nest with beautiful eggs in it."

Mary frowned and shook her head. "No!"

Apparently, something more serious. What then? "You finished your rows in the vineyard faster than the men."

Her face lit up. "No, but you're closer."

"It has something to do with Abba or Zar?"

She giggled. "No."

"With Asher?"

"Yes!" She clapped her hands in front of her chest.

She laughed. "Then I've no idea, Mary."

"He talked to Abba."

"He talks to Abba all the time, Mary." She returned to kneading her dough.

"Yes, but he asked him a question. A *very particular* question."

"He did?" Her hands stilled. "You mean, Asher asked Abba if he could—"

"Yes!" Mary jumped up and down. "Yes! Isn't it wonderful?"

"Oh, I'm so happy! Yes, this is very good news indeed. Did they talk about when? And where will he live? Could he live here, do you think? I'd hate for us to be split up."

Mary's face clouded for the briefest moment. "No, they didn't discuss any of that. Maybe when he comes to sign the *ketubah*."

Martha nodded. That made sense.

"I think you need to talk to him first, though."

"Me? Why would he need to talk to me?"

"Don't be silly." Mary laughed. "Why wouldn't he?"

Martha watched Mary dance away, grinning and laughing. *She has no idea how her life is about to change.*

Martha had a lot to teach her in the coming months. But first, she had to talk to Asher, though she had no idea why. Perhaps she could take the morning meal to the vineyard and see him then.

Martha strolled to the vineyard, her eyes on the basket perched on her hip, and nearly slammed into Asher. Hand to her chest, she backed away. "I'm so sorry. I wasn't watching where I was going. Forgive me."

He nodded silently and tried to go around her.

"Wait! I brought your morning meal." She held out the basket loaded with cheese and still-steaming bread. "I know you're all very busy, so I thought I'd bring it to you."

He only glanced at it before mumbling and trying again to pass her. "I'm not hungry."

He had to know it was an accident. Had she in some other way offended him so badly he refused to talk to her? If he was to be her brother-in-law, they'd have to repair this rift now. Maybe if she brought up the wedding, showed him she was happy for him.

"Mary said I'm supposed to talk to you."

He halted and turned to face her. "About what?"

"About your talk with Abba."

He frowned. "What about it?"

"I'm not really sure. She just said I needed to talk to you. Maybe she wants me to arrange a time for you to come sign the ketubah."

Pain twisted his face. "Why would I need to do that?"

She chuckled lightly. "Asher, I know you talked to my abba about marrying her. And I saw how happy she was. I'm very happy for both of you."

His brows twisted and then his face softened. "You think I was talking to your abba about your achot?"

She shrugged. "Of course." She chuckled. "You wouldn't be the first. I'm glad she finally said yes."

He blew out a sharp breath. "That's not what we were discussing."

She replayed the conversation in her mind. Abba and Asher talking, Mary giddy, a ketubah... "But she said..."

"I wasn't asking him about *her*. I was talking to Simon about *you*."

All the breath left her lungs. "Me? Why?"

He held his hands out, palms up. "Because I want to marry you. Why else?"

"But why would you want to marry me? Mary is beautiful, smart, young—"

"She's a child!" He threw his hands in the air and let them slap to his thighs. He closed his eyes and drew in a deep breath. "I understand Mary is a wonderful person. And yes, she is smart and beautiful, but she's barely a woman. And she talks too much, and she can't stand still, and she panics easily." He wandered toward the olive tree at the edge of the vineyard, beckoning her to follow him. He sat in the shade and smoothed out a space beside him.

She sat and placed the basket between them.

He grabbed a round of bread but made no move to eat it. "I married someone like her, when I was also very young. And we learned and we grew. We shared joys and sorrows. We made mistakes and learned how to build a life. Then it all disappeared."

Staring in the distance, he said, "I came here because I didn't want to marry again. I wanted a simple life, alone."

He shifted his gaze to her. "Then I met you, and for the first time in three years, I thought about marrying again." His eyes held hers, a soft smile growing. "It surprised me. Pleasantly."

Her cheeks burned, but she said nothing.

"But if I do marry, I don't want to start all over. I want someone who has something to talk about late at night when we can't sleep. Someone who can see beyond tomorrow. Who can solve problems with me and has the strength to endure whatever Adonai has in store for us."

He set the uneaten bread aside and brushed his hands together before locking them around one knee.

"You are the strongest person I've ever met. If I marry, I want to marry you."

"You know I'm a divorced woman. Why would you do that to yourself?"

"Do what? My *reputation* won't be damaged." He laughed. "Simon says everyone in the village knows the real truth. That my cousin and my uncle are fools. There was no reason for him to end the betrothal." He made a face. "My uncle has always been so concerned with what others think of him. He passed up what could have been Adonai's greatest gift to his family when he passed you up."

She looked away. No one, except Abba, had ever spoken of her that way. The suitors who asked for Mary had proved to her she was less desirable than her younger achot.

She faced him again. "Tell me about her."

"Who? My wife?" His brows furrowed. "Why do you want to know?"

"She was a part of your life. She helped make you who you are. I'd like to know her."

He burst into a smile. "You are not only the strongest woman I know, you are also the wisest." He picked up a piece of cheese, bit off a small chunk, and swallowed. "Leah was much like Mary, young and beautiful. She was my cousin, though I'd met her only twice before we signed the ketubah. Then I didn't see her again for a year. When we married, we had to get to know each other, and that took a while." He ate another bite of cheese while he thought.

His face clouded just a bit. "Leah wasn't strong, like you. It took a long time for her to be with child, and we lost several babies very early. It destroyed her. It devastated me too, not only because we lost a child but because I saw what it did to her. She saw it as a punishment from Adonai and was terrified I'd divorce her, no matter how many times I told her how much I loved her and would never leave her. Every time we lost a baby, I watched her sink into herself. When she finally carried a baby to the time of delivery, we were…" His face lit up at the memory. "We were so happy. When she carried the baby for longer than three months, it was like she finally came to life. She was an entirely different person."

He paused, ripping off pieces of cheese and dropping them into the basket. "We got closer to the time for her to be delivered, and it was a glorious time. She loved every sunrise, every fluffy cloud. Suddenly, about a month before, the baby stopped moving. The midwife said the babe had likely died inside her and we would have to wait for it to be delivered. That took over two weeks. I saw her die a little more each day." He looked away, beyond the vineyards. "It was a very difficult delivery." His voice lowered. "Leah didn't have the strength to survive it."

No wonder he didn't want to risk marriage again. "Asher, I'm so sorry. That must have been agonizing."

"It was. So, I determined to never risk such pain again. Much like you have."

His words hit her hard. He was right. She hadn't done it on purpose, but she had decided to avoid the risk even if it meant losing out on possible joy.

"We can take this risk together. Will you marry me?"

She grinned. "Don't you have to ask my abba?"

He laughed. "I already did."

She remembered Asher's face when he saw her earlier. Why was he so glum? "Did he not give you his permission?"

"Oh, he gave me *his*. He just doubted you'd give me yours. Even Mary said you've stated repeatedly you'd never marry."

Martha remembered her dancing around the common room. "Then why was she so happy?"

"I don't know. She told you I asked for you?"

Martha thought back through her conversation earlier. "You know, I don't think she ever did. I just assumed she meant herself, and I guess she assumed I knew she meant me."

"I'm glad it got straightened out." He glanced around and leaned in to kiss her cheek.

Her face heated again. "Asher, are you sure you want to marry again? I mean, to me? I'm older, and I have no idea if—"

He placed his hands on her cheeks. "I'm not marrying you just to have children. If Adonai blesses us with children, I will praise Him. If He doesn't, I will still praise Him because He'll have blessed me enough by giving me you."

He was right. A husband like Asher was blessing enough in itself. How could she ask for more?

CHAPTER SEVENTEEN

*He who finds a wife finds what is good
and receives favor from the L*ORD*.*
—Proverbs 18:22 (NIV)

Tishri 25
Four days after the Feast of Tabernacles

Mary felt the panic rising within her. "Adah, help me!"

Adah hurried to assist her. "What's wrong?"

"My bread is falling apart! I don't know what I did. I made the dough just like I've made it a thousand times—the way Martha showed me."

Adah broke off a chunk of bread and winced as it crumbled. She turned to Mary with an exaggerated smile. "Why don't you go help your achot get ready?" She glanced at the sun, just past its apex. "The sun is already on its journey to the west. Has she even immersed yet?"

"I don't know." Mary scanned the common room bustling with women cooking the wedding feast. Martha had been banished, but it would be just like her to find a way in. She wasn't there. Mary checked the courtyard, where more women—and young girls—showed their love and appreciation for Martha by decorating every tree branch and wall in sight. Not there either.

Had she snuck by? Was she still in her chamber? Mary had been so intent on cooking something—anything—delicious for Martha, she'd not paid attention to anything else. She was supposed to make sure Martha was ready in time, and now she failed in that as well.

She hurried to the corner of the common room and paused at the door of their chamber—which would after today be Mary's alone—and knocked. "Martha?"

Silence greeted her. She pushed the door open just enough to poke her head in. "Achot? Are you in here?"

"I'm here." Her voice seemed so small.

Mary entered the room and crossed to the bed, where Martha sat staring at nothing. Her breath caught in her throat. "Are you ill? Is there anything I can help you with?"

She slowly shook her head. "I don't know how to do this."

Mary moved to their bed and sat, placing her hand on Martha's back. "Do what?"

"Be a wife. I'd accepted I would never marry, and now that it's happened, and happened so fast… I don't want Asher to be disappointed. Again."

Mary gently rubbed Martha's back. "Asher is never going to be disappointed with you. Unless you don't marry him." She giggled.

That didn't help. Tears fell from Martha's lashes and dropped to her hands.

Try something else. "Remember when Abba became ill?"

Martha raised her head, her eyes wide with horror. "Of course. Why are you bringing that up now? Today of all days?"

"What did you do after we took him to the bet?"

"Cried."

"After that?"

Martha jumped to her feet. Her hands balled into fists. "I don't remember! Why is this important?"

"You made stew."

"What?" Martha's brows furrowed.

"You made stew. The most delicious bowl you've ever made, so we could eat. Then you took him some."

"I don't understand." Martha folded her arms across her chest.

Mary rose to face her, placing her hands gently on Martha's upper arms. "You did what you always do so perfectly. You didn't let what happened stop you, and you took care of us. Because that's what you do. It's who you are."

She scoffed. "That's what all women do. That's—"

Mary shook her head violently. "No, no, it's not. When Adah's baby was sick, who fed her family? You did, because Adah could only cry. When Hannah—"

Martha nodded. "Yes, yes. But is that enough? What if—"

"It's enough. It's perfect."

Martha frowned, her disbelief evident.

"And now you have someone else to care for, someone who thinks the sun shines when you smile, and the rain comes when you are sad."

Finally, a small smile appeared. "He does, doesn't he?"

"Adonai made you for each other. I don't know why it took longer than for others, but you're both here now."

Martha smiled. "I guess you're right."

"Now let's get you immersed and dressed."

Martha stepped into the mikveh southeast of the village. Long ago, the residents of Bethany had built a small, simple ritual bath, since the community spent so much time caring for the sick and were often unclean. Most of the time, it mattered little, since being unclean only meant you couldn't enter the temple grounds. But women needed to immerse each month, and the mikveh allowed anyone to immerse after sunset when needed, purifying themselves once again.

The mikveh wasn't much wider than a man was tall, but it was deep enough for the water to come to a woman's neck or a man's chest. It was enclosed by a roofed, three-sided shelter made of reeds, and a fabric door made the fourth wall for privacy.

Martha reached the floor of the pool, bent at the knees, and allowed the water to cover her. She rose, then immersed twice more. "Blessed are You, Adonai our God, King of the Universe," she whispered, "who has sanctified us with *mitzvot* and commanded us concerning immersion." She wiped the water from her face and then slid her hands down her hair.

At the top of the steps, Mary handed her a towel. As Martha dried herself, she studied the blue dress Adah had lent her for the wedding. Adah's family was quite wealthy, and her mother was particularly upset when she moved to Bethany to live simply and serve with her new husband. Like most wedding tunics, it was bordered in blue, but this one was made of fine linen.

Martha handed the towel to Mary as she fingered the cloth. Never had she felt anything so soft. As she slipped it over her head, its hem fluttered to her feet. Adah was a head taller than Martha, but she pulled some of the fabric over the blue sash until it no longer dragged the ground. Most of the blue was hidden, but it was either that or trip over the hem.

Mary moved behind her, arranging the dress so that most of the excess hung in back, showing off the blue linen at her waist. She stepped to the front and inspected the dress. "There." She flashed a bright smile.

"Todah." She rubbed her hands down the dress. "It's so beautiful."

"You're beautiful, Martha. It's not the dress, it's you."

Martha's face warmed. She wasn't used to being complimented.

Mary's smile faded. "I know this isn't the day you would have wanted."

Martha jerked her gaze to Mary. "What do you mean?"

"Imma. *She* should be here, helping you. Not me."

Martha's heart broke. Did Mary really think Martha didn't want her here? "Oh Mary, no." She reached for her hand and pulled her close. "Of course I wish she could have been here, but that doesn't mean I don't want you to be part of this too. I can't imagine doing this without you." She enveloped her in a fierce embrace. "I *wouldn't* be doing this without you. I'd still be sitting on the bed if you hadn't come in."

"Do you mean that? You'd still want me helping you?"

"Of course. You're my only achot, and my favorite person in the world."

Mary pulled back, grinning. "I hope you have a new favorite now."

She nodded. "But there will always be something special between us. We share a life here in Bethany that most will never know. We know what it's like to live to serve others, and unlike most of the women here, we were born into this life. There isn't anyone else I can share that with."

Mary stared at the floor. "I know I wasn't always the easiest person when I was young."

Martha smiled. "Only when you were young?"

"Even now. But all that I do right is because of you. Because you gave up so much of your life—willingly—to make me the woman I am now."

Martha waited until Mary raised her face and caught her gaze. "*No*. It's because of Adonai. He designed you to be who exactly you are, and He didn't let me destroy it."

Mary kissed her cheek. "I love you, achoti."

"I love you too."

Mary stepped away suddenly. "I almost forgot. Just a moment." She picked up a wooden box and lifted the lid. "Asher sent this for you." She removed the lid and held the box out.

Martha gasped as she eyed a wide silver cuff bracelet. She picked it up, slipped it over her hand and let it sit on her wrist as she slowly turned it to see all sides. "It's exquisite," she whispered. "How, when did he get this?"

"He still had the money he brought from home when he moved here. He went to the city a month ago and asked a silversmith to make it. It took longer than he promised, and Asher was beside himself. It was kind of funny."

"Did Abba know about this?"

"Of course. And look—your name is on there." Mary twisted the bracelet until she found the part she sought, then pointed to it. "Here—Martha. Now sit and let me comb your hair."

Martha did as he was told and studied the silver she held. Words ran along the outside. *An excellent wife, who can find? For her worth is far above jewels.*

An excellent wife. Is that how he saw her? Tears welled up, whether from anxiety or gratitude, she couldn't tell.

Could she live up to his expectations?

CHAPTER EIGHTEEN

Though one may be overpowered,
two can defend themselves.
A cord of three strands is not quickly broken.
—Ecclesiastes 4:12 (NIV)

Surrounded by the women of the village, Martha dipped her bread into the bowl of lentil stew. The flavors of garlic, salt, and pepper danced on her tongue. Bowls of black olives, plump grapes, freshly picked dates, and ripe figs nestled among amphorae of honeyed wine and platters heaped with bread, sliced melon, and roasted fish.

How many times had she prepared such a feast for others? How many times had the dream of her own feast been alive only to die? It was almost too much to believe it was really happening.

Martha ripped off a piece of bread and placed it on her tongue. "It's good. Did you make it, achoti?"

"I helped." Mary grimaced. "Adah had to fix it."

Martha rubbed her back. "I'm sure she didn't have to do much."

"Yes she did. It would have been terrible if she didn't."

"It wouldn't be terrible because it would have been baked by you, just for me. I know how much it worries you to cook, and I am honored you would do this for me."

Mary's cheeks pinked, a rare occurrence. "I'm glad you're staying in our house. I know you wouldn't have been far, but still."

The sun slid behind the mount. It wouldn't be long before the brilliant reds and purples of a harvest evening would tell them the sun had finally dipped below the horizon.

Abba tapped her on the shoulder and beckoned her.

She rose and stepped away from the group, scanning the courtyard. There wasn't really anywhere they could be alone, and there wouldn't be anytime soon, as the feasting would last all night.

"Walk with me." He headed toward the center of the village, to the well.

They soon reached it, and he leaned backward against it. He studied her face, a wistful smile on his own. "You look just like your imma did the day I married her." He sniffled. "I know everyone says Mary is the pretty one, but you always reminded me of her."

"I never knew that."

"I never said. The thought always brought a tear to my eyes." She placed her hand on his cheek. "I'm sorry, Abba."

"I'm not." He took her hand in both of his. "You know, if you look back on all that has happened, not just in the last two years, but even all the way back, you can see Adonai had His hand in all of it."

"What do you mean?"

"This is what He planned. From the start. I don't know why, but *this* is His plan."

She laughed dryly. "Why couldn't He have just brought Asher and skipped Daniel?"

"I don't know. Maybe Asher wasn't ready yet. Maybe his wife needed him for a while. We don't always know why. I don't know why your imma died, and probably never will. But even when we have no answers, we can trust that He does."

She didn't like being without answers, never had. She liked evidence.

"Could you ever have imagined that my becoming ill could be a good thing?" he asked.

Twice in one day this had been brought up. "Of course not! It was a horrible thing!" How could he even say that?

"Yes, but if that hadn't happened, we would never have known the joy of my being made clean, never have seen the power of Adonai working through the One He sent. And I would take ten thousand days of being unclean to experience that."

She hadn't thought of it that way.

"Solomon said, 'He has made everything beautiful in its time.' His ways are too hard for us to understand, yet we must trust Him. And His timing."

"I'll try to remember that, Abba."

"Good, motek." He pulled her close. "And remember I love you."

"I will."

He pointed over her shoulder. "I think your *ahuvi* has come for you."

She turned to see Asher, in Yoash's fine linen tunic, strolling toward her. Her heart fluttered as he neared, smiling. How handsome he was!

But as pleasing as his face was, what drew her to him, what had from the start, was his heart. His compassion, his integrity, his love for Adonai and His law.

She didn't know as much of the Scriptures as Mary did, or even as much as Asher or Abba. But one sentence came to mind, more of Solomon's words.

"I have found the one whom my soul loves."

Mary watched Martha walk toward the house with Asher.

Abba stopped at the tables on his way back, grabbing a cup of wine and reaching her at about the same time Lazarus approached, his hands cupped and filled with raisin cakes. "These are the last of Martha's cakes." He held out his hands. "I scooped them up before anyone else could."

"How many have you had already?" Mary laughed.

"None!"

She raised a brow.

"None. Truly. Today, anyway. I did steal a few when she baked them yesterday."

"I'm surprised there were any left if you were around." Abba popped one in his mouth.

"I think she started hiding them from me." Lazarus laughed.

"I'm so glad she's staying in our house," Mary said.

"It was incredibly generous of Asher to give the house to Bethany," Abba said.

"He did?" Zar asked. "I thought he sold it to us."

"For a denarius." Abba laughed. "I think the village owns all of them now, so we shouldn't have any more situations like we did with Daniel and Enoch. We decide who can live there from now on."

"Who will live there? Has it been decided?"

"Yes. Yoash and his brother and their families will. With two already married and five children, and his brother marrying soon, his abba's house is too crowded, and there's no more room for them to keep adding to it."

"I didn't know his brother was marrying!" Zar said.

Mary scoffed. "Everyone knows that."

"Not everyone, obviously," he said.

"You just don't pay attention," she smirked.

Abba raised his hand. "Be that as it may, he and his new bride will share the house with Yoash and Hannah."

"How many brothers are left?" asked Mary.

Abba held up two fingers. "There are two left to marry."

Mary looked toward the southeast end of their home, where Asher had been building the room they would live in. "Have you seen it?" she asked.

"The inside? No." Lazarus shook his head. "Once we finished the outside, only he worked on it. He's kept it secret. But if he's good enough to work on the temple, I imagine it's quite lovely."

"I'm sure it is." It had to be, as much as he loved Martha and as much time as he'd put into it. But no matter how beautiful it was, it could never be more than she deserved.

Asher neared Martha, coming to stand only a hand's breadth away.

"Shalom, *ahuvati*," he whispered. His hands on her face, he leaned in and kissed her. His lips were soft and his touch tender, and warmth shot all the way down to her sandals. "You're so beautiful."

"Todah," she managed, her voice weak.

He chuckled softly. "Come. I want to show you what I made for you." He took her hand, and they wandered toward the house.

"You're sure you're all right living in our house? It's not usually how it's done."

"But everything is different in Bethany, isn't it?" He grinned.

"Not everything. But yes."

"It makes sense. Why take you away from Mary just to have you live all alone? And that house is far too big for two people. It's better for everyone this way."

"But you just gave it away."

"I won't need it anymore, will I? Now come inside with me." He veered to the right past the pomegranate tree, to the back of the house, to the new room he'd built on the southeast side of the house.

He stood at the door on the east wall. "Now close your eyes."

She did, and the door clicked then swung open. He took her hand and pulled her forward.

"All right, you can look now."

She opened her eyes to a room about twice as big as the one she'd shared with Mary. A bed nearly filled the left side, and a chest sat on the floor at its foot. Several small niches had been built into the walls to hold oil lamps.

A door on the opposite wall led to the hall of guest rooms. "You can go out this way too."

She peered out the inner door. A few steps to the right would put her in the common room.

He closed the door and pointed to a shelf on the wall beside it. "And Mary made me do this. It's acacia wood."

Mary's unbroken alabaster jar sat on it.

"But it's hers!"

"She wants you to have it. And look." Asher pointed above the bed. Wide, short windows graced two walls above the bed, allowing the faint woody scent of the massive, ancient olive tree to waft through the room. The gnarled trunk could be seen from both openings, its deeply grooved wood supporting drooping branches full of silver-green oblong leaves.

"My tree!"

"I made sure you could see it from anywhere in the room, even from the bed."

"It's marvelous, Asher. You made all this?"

Love and pride lit his face. "Simon and Zar helped with the walls and roof, but I made the bed and the chest."

She knelt before the chest and ran her fingers over the top. Graceful olive branches intertwined across the top, their sleek leaves extending on either side in perfect order, and round, fat olives were carved deep into the wood. She looked up to meet his gaze. "Oh, Asher, it's…it's astonishing."

"Mary said your favorite line in all the scriptures is from a mizmor. 'But I am like an olive tree flourishing in the house of God; I trust in God's unfailing love for ever and ever.' I wanted you to be able to see this and be reminded of His love for us every day." He laughed. "Even though you have a real one outside your window."

She stood and surveyed the room. "I can't believe you did all this in such a short time. When did you ever sleep?"

He laughed. "Sleep is overvalued." He wrapped his arms around her waist and pulled her toward him. "Remember, whatever happens, we can face it together. You, me, and Adonai. We have to remember what He told Isaiah, 'So do not fear, for I am with you; do not be dismayed, for I am your God. I will strengthen you and help you; I will uphold you with my righteous right hand.'"

"I'll remember."

Just six months ago, everything was so different. Abba was in the bet with tsara'at. She was a divorced woman, who believed she would never know the joy of a husband and children.

Now everything had changed, and all because of the Rabbi. He'd restored Abba's health, returned him to his family, allowed him to once again be part of the community and to worship Adonai in His holy temple.

But He'd healed more than just Abba.

He'd healed the entire family.

He'd healed her when she didn't even realize how much she needed healing, and He'd given her more than she could ever have asked for.

CHAPTER NINETEEN

Then Jesus went up on a mountainside and sat down with his disciples. The Jewish Passover Festival was near.
—John 6:3–4 (NIV)

Nisan 23

Martha awakened to find Asher on his side, head resting on his raised fist, watching her and grinning. She laughed. "What are you doing?"

"Waiting."

"For what?"

"For you to wake up."

She rolled over and closed her eyes. "I'm not waking up yet. We had a long week of guests, and I want to sleep just a few moments longer. There's bread and wine on the table."

"Yesterday's bread."

She laughed. "There will be fresh loaves soon."

"I'm not hungry." He leaned in and softly kissed her. "I was thinking. I know all your family, but you know none of mine."

She opened one eye. "I'd love to, but they don't live here."

"Exactly. I think we should go visit my sister."

She opened the other eye and raised up on one elbow, mirroring him. "Go *where*?"

"To Gennesaret. I want her to see how Adonai has blessed me. I think they were a little worried about me when I left."

She placed her hand on his cheek. "She must love you very much."

"She does. And she'll love you as well."

"Do you think so?"

He rolled onto his back and tucked his hands under his head. "Why wouldn't she?"

"I don't know. I'm older than most brides. I haven't given you a child." *Yet.*

"It's only been six months!"

"Seven."

He laughed then stretched to kiss her cheek. "Trust me."

"All right."

His brows raised. "Just like that? All right?"

She nodded. "You've given me no reason not to trust you." She paused. "Would it be just the two of us?"

"The others can go if they want to. I'm fine either way."

"I can't imagine Mary not going."

He chuckled. "Me either."

She pondered the plan for a moment. "When?"

"I think we have two options. We can go now right after Shavuot. The barley harvest will be over, and Bethany doesn't grow wheat except for that tiny plot we use for the Shavuot offerings, so we wouldn't be missed for a couple of weeks. And it's not terribly hot yet. The other option is to wait until after the grape harvest and the Feast of Tabernacles. But then there's the olive harvest and we run into the chance of rain."

"Let's go sooner then." Martha rose and slipped on a tunic.

"I thought you weren't getting up yet."

"I'm awake *now*." She grinned. "How long is the journey?"

"Six days, maybe seven."

Her hands stilled as she tied her sash. She'd always heard how long the trip from Galilee was, but she'd never really stopped to think about how hard it must be. "Where will we stop to sleep?"

"I'm not sure." He sat up and gave her an exaggerated shrug. "But I've heard there are people who offer hospitality to those on their way to and from Jerusalem. Even to total strangers, if you can believe such nonsense."

She grabbed a pillow and threw it at him. "Very funny."

Laughing, he ducked to one side before the flying object hit his head. "Well, you asked."

She frowned and secured the sash around her waist. "I've never been farther than the temple."

"And yet your life revolves around travel." He rose, grabbing his tunic from the end of the bed.

"I suppose."

"I've met many hosts on my trips to Jerusalem. Some I've stayed with every year, the way some people return to you year after year. We shouldn't ever have to stay with someone I don't know. Because who would ever do something so odd?"

"You can make your own bread this morning." She smirked as she headed for the door.

He grabbed her as she passed and pulled her close. "I'm sorry. I was only teasing. Forgive me?"

She smiled. "Nothing to forgive." She wriggled from his embrace. "But I do have work to do. It's my day to visit the bet."

He followed her out of the room, kissed her cheek as she stood at her table, and headed for the barley field.

Martha knelt at the cistern in the corner and dipped a small pitcher inside, bringing up water. She returned to the table, then pulled a large bowl toward her and poured in flour, water, and some leaven and began mixing.

Three children burst through the courtyard and into the room.

"Martha! Martha! We want raisin cakes!"

She grinned and bent at the waist, hands on her knees. "Is that how you ask for a treat?"

Selah hurried to catch them. "I'm so sorry. Imma is with Hannah and they just got away from me." She turned to her brothers. "Boys! You know better! You can't just barge into someone's house!"

"Hannah's baby is coming?" Adah was the village midwife.

"They came to get her in the middle of the night."

"Have you had anything else to eat?" asked Martha.

Selah nodded. "There was bread left from yesterday."

"Come back for fresh bread in a bit. And if Adah doesn't return by evening, come here to eat." She bent at the waist, her hands on her knees. "You boys know you are always most welcome to my treats, but only if you ask properly."

"May we have some, please?" The two oldest spoke in unison, but the youngest remained silent.

"David? What about you?"

Martha didn't expect much, as he was barely talking. But it was never too early to learn to say please.

"Pwease?"

Martha laughed. "Very good." She reached for a basket at the back of the table and withdrew four cakes, then distributed them.

Eager hands nearly snatched them from her open palm.

"What do you say now?" asked Selah.

"Todah," they answered in unison and ran off.

"Selah, will you come by later to make bread?"

"If I can. I have to watch the boys."

"Mary would be delighted to watch them and let you cook."

"All right." Selah nodded as she steered her brothers out of the courtyard, David's tiny hand in hers.

Martha smiled as her hand went instinctively to her belly.

As she kneaded the soft dough, she counted in her mind again, although she already knew the answer.

It had been ten weeks and one day since her last time of blood. Too early to truly believe she was pregnant. Too late to say she wasn't.

But until she was certain, one way or the other, she would keep this information to herself.

Mary pulled on the rope to raise the heavy bag from the well, sloshing some of the water out as she poured it into the jar.

"Careful!" Martha scolded.

"I'm sorry! At least none of it spilled onto the ground, just back down the well."

"You're making more work for us, and we still have to get the evening meal ready."

Mary studied her achot. It was unlike Martha to scold her over anything, especially something so trivial. "Why are you so touchy?"

"I'm not!" She sighed. "It's just—"

"I must speak with you." Gershom approached.

"To us? Why?" asked Mary. Why couldn't he leave them alone?

"I've just come from the temple. Your names came up."

"*Our* names?" Martha placed her hand on her chest.

"Both of you. Along with your abba and your ach."

"For what reason?" she asked.

"Your association with the so-called Rabbi from Galilee has been noted. You would all be better off staying far away from Him."

"He hasn't even been here in almost a year!" said Mary.

"The next time He comes here, send Him away."

Asher hurried toward them. "What's going on here?"

Gershom huffed. "Finally, a man. Perhaps I can have a reasonable conversation with *him*."

Martha gestured to the priest. "He wants us to send Yeshua away if He returns."

"What? Why would we do that?" asked Asher.

Mary stepped closer to Gershom. "We have *never* sent anyone away, and we *never* will. We will show mercy to anyone who—"

"Not to *Him*!" The priest's voice was sharp.

"May I ask why not?" asked Mary.

"He is a blasphemer and a magician." Gershom ignored Mary, directing his answer to Asher. "So while you're reciting the commands of our God, remember those which forbid the magic arts from being practiced among us."

Mary's hands folded into fists. "He does not practice magic arts, or sorcery, or witchcraft, or anything else unholy!"

Gershom looked at Mary, then at Martha, and finally at Asher. "You need to control these women before they drag you down with them."

Asher wrapped his arm around Martha's waist and drew her to his side. "This woman has already brought me closer to Adonai, and we've been married less than a year." He glanced at Mary. "And this one knows the sacred texts better than you or I or anyone else in this village."

His face twisted into disdain. "I fear it's already too late for you. For all of you." He turned on his heel but spun immediately back to face them. "I almost forgot." The contempt morphed into a wicked form of glee. "And though I doubt it, perhaps this will change your behavior. You may have heard of the man who preached baptism and repentance in the wilderness?"

"They call him John," Mary said.

Gershom nodded. "He is apparently related to your Rabbi."

"I believe they're cousins," added Asher.

Gershom allowed a smug smirk. "That's correct. And this cousin was just executed by Antipas."

Mary's stomach roiled and her knees buckled. She remembered the pain in Yeshua's eyes when He talked about John in prison.

"Why?" Martha's voice broke. "What had he done that could earn him such a punishment?"

"Treason." Gershom sneered. "Antipas reasoned he might start a rebellion and bring the wrath of the Romans upon us."

Rebellion? Mary struggled not to laugh. Any revolt would be due to Herod's actions, not Yeshua's. "You're sure it wasn't because Herod married his brother's wife and John identified his sin in public?"

"Mary!" whispered Martha.

Gershom jutted out his jaw. "Even if Herod did such a thing, it was not the business of this preacher."

"Why are you defending this man?" asked Asher. "He's not even Jewish! He obeys none of our laws. His palace walls are lined with idols."

Gershom waved his hand. "I'll hear no more of this talk. I'll simply warn you once again. Stay away from this so-called Rabbi, and do not allow Him into your home." He stormed off, muttering to himself.

The trio walked back to the house in silence, but Gershom's words—and their inescapable implication—rang in Mary's ears.

If John is dead, what kind of danger does Yeshua face?

CHAPTER TWENTY

But Herod said, "I beheaded John. Who, then, is this I hear such things about?" And he tried to see him.
—Luke 9:9 (NIV)

As the evening drew to a close, the setting sun splashed brilliant purples and pinks across the western sky. Mary rolled up the sleeping mats and laid them in a long, low woven box in a corner of the roof. She swept the floor then gathered some left-behind plates and cups into a basket she carried to the top of the stairs. She straightened and looked toward the dirt path that led from Bethany to the crest of the olive-tree covered mountain. Most of their guests had left as soon as the sun dared venture above the horizon, taking some of Martha's fresh bread along with some cheese and dried grapes Mary had packed for them. The remaining three or four, who lived only a day away in Jericho, waited until the spring morning was fully lit.

But the road that led their guests out of Bethany also brought them into it. Why hadn't Rabbi Yeshua come this year? It wasn't like Him to miss Pesach, or any of the feasts. Only something very serious could have kept Him away.

Adonai's commandments required every male to appear in Jerusalem, although the priests had established exemptions for those who lived more than a day's journey away. But Yeshua, like most Galilean men, had come that far before. In fact, Yeshua had said He'd made that journey every year of His life. Why miss this year?

Would they ever find out? Or would they never see Him again? Surely, if He was the Mashiach, He wouldn't just disappear.

Footsteps on the stairs shook Mary from her thoughts.

Martha stepped onto the roof, a large platter held with one hand and resting on her hip, an amphora dangling from the fingers of her other hand. She approached Mary. "Help me with this?"

The scent of fresh roasted vegetables and fish reached Mary's nose as she took the pottery dish from her sister.

Martha placed the amphora next to the platter on the round leather mat that served as a table. "Let's get the rest." She turned and hurried back to the stairs.

Mary grabbed a few more cups sitting on the low wall around the roof and hurried down the stairs. Martha passed her as she entered the common room, so Mary quickly set the soiled cups on the worktable and grabbed the platter full of dried figs and dates before taking the stairs two at a time.

The men had beaten them to the roof and were already sitting around the mat. After eight nights hosting guests, tonight would be a relaxing meal with just the family. A gentle breeze cooled the air and refreshed their weary bodies. The slopes of the mount were covered in trees dotted with tiny white flowers, and the scent of the emerging olive blossoms could only be detected due to their sheer numbers.

"It's always nice when it's just us." Abba smiled at the small group. "Let's thank Adonai."

Mary closed her eyes, ready to once again hear the quiet voice she'd missed for the last week.

"Blessed are You, Adonai our God, King of the universe, who brings forth bread from the earth."

"Amen," all repeated.

Martha reached for the bowls and filled each with stew.

Mary took them from her and handed them to the others. "I missed having the Rabbi here for Pesach."

"Me too." Lazarus shrugged his shoulders as he reached for a loaf of bread and ripped off a large piece. "But you heard what Gershom said. It's not safe. I'm not surprised He didn't come."

"Will He never come again?" Mary asked.

Abba reached for a round of bread. "He will. I'm sure of it. But this is not the time for Him."

"Do you think He knows about John?" Zar asked.

"It's hard to say," Abba said. "Galileans only come to the city for the feasts, so someone from there would have had to be here in the weeks before Pesach, heard about John, realized he was Yeshua's cousin, returned to whatever town Yeshua is in now, and told Him."

Asher cleared his throat. "Martha and I talked about going to Galilee to see my family. We could try to find Him while we're there."

Mary frowned. "When were you thinking of going?"

"I only brought it up this morning, so we haven't made any plans. We thought about after Shavuot, so we would be here for the barley harvest."

"I think you should go now."

"You don't need us for the harvest?" Asher asked.

"We can manage without you. I think we should try to let Him know, just in case He already doesn't," Abba said. "No need for Him to put Himself in danger."

"Do you think you could find Him?" asked Mary.

"It's possible." Asher nodded. "But Galilee is a very big place. He could be in any one of a hundred towns. I wouldn't go there just to find Him, but since we're going anyway, we can try."

"Just you two are going?" How she'd love to join them! But he likely wanted to go with just Martha.

"No, anyone is welcome to join us," he said.

Excitement bubbled up within Mary. She'd never been farther from Bethany than the temple, but now she had a chance to see an entirely different part of Israel. "I'd love to join you, if that's really all right with you."

"Of course you can come." Martha squeezed her hand.

"More is always better when traveling," Abba said. "Safer. How long do you plan to be gone?"

"Not too long, right?" Martha looked to her husband.

He nodded. "We'd be back at least by Shavuot but probably much sooner."

"Then I guess you'd better get started." Abba smiled.

"We should leave the day after Shabbat. Then we have six days to get there. Otherwise we'd have to spend Shabbat somewhere on the way."

The day after Shabbat was six days away—an eternity. Leaving tonight wouldn't be soon enough for Mary, but she had no choice. She'd have to wait.

CHAPTER TWENTY-ONE

Then he went down to Capernaum, a town in Galilee, and on the Sabbath he taught the people. They were amazed at his teaching, because his words had authority.
—Luke 4:31–32 (NIV)

Iyyar 5

The last five days had been long and hard. Long hours of walking, walking, walking broken only by sleeping in strange houses. Martha's feet ached, and the bag she carried cut a groove in her shoulder. Thank Adonai the nausea she'd had before they left had vanished.

She had always tried to provide the best for the guests, but she would have much more empathy for them now.

The village of Gennesaret was not much bigger than Bethany. It sat on a small, narrow plain of the same name that ran along the shore of the lake. They'd avoided Antipas's palace in Tiberias and circled west, wide of the lake, before turning east. Streams flowed from the hills to the sea, dumping not only water but rich soil onto the little plain.

"I've never seen so much color! Look at all the flowers!" Mary spun in a circle as she walked. "And vineyards, and olive groves, and so many trees!" She laughed.

"That's why the rabbis called this area 'the Garden of God,'" said Asher.

They turned off the road and picked their way down a rocky path to the village. Martha reached for his hand to steady her steps. "Where is your house?"

"Down by the sea. We're almost there."

She looked at the sun, behind them in the west. "We'll be there before the sun sets?"

"Yes, don't worry. We'll be safely on my achot's roof before Shabbat begins."

Mary drew up beside her. "We get to see the lake! Aren't you excited?"

Martha laughed. "Not as much as you."

Asher led them to a house at the end of the road, sitting next to the shore. He knocked on the door. "Achot?"

A loud crash sounded from inside.

Asher's eyes widened. "Tabitha? Are you all right?"

The door flew open, and a woman ran out. "Asher!" She wrapped her arms around his neck, nearly knocking him over. "What are you doing here?"

Asher patted her back and extricated himself from her embrace. "I came to see you." He grasped Martha's hand and drew her near. "I want you to meet my wife."

Her eyes flew to Martha, and she burst into a grin. "Your *wife*?" She wrapped her arms around Martha and squeezed her tight.

Martha gasped as it seemed all the air was forced from her lungs. She stared at a laughing Asher over Tabitha's shoulder.

He tapped her shoulder. "All right, achot. She can't breathe."

Tabitha pulled back, but kept one arm around Martha. "What happened to 'never again'?"

He shrugged. "I have no idea. It wasn't my plan. Why do you think I went to a tiny village on the side of a mountain?"

She shook a finger at him, laughing. "I told you. You can't hide from Adonai."

"I guess you were right." He smiled sweetly at Martha. "Turns out He was sending me to her."

Martha laughed. "Perhaps He could have let me in on the plan. Might have been easier to bear."

Tabitha peered behind Martha to study Mary. "And who is this?" Her eyes flitted from one to the other. "Her achot, I'm guessing?"

Mary nodded. "I'm Mary. And I knew he was for her the moment I met him."

"Did you?" Tabitha asked, laughing.

"Martha thought I was sent for *her*." Asher laughed as he jerked a thumb toward Mary.

Mary grinned. "I've always been smarter than she is about things like that."

Martha smacked Mary's arm. "You hush."

"Well, we'll have plenty of time to talk about all this later. I think I'll put you on the roof. It's lovely this time of year. You can hear the sea birds and the waves. That all right with you, Ash? Back on the roof?"

"I always loved it there."

"Why don't you go up and rest for a bit? Joel will be home soon."

Martha and Asher followed Mary up the stairs to the roof. "Tabitha was right. It is lovely," Martha said.

Mary wheeled to face them. "What did she mean?"

"What did who mean?" Martha asked.

"Your sister. She asked if it was all right with you to be back on the roof."

"Oh." He shrugged. "I grew up in this house. I slept up here almost every night."

"You didn't tell us that."

"I'm sorry. It's just been her house for so long. I don't even think of it as ever being mine anymore."

"You slept up here every night? Even in the rainy season?"

"It rarely rains at night, but if it did I'd sleep inside on the floor of my brothers' room."

"Was there no room inside?"

"My parents fought…a lot. My abba was a very angry man. He yelled at all of us but especially my imma. It was just easier to stay out of the way."

"How many brothers do you have? And where are they?"

"I have four brothers, all much older than I am. They married and left home as soon as they could." He shrugged. "Can't say I blame them. Anyway, I loved it up here. I'd lie here and count the stars to shut out the noise."

Martha placed her hand on his shoulder. "I'm so sorry, ahuvi."

He kissed her cheek. "It's all right. It worked out fine."

Mary helped Tabitha carry the meal to the roof and place the food on the mat, then sat on a cushion between Martha and Tabitha.

"Where's Joel?" Mary asked.

"At the synagogue," Tabitha said. "He should be on his way, though. He's always here by sunset, at least. He loves being up here this time of day."

"I don't blame him." Mary watched the fishermen shove their boats into the lake and clamber aboard. She pointed toward the shore. "What are they doing?"

"They're going to fish."

Her jaw dropped. "At night?"

He nodded. "Their nets are made of flax or linen. The fish can see them in the bright sun and just swim right around them."

"They can also avoid the heat," added Tabitha. "Not so bad this time of year, but in summer? That sun will burn the skin off your body."

"It's lovely up here," Martha said. "The sea is beautiful. I could watch it all day."

Tabitha nodded. "It is, isn't it? We forget that sometimes, seeing it every day. But I must admit it's one of Adonai's most wonderful creations." They watched the sea for a few long moments, soft waves lapping against the rocky shore. "Don't let it fool you, though. It can change in a moment, from gentle to deadly."

All heads jerked toward the stairs as heavy footfalls drew their attention.

"Oh dear." Tabitha grimaced. "He must have had a bad day. I don't hear that very often."

Joel stepped onto the roof and crossed to them, his face dark. He growled as he dropped down next to his wife and snatched a cup of wine.

Tabitha placed her hand on his arm. "Ahuvi, what's the matter?"

"Did you hear those ridiculous rumors about what happened just north of here?"

"What rumors?"

"About that new Rabbi, the one who spends so much time in Capernaum."

The new Rabbi? Mary's heart sped up, and she leaned nearer.

Joel scowled. "There are always outrageous stories about Him. It seems a new one every week."

"What kind of stories?" Mary asked.

"Supposedly He helped His talmidim catch a load of fish so large He nearly sank their boat. They also say He once changed water to wine. But mostly, it's healings. Paralytics. Demoniacs. Lepers." He laughed derisively. "Not one leper has been healed in Israel since Naaman."

Mary grabbed Martha's hand and squeezed. "It's Rabbi Yeshua! It must be!"

"Who?" Tabitha asked.

"Yes, Yeshua." Joel's voice was sharp. "I think that is the name. Why? Do you know of Him?"

Martha nodded, her face bright. "We know Him very well. He's stayed at our house."

Tabitha's brow furrowed. "Why would He stay at your house?"

"Martha and her family are hosts in Bethany," Asher said. "Travelers, most of them Galileans, stay with them when they come to Jerusalem for—"

Joel rested his forearms on his legs, leaning nearer. "Then this Rabbi, He's stayed with you?"

"He's stayed with us many times, whenever He comes to Jerusalem for a feast." Mary thought a couple of weeks back to Pesach, when she'd looked for Him every day, but never saw Him. "But He didn't come this time, so..." Her voice trailed off as she thought of all the reasons—most of them bad—that would keep Him away.

"You must know Him well then." Joel's voice softened. What do you think of Him?"

How to describe Him? Healer? Prophet? Rabbi?

Mashiach?

"I think He was sent by Adonai." Before Mary could answer, Martha pronounced her judgment.

"You do?" asked Tabitha.

"I mentioned to Martha that I wanted to come to see you." Asher set his empty cup aside. "When we decided to come, we thought we might try to find Him while we were up here."

"You mean because He didn't come for Pesach? Many Galileans don't."

Asher nodded. "After what happened to John, well, we've been worried."

"John?" asked Joel.

"The one they call the baptizer. You've heard of him, surely?"

"Oh yes." Tabitha nodded. "The one that lives in the wilderness. Wasn't he arrested?"

"Yes, he was. By Herod," Mary said. Her throat burned.

"Are you afraid Herod will arrest this Rabbi of yours?" Joel asked.

"John wasn't just arrested." Asher fixed his gaze on his brother-in-law. "Herod killed him."

Tabitha's eyes grew as big as the figs in front of them. "What?"

"He beheaded him," Mary said.

"Whatever for?" Tabitha spread her hands to her sides.

"Antipas said he was guilty of treason." Asher scoffed. "He said he feared John's activities would bring the wrath of the Romans upon us. But we think it was because John publicly criticized Herod for marrying Herodias, because she was his brother's wife."

"And if John was killed because Herod didn't like what he had to say, what's to stop him from killing Yeshua?" asked Martha.

"Herod is no descendant of David, and he doesn't belong on the throne, but just because he isn't righteous doesn't mean that your Rabbi is," Joel said.

"So you came here to make sure He's all right?" Tabitha reached for his cup.

Martha swallowed a bite of fish. "Our brother says most of the Pharisees are not very happy with Him. They've even talked about stoning Him."

"Talked about it! They've tried to! More than once." Mary's voice came out louder than she intended.

"Well, what did He do to deserve that?" Joel asked.

Mary tried to hide her disgust. "He only gave a blind man back his sight, and a lame man is now walking again."

"Trickery!" Joel laughed. "Or worse, the work of demons. I've seen men who call themselves rabbis do that before. They think such things will gain them followers, and it does, but they all fall away as soon as the deception is revealed."

Mary rose up on her knees. How dare they speak of Yeshua in that way! "It is most definitely not trickery. We know the man He healed. He hadn't walked or even stood upright since Abba was a small child. Now we see him in Jerusalem all the time. And even if you think so, He healed our abba, and no one can ever tell me He didn't." She punctuated her statement with a jab in the air and sat back.

Martha squeezed her hand. "Our abba had leprosy, but Yeshua healed him. Both his illness and his cleansing were verified by priests." Martha spoke softly and calmly as if she were trying to make up for Mary's unnecessary emotion.

Joel stopped chewing and fixed his gaze on Asher for a long, silent moment. "Her abba was cleansed of leprosy?" His voice still held disbelief, but the condescension from before had vanished. Joel obviously held Asher—and apparently anyone Asher loved—in high regard.

"Yes, he was. And the priest who pronounced him clean was the same priest who sent him away. I can guarantee you he did not want to do anything that would help Yeshua. He is no friend of the Rabbi, but even he couldn't deny it."

Joel set his bread down as he pondered their words. "All I've heard about this man are rumors. I've heard what the Pharisees in Capernaum have to say, which is not flattering, as you may well imagine. I've never met Him or anyone who knows Him. I trust you, and I believe you speak the truth, but at the same time, I can't believe it."

Asher grinned. "He does that to people."

"Perhaps we can pay a visit to the synagogue leader in Capernaum. See what he has to say about all this."

"You know this synagogue leader?" Asher asked.

Joel nodded. "I know him well. He was the leader here in our synagogue before Capernaum stole him away. I trust him too."

"Sounds like a good idea then," Asher agreed.

"Tomorrow is Shabbat, so we'll leave the next day at midday. It's not a long walk."

It should be a good idea, but Mary worried. Yeshua had upset as many synagogue leaders as Pharisees. Would the synagogue leader defend Him—or side with the leaders who want Him stoned?

CHAPTER TWENTY-TWO

An honest answer is like a kiss on the lips.
—Proverbs 24:26 (NIV)

Iyyar 8

Mary gasped as they entered the market in Capernaum. Too bad Martha chose to stay home with Tabitha—she would have loved it. She said she went to the market often enough at home, and perhaps she was right, but Mary couldn't get enough of the sounds, the scents, the colors, the people. "It's so huge! Almost as big as Jerusalem's."

"It serves a large area," Joel said. "People like us come from all over. Capernaum is one of the biggest cities in Galilee, and merchants from the entire region bring goods here to sell."

Enormous, brightly dyed cloths of blue, deep red, and sun yellow stretched out to poles from the walls, offering shade to vendors and buyers alike.

She cringed as four Roman soldiers strutted past them on their way to the city gates. "I didn't expect so many soldiers."

"There's a Roman barracks here, on the other side of the city," Joel said. "So there are always a great number of soldiers all over the city, especially in the market. They don't usually bother us unless a fight breaks out."

"Where's the synagogue?" Mary asked. Shopping could wait. It was far more important that she and Asher hear what this friend of Joel's had to say about Yeshua.

"There are several in a city this size. My friend's is just down the street." Joel gestured to his left. "We can go there first, or to the market, whichever you prefer."

"The synagogue," Mary said.

Joel flashed her a bemused smile. "You don't want to see what they have in the market?"

She shook her head. "The synagogue." She'd never enjoy the shops until she knew what the leader had to say.

They hadn't strolled far along the street when a deep voice caught their attention. "Joel!"

The three turned and scanned the road to see who called.

"Joel! Here!" A short, balding, animated man waved from across the road. The voice was much bigger than should fit in such a small body.

Joel laughed as the man hurried toward them. "Jairus! Shalom!"

"Shalom!" Jairus wrapped Joel in a fervent embrace then pulled back, one arm still around Joel's shoulder. "Here to enjoy the market?"

"Perhaps later, but first we came to visit you. Let me introduce my wife's ach, Asher, and his wife's achot, Mary."

"Shalom to you all." A bright smile consumed his face, as if they were friends he'd finally found again after decades of searching. "Is there something I can do for you? Is your synagogue in need of something?"

Joel winced. "No, um, we want to speak to you about the Rabbi, Yeshua. I know He spends a lot of time here, and I was hoping you can tell us about Him."

"Oh, I'd be delighted!"

The joy on Jairus's face was overwhelming. Even Joel had to recognize it, though he likely didn't realize, as Mary did, that it was the joy of one who had encountered Yeshua.

"So you think He is a genuine healer?" Joel asked.

"Oh, He's far more than that, my friend. I believe He is the Son of God."

It was all Mary could do to keep from cheering right there in the middle of the street.

"What makes you say that?"

"Why don't you come to my house and see? Deborah will be so happy to see you."

"Are you sure you want guests?" Joel lowered his voice. "How is your daughter?"

Jairus laughed, a deep and hearty sound that caused several bystanders to look their way. "Just come and see."

The long journey had caught up with her, and Martha had decided to skip Capernaum's market in favor of rest. But she'd never intended to fall asleep and leave the work to Tabitha. She peered up at the sun, halfway down to its own western resting place, and hurried downstairs. The scent of roasted fish engulfed her as she entered the common room. A wave of nausea bubbled up, and she suppressed a gag. She covered her mouth with her hand and ran from the room in time to vomit in the backyard. She stood and dragged her hand across her mouth.

Tabitha approached with a cloth and a pottery cup. "Here."

Martha accepted the cloth and cleaned her hand and mouth.

"Drink it."

Martha sipped the heavily honeyed wine. The sweetness chased away the sour taste, and the honey soothed her stomach.

"Are you all right?" Tabitha searched her face.

She nodded. "I don't know what came over me."

Tabitha frowned. "You don't?"

She pursed her lips. "I may have some idea."

"When did you last bleed?"

"Eleven weeks." And five days. Martha had counted every one of them.

Tabitha's eyes widened. "And you haven't said anything yet?"

Martha's cheeks heated, but she remained quiet.

"Not even to Asher?" Her eyes widened. "You couldn't have. Because that would have been the first thing out of his mouth if you had."

"I'm afraid to."

Tabitha took the empty cup. "Afraid of what? His reaction?"

"Of course not." She breathed deeply. "Afraid it won't happen, and he'll be disappointed—again. I know what happened before, and I don't want him to hurt like that again."

"Oh, Martha." She tipped her head toward the house. "Come sit down."

She crinkled her nose. "I'm sure your fish is wonderful, but I can't. I'm sorry. We don't get fresh fish very often. Only salted fish is available in our market."

Tabitha laughed. "Then let's go sit by the water. When I was pregnant, the sea air helped my nausea." She pointed toward the shore. "There are two large rocks just there. Have a seat and I'll bring you some more wine."

Martha made her way out of the courtyard and toward the water. Fishing boats dotted the shore. Large white-headed birds, their wide wings lined in black, soared over the water, screeching greetings to each other.

Tabitha appeared beside her, a cup in each hand. "Majestic, aren't they?"

Martha took the newly filled cup. "I've never seen anything like them."

"You have to tell him, you know." She steered Martha toward the rocks and sat on one.

Martha sat facing her, the cup cradled in both hands. "But what if—"

"He can handle it. He's handled it before. But even if not, is deception a better alternative? Is that a good way to start your marriage?"

"I suppose not."

"I once lied to my husband. I didn't want to tell him some bad news about my family. It turned out the news was far less important than what happened to us. It took him years for him to completely trust me again."

Martha recoiled, straightening her shoulders. "But I'm not lying."

"No, but I don't think the results will be much different. Even if it's good news you're withholding, not bad, and even if it's done to protect him. It's just not a good idea."

She relaxed. "I know you're right. I've known it all along, I think. I'm probably trying to protect myself as much as him. If I don't say it aloud…"

"It doesn't exist."

Martha grinned. "Something like that."

"And yet it does. And Asher has a right to know about it."

Tabitha was right. But what would he say when she told him she'd been keeping something this important from him?

Mary followed the men into Jairus's house. A girl just short of womanhood sat in the courtyard with her imma, spinning wool.

The woman—Deborah?—rose to meet them. "Joel! It's been so long. I'm so glad to see you. And where is Tabitha?"

"We didn't want to bother you. You have so much…" Joel halted in midstep. "Is this Esther?" He pointed to the girl.

"It is." Deborah beamed. "I'll get us some wine. You have a long story ahead." She beckoned to the girl, and they disappeared inside the house.

Joel's brows knit together. "But I thought she was ill. Very ill."

"She was," Jairus answered. "In fact, she was at the point of death."

"Then what happened?" Joel asked.

Mary could hardly keep silent. *I know what happened. Yeshua happened.*

"You know, I'd heard all the stories. And I thought, what can it hurt? So I went to find Him, this Rabbi I'd heard so many rumors about, and I fell at His feet and begged Him to come heal her."

"And He did?"

Jairus chuckled. "Eventually."

"What does that mean?" Joel threw his hands in the air.

Even Mary could tell he was growing frustrated—probably much like Martha often felt with her.

"Sit, sit." Jairus lowered himself to the blanket on the ground as Deborah returned with cups and an amphora. Esther held a bowl of pistachios, which she placed in the center of them. "He was on the way to our house when we were interrupted by a woman who was herself quite ill. And He stopped to deal with *her*!" His face clouded. "I'm ashamed to admit, I was incensed."

"An honest reaction, ahuvi." Deborah handed him a cup of wine.

"I thought, 'This woman is alive, and my daughter is dying!' But then I saw her face, and she was in such pain. She said she'd been unclean for twelve years, which is the same amount of time Esther has been alive. To be unclean all that time, separated from the people of Adonai... Forgive me." He sniffled and wiped his eyes. "And all she did was touch the hem of His robe, and He said she was clean! I was certain then He could heal Esther. We headed here again, but on the way..." His voice broke, and his eyes misted.

"While Joel was gone, Esther... She took her last breath." Deborah took over the story. "I sent someone to tell him he should come home. Mourners showed up, hired by some of the Pharisees. I know they were trying to show Joel respect as the head of the synagogue, but I hated the sound of them. I couldn't even grieve myself for all their noise."

Mary had never been around professional mourners. No resident of Bethany could afford them, and those in the bet... they rarely had anyone who cared enough.

"The men stopped us in the street and told me Esther... they told me not to bother the Rabbi anymore. I felt like my heart had been ripped from my body. Despair threatened to destroy me. I fell to my knees again. But He knelt with me, and raised my face to His and said, 'Don't be afraid; just believe, and she will be healed.'"

"And did you? Believe?" asked Joel.

"Of course he did! Look at her! She's most certainly alive!" Mary laughed.

Jairus narrowed an eye at her. "You know Him, don't you? I can tell by the look on your face."

"Yes! We do! Very well. He—"

"Finish the story!" Joel roared.

Mary glanced at Asher, who only grinned.

"We arrived, and He told all the mourners to hush. Said she was only asleep, which, as you can imagine, brought a flurry of scorn and laughter. He ordered all of them from the house and allowed only Deborah, me, and three of His talmidim in with Him. And then He simply told her to wake up."

"And she did!" Deborah reached for Esther's hand.

"Maybe she *was* only asleep," Joel said.

Deborah shook her head. "She was not asleep. There was no breath, no movement, her eyes were open… She was gone."

"And the other woman?" Mary asked. "Did you know her? Was she from here?"

"I didn't know her. She lived at the very edge of the city. She never left her house—she couldn't. She was unclean. But she'll be here on Shabbat, if you want to meet her."

Joel was silent on the short walk back to his village, but Mary all but ran. Martha had to hear about this.

The sun cast long shadows over the lake as Asher hurried toward the women sitting at the edge of the river.

Martha winced. Time to tell him the truth.

He drew close to them and stood behind his sister, aiming a soft smile at Martha. "There you are. I've been looking for you. So is Mary, but I told her I got to see you first. We have quite a story to tell you while we eat."

Martha studied her fingernails.

"Is something wrong? Why are you two out here?"

Tabitha rose. "I guess it's a good day for stories. I'll go… um…finish the fish." She hurried away, and Asher took her seat.

"Martha? Is everything all right?" He glanced at his hastily retreating sibling. "She didn't say anything to you, did she? Something to hurt you? I know sometimes she's blunt, but—"

Martha leaned over and grabbed his hands. "No, of course not. She's wonderful. A lot like you, in many ways."

"Then what?"

"I have to tell you… I have to confess something to you and hope you will forgive me."

"Whatever it is, I'm sure it's nothing. I can't think of anything you could do I wouldn't forgive. If it even needs to be forgiven in the first place."

She could only hope that was true. "I… I am carrying your child."

His face lit up like the sun escaping a cloud. "Martha, that's wonderful!" He slid off the rock to his knees, kneeling before her, then placed his hands on her cheeks and kissed her. He sat back, his hands holding hers. "That's marvelous news. What could possibly need to be forgiven about that?"

The easy part was over. She sucked in a breath. "I've known for a while, but I didn't tell you."

His face clouded a bit, and he backed up onto the rock again. "How long?"

"Over two months. Almost three."

"Two months?" The disbelief in his voice skewered her heart. All her plans to keep him from being hurt had come to nothing. That pain was there, written on his face, and she had been the scribe.

He rose to pace at the water's edge, rubbing the back of his neck. At length he stopped and turned to face her. "Why?"

She raised her face to meet his gaze. "I wanted to wait until I was sure. I didn't want you to be disappointed like…like before."

His face relaxed a bit, and he knelt before her again, his hands on her arms. "Martha, yes, I was disappointed my baby did not live. But what saddened me more was watching Leah wither away. She couldn't trust Adonai to care for her, and she couldn't trust me to love her anyway."

"I do trust you. And I love you. I was only trying to protect you."

"I appreciate the sentiment, ahuvati. I do." He allowed a soft chuckle. "But Martha, we can't avoid pain in this life. You should know that more than most. And we can't hold the truth prisoner, no matter how good the intentions or the reasons are. The truth will always become known, somehow. So promise me you will always tell me the truth. All of it."

"I promise." She swiped away a tear. "I'm so sorry. Forgive me?"

He placed his hand on her cheek. "As I've heard you and Mary say so often, nothing to forgive."

CHAPTER TWENTY-THREE

*And these are but the outer fringe of his works;
how faint the whisper we hear of him!
Who then can understand the thunder of his power?*
—Job 26:14 (NIV)

Iyyar 15

Martha flinched and wiped her cheek. She pulled away wet fingers. Was that rain?

She sat up as several more drops landed on her head. "Asher!"

No response.

"Asher!"

He grunted and rolled to face away from her.

She shook his arm. "Asher, wake up!"

He rolled onto his back. "What? What is it?"

"It's raining!"

He looked at the moonlit sky. "No, it's not."

"Then what's this?" She swiped a drop from his cheek.

Mary bolted upright. "It's raining!" She rose and snatched her mat and blanket. "I'm going inside." She ran for the stairs and disappeared behind the wall.

Martha giggled. "Me too. Stay here and get drenched if you want. I'm taking the blanket, though."

She rose and followed Mary, mat and blanket in hand.

Mary had already spread her mat along the back wall of the common room and lay facing it.

Martha tossed her mat nearby and dropped the blanket on it, then headed for the edge of the covered part of the common room.

Dark clouds gathered above the center of the lake, but the waves lapping along the shore were no more than they'd been all day.

"It looks like the storm is way out there. Perhaps it won't reach us after all."

Asher laughed as he followed them in. "Oh, no. It will be here soon enough. The wind is churning up waves out there large enough to sink any one of these boats easily. But all that energy has to go somewhere, so the waves will spread out from the center and reach every part of the shore, all the way around the lake. Over there, on the east side, they won't do much damage because high mountains reach right down to the shore. But here… It doesn't happen often, but the waves can destroy the boats, even homes."

"But earlier, when we were eating, there were no clouds, no dark skies. It was a beautiful night."

"I know. It happens quite suddenly. Only after the rains, though, when it's hotter on the eastern shore than it is here. My abba used to say the hot winds and the cold winds were battling in the sky." He chuckled softly.

A wave crashed against the rocks, splashing water into the courtyard.

"Oh!" Martha jumped back. "The waves are getting higher. And stronger."

The wind grew fiercer, bending the olive and fig trees low as if they were bowing to an invisible monarch. The rain pelted the sea, the rocks, and the ground, and the air chilled in a moment.

"Will the boats be safe?"

"The fishermen know that though a furious storm is unlikely, it would destroy their vessels. They're all on their way back to shore."

A bolt of lightning lit up the sky, and Martha shuddered. Thunder rolled before the sky darkened again.

"Blessed are You, Adonai our God, King of the universe, who performs the work of creation," whispered Martha.

"Blessed are You, Adonai our Lord, King of the universe, whose power and might fill the world." Asher recited the blessing of thunder, the twin to her blessing of the lightning.

"Adonai, keep all those safe on the lake tonight."

Iyyar 16

Gazing at the sea from the roof of Tabitha's house, Martha hugged herself against the chill of the early morning. The sun hadn't yet burned away the mist that settled over the low-lying sea. The air was wetter and colder than she was used to, but the scent soothed her mind, and somehow, her body.

Warmth enveloped her, and she felt a blanket drape her shoulders, and arms wrapping around her from behind.

"You came back up?" Asher whispered.

She nodded as his hand slid from her waist to her belly.

"How are you feeling?"

"Much better." She placed her arms on his and leaned back against his chest. "The storm is over. Look, the water is as calm as glass."

They watched in silence for a few moments.

"I spent many mornings on this roof watching the boats come in," Asher said.

"You did?"

His chin bumped against her shoulder as he nodded. "Nothing has changed."

"Nothing? Tell me about it."

"Let's see. That boat"—he pointed to the left—"belongs to old Amos. Or it used to. Looks like his sons are manning it now. The one next to it is Bildad's. The next one is Gideon's. And on the right, that one was Jabez's. He died just before I left, so I don't know who's running it now."

"So a few changes then." She chuckled.

"A few."

She squinted at the lake, then pointed out a boat just offshore. "Why is that one still out?"

"I don't know. I hope no one is injured." He stepped out from behind her and moved closer to the edge.

She moved to stand beside him. "Should we go see if they need help? There doesn't appear to be anyone else around."

"I'm sure they're all right, but I'll go check." He kissed her cheek and headed toward the stairs, grabbing his cloak on the way.

Martha followed him down and found Tabitha and Mary by the fire. She knelt beside them and picked up a hand stone. She poured kernels of barley on the quern and began grinding the grain into flour.

"How are you feeling today?"

"Much better. Todah for asking."

"Your nausea should be over for the most part. At least that's the way it happens for most wom—"

"Tabitha!" Joel bellowed.

They hurried to the courtyard, where Joel stood by the knee-high wall, arms crossed, facing the lake.

Tabitha stood beside him, studying her husband. "Joel, what's wrong?"

"What on earth is he doing?" he growled.

"Who? What are you talking about?" she asked.

Joel pointed to the shore. "He's bringing a boatload of people to our home!"

"Who is?" Tabitha scanned the shore.

"Your ach."

Martha stepped closer to the wall and tried to see what had upset Joel so much. At first she saw nothing other than Asher strolling toward them, but beyond him, on the shore, a boat had anchored, and a large group of men clambered out. Had they gone back out after the storm passed? Or had they never come in?

Asher neared them, grinning, and extended his arm. "Look who I found."

She stepped closer. The group seemed familiar, but in the dusky light it was hard to make out faces. A familiar, gentle laugh sounded, and her breath came faster as she recognized the gait of one of the men.

Yeshua and His talmidim.

Mary rushed to meet Him, and His face brightened.

"Ah, my favorite family!"

She wrapped Him in a hug. "What are You doing here? Why did You arrive by boat?"

Martha wasn't far behind her sister, and Yeshua embraced her too. "Martha, I'm so happy to see you."

He continued walking toward the house, where Joel and Tabitha stood with mouths open.

"We came from Bethsaida. We meant to land in Capernaum, but we ran into a little wind."

"That's not all that happened," John muttered as he passed them.

"What does he mean?" Mary asked Yeshua.

"Ignore him. We've been on the lake most of the night."

"We hoped to find You!" Mary said.

He laughed. "You did."

John neared Martha again and jerked a thumb at Asher. "He said this is his sister's house and that we were welcome to stay. But the Rabbi would like to talk to her and her husband first."

"Of course. Let me introduce you." She led John to the couple, Yeshua only a step or two behind.

"This is my home. May I help you?"

"Shalom, Joel. I'm Yeshua. These are My students. Asher has offered us a place to stay tonight, but I realize it's not his house."

"You know him?" Joel couldn't hide the surprise in his voice.

He smiled. "Very well. And Mary and Martha as well. I've stayed with them many times."

"Then of course. Welcome to my home. Come in, and we'll get You some food and then You can rest. You must be exhausted."

"We won't be here long. We need to return to Capernaum."

"As You wish, but You may remain as long as You like."

"Todah, Joel. That's very generous."

"Why don't You go to the roof? Unless You'd rather not face the sea." He chuckled.

Yeshua laughed with him. "The roof will be nice."

"I'll bring some water for Your feet."

Tabitha approached and steered the women back inside. "We have thirteen hungry men to feed."

Martha's heart sank. It would take them hours to grind enough flour, let alone make and cook the bread. She was suddenly very thankful for the mill at home.

"I have flour saved for just such an occasion. I'll bring it from the storeroom. You girls get the oven nice and hot. I'll also bring some dried fruit and olives." She disappeared, reappearing later with several jars in the crook of her arm and cheese wrapped in cloth in her other. "Those boys will be hungry if they were rowing against the wind all night. I know what 'a little wind' is like on that lake."

Mary took a large basket of bread and the fruit to the roof. "More is coming."

"Todah, Mary," John said.

James nodded. "Yes, todah."

"I'll be right back."

"We know He's here," called a woman from the street.

"Bring out the Rabbi," yelled another.

Mary ran to the edge of the roof and peered over the edge. Her breath stilled. "Oh no."

"What's wrong?" asked James.

"I think there are some people here looking for You, Yeshua."

Yeshua silently stuffed the last bite of bread in His mouth and grabbed another before heading down the stairs.

Mary returned to the group. "He doesn't seem very happy. Or maybe He just needs rest?"

"I think it saddens Him that people come only for the healings," Simon said. "They don't really want to hear what He has to say, but His love and compassion for the people won't let Him ignore them."

The others grabbed what bread remained and followed their Teacher.

"Wait, will you be back?" called Mary.

James shrugged. "This could last most of the day."

CHAPTER TWENTY-FOUR

*When they had crossed over, they landed at Gennesaret
and anchored there.*
—Mark 6:53 (NIV)

Mary, Martha, and the others stood on the roof overlooking the never-ending crowd that lined the main road and trailed east. Men, women, children, babies. Some on crutches, some limping, some carried by family or friends. Others, apparently blind, led by the arm. It was like nothing they'd ever seen before.

"Where did they all come from?" Mary asked. "They can't all be from Gennesaret."

"Oh, no," answered Tabitha. "This is many times the population of this little town."

Joel gestured at the people. "A lot of them are farmers. I can tell by their dress. They must be from much farther inland."

"How do you think they heard?" asked Martha.

"He's been spending a great deal of His time in Capernaum." Joel shrugged. "Jairus said the city has been inundated with those who follow Him. Thousands, really. And the Rabbi said they'd planned to return there, so my guess is when they didn't show up, the crowds followed Him here."

"But how would they know He was here? Specifically?" asked Mary. "He could have landed anywhere along the coast."

"Maybe they were on the roof, looking for Him, the way we are now." Asher gestured up and down the shore. "We can see all the way to Capernaum and Magdala on a clear day. It would take only one person to figure out where He was headed and tell everyone else. It's not much farther from here to Capernaum than it is from Bethany to Jerusalem."

Tabitha's eyes widened. "You're that close to the temple?"

"Oh yes, just on the other side of the mount. Less than an hour's walk. That's why so many stay in Bethany or Bethphage or even camp on the slopes when the city is full."

"It's much more pleasant than being in a crowded city," added Martha.

"We should get back down. They'll be gone some time, and they'll need even more food than before."

The sun was past its apex when James, John, Simon, and Andrew slipped away from the crowd.

"Some of the talmidim are coming!" Mary pointed to the trio. "I'm sure they're hungry."

"And exhausted," Asher said. "Don't forget they were fighting the wind all night."

"Oh, those poor men! They must be asleep on their feet!" Tabitha said. "Let's get that bread baking, girls. Joel, do we have enough wine?"

He nodded. "Asher and I brought some in from the storeroom, along with some more olives and some oil."

"Thank you. That was very thoughtful." Tabitha patted his arm.

"I'm learning." He chuckled just as the men stumbled into the courtyard.

"Here, sit." Mary pointed to a low table in the courtyard. She set a full basket on it and the men half sat, half collapsed to the ground.

Asher approached with a pitcher and bowl, and a cloth slung over one arm. He set it at one end of the table. "For your feet."

"Thank you," mumbled Andrew as he reached for the bowl.

Mary watched as the men took turns washing the dust from their feet, setting their sandals aside. Heavy eyelids drooped over bloodshot, red-rimmed eyes, and slow, deliberate movements attested to heavy limbs. Rumpled clothing and hair wet with sweat attested to the difficult work of not only last night, but this morning as well.

Mary set a bowl of olives before them. "Will the others be coming after you are done?"

Simon shrugged. "I don't know. He just told us to come eat and rest a bit."

"Sit with us, please. You can help keep us awake." James chuckled.

Mary sat at the other end of the table while Martha began filling cups with honeyed wine. "And the others? Do they not need food?"

"They may come get something to eat and return to help. But I think He wanted us to rest, as we did most of the rowing last night."

Mary frowned. Why only those four?

Andrew seemed to read her mind. "We're the most experienced fishermen. We were all awake all night, except for Him."

Martha sat beside Mary. "I don't understand. He wasn't with you, or He wasn't awake?"

"He joined us later," John answered. "He'd stayed behind to pray, and we assumed He'd meet us in Bethsaida."

"He didn't?" Mary asked.

"In the darkest of the night, the wind picked up. I've been a fisherman since I could walk, and I've rarely felt wind that strong. And never while in a boat." Andrew sat up straighter, the story energizing him. "We rowed, and rowed, and finally we put two men to each oar. We tried to get to Capernaum but we kept getting pushed west."

Mary watched Simon, who had been strangely silent since they arrived, and hadn't eaten a single bite.

"Then, near dawn, we saw…something…on that lake." James continued the tale. "It looked like a man, but that made no sense. A man, in the middle of the lake?"

"It made no sense *at the time*," added John.

"It was Yeshua!" Andrew's arms flailed. "He was walking on the water! Just as easily as if it was solid ground. And we were afraid, I can tell you. We thought it the spirit of a dead man."

"But He called to us!" James added. "He said, 'It's me. Don't be afraid.' And our fear vanished."

"Then what?"

"Then He climbed into the boat, and the wind stopped, as if someone had blown out a flame." Simon's tone seemed to put a stop to the story, or at least head it off in a different direction.

Mary looked at each one, but the men concentrated on their food. "Why do I feel we're missing something?"

"You're missing nothing. Except that now we truly know who He is." Simon drained his cup and stood. "I'm going to do as the Rabbi instructed and try to sleep." He tromped toward the stairs.

"There are mats and blankets up there," Martha called.

The other three whispered among themselves. "If He didn't tell, we shouldn't," said John.

"It will become known, no matter what," Andrew said.

Mary had had enough. "What are you taking about?"

The three exchanged long looks, and then Andrew faced them. "Simon walked on the water too."

Mary gasped.

"He what?" asked Martha.

"When Yeshua called out and said, 'It is me,' Simon said, 'If it's really You, tell me to come to You.' Yeshua stretched out His hand and said, 'Come.' And he did! Simon *walked to Him.*" James shook his head. "It was the most astonishing thing I have ever seen. I mean, we see Yeshua work wonders all the time, like today. But He is sent by Adonai. This was *Simon*. One of us."

Mary leaned forward. "How far did he walk?"

"A few steps," said John. "The wind picked up even harder, and he began to sink. Yeshua pulled him back up and they got in the boat."

"But it was more than any of us did," said Andrew.

Yeshua walking on water. *Simon* walking on water. Thousands of people healed before her eyes.

Yeshua was of God, Mary knew that.

But who was He, exactly? More than a prophet. More than a rabbi.

And what did Simon mean when he said, "Now we truly know who He truly is"?

Iyyar 25

Martha placed her hand on her belly. Though it was still as flat as it always had been, it all seemed more real since she'd told Asher. Mary was as excited as they were and talked about her new niece or nephew almost as much as she talked about Yeshua.

Asher fell into step beside her. "Are you feeling all right?"

"Yes, actually I'm feeling better than I did on the way here."

He halted, grasping her arm. "Is that all right? Does that mean something's wrong? Do we need to stop for the night?"

She laughed. "Tabitha said it's quite normal. In fact, she told me that the next three months should be the easiest part. Which is good, since all the summer work will be upon us soon."

"You need to take it easy. We'll have to find something for you to do that's not terribly strenuous."

She laughed again. "Asher, women have been harvesting *and* having babies since Adonai gave breath to Eve. I'll be just fine."

She was far more concerned about the events of the last week. They would not leave Martha alone. She'd heard of the healings, she'd even seen Him heal Abba.

But to see so many people healed of so many things in one day...

Many of those touched by the Rabbi had been carried to Him, unable to walk. And like the man by the pool of Bethesda, they arose, picked up their mats, and walked away. The blind saw again—or for the first time—and marveled at the rippling waters of the lake, the colors of the sky, and the fruit of the trees that seemed to be so abundant in this area. Those who were deaf heard the praises of others and joined in with their own, while others spoke for the first time. Children, small and frail and who had been ill much of their lives, laughed and jumped while their immas cried for joy. Limbs were straightened, skin was cleared, strength was restored.

Miracles that happened one at a time were easier to understand. They were woven into the fabric of all the other things about the Rabbi. But seeing hundreds of people cured of diseases and injuries and lifelong sorrows was an entirely different matter. These were not works that could be overshadowed by teaching and confrontations with the Jewish leaders. This time the wondrous works were all there was. They couldn't be ignored or explained away or even tucked in the back of one's mind.

And then there was the storm that stopped so suddenly, not to mention Simon walking on the lake along with Yeshua.

This time the very nature of life and creation itself had been challenged and upended. No mere rabbi, no prophet, was capable of that.

There was only one answer.

Yeshua was the Promised One of Adonai, the Redeemer.

The Mashiach.

CHAPTER TWENTY-FIVE

*However, after his brothers had left for the festival,
he went also, not publicly, but in secret.*
—John 7:10 (NIV)

Tishri 14

"Rabbi!" Mary looked up from her water jug at the well. Her joy at seeing Yeshua and His students was muted by worry for His safety. She set aside the jar and rushed to meet Him. "We weren't expecting You!"

"Shall I go?" He grinned as He spread His arms to receive her.

"Of course not! We've missed You. All of you." She stepped back. "But are You sure it's safe for You to be here?"

Yeshua nodded. "It is not yet My time, and I am perfectly safe until it is." She shoved away the thoughts the word *until* brought to mind.

"Then we're glad You're here now. Come!" She slipped her arm though His and led them to the house.

The *sukkah* Abba and Lazarus had constructed, and that Mary and the children had decorated, occupied almost the entire courtyard.

John whistled. "It's enormous! I've never seen one so large."

"We always make it as big as we can, and we've never had trouble filling up. Until this year." Mary laughed. "Adonai must have been saving room for you."

Mary stepped into the common room. "They're here!"

Martha dropped her knife and hurried outside. "Rabbi! I'm so glad You were able to come. We feared You might have to remain in Galilee again."

"I'm glad to see you. Both of you." His eyes sparkled.

Her cheeks pinked, and she placed her hand on her very round belly. "Todah. It's all almost ready." She pointed to table waiting in the sukkah. "Please sit. There are nuts and cheese on the table, and the fish will be ready soon."

A soft breeze blew down the mount, bringing with it the scent of ripe olives and freshly pressed oil. Martha glanced up the road as she carried platters of roasted fish sprinkled with soft goat cheese from the common room to the table in the courtyard. Sukkot occupied courtyards, roofs, the street, and even the mount itself. Oil lamps twinkled from Bethany to Jerusalem, as if the stars in the sky had fallen to earth.

Lazarus and Asher lit the last of the oil lamps Martha had placed the length of the table as she set the fish next to baskets stacked high with hot bread. Bowls overflowing with fat grapes, ripe figs, black olives, almonds, dates, and pistachios completed the meal. Mary followed her, a pitcher of honeyed wine in each hand.

"Let us say the blessing," Abba said.

All rose and spread their hands, faces to heaven. "Blessed are You," the group recited, "Adonai our God, King of the Universe, who has made us holy by mitzvot and has instructed us to dwell in the sukkah."

As they sat on the cushions, Abba selected a round of bread and passed the basket to his left.

"Martha, thank you. This is another excellent meal. Especially after months on the road." Yeshua took bread and passed the basket.

Her heart warmed at His public praise. "Todah rabah."

The meal was nearly over when Yeshua cleared His throat. "There are some things I must tell you. You have been as much a home as I have had in these last few years. Bethany is as close to the kingdom of Adonai here on earth as is possible. You feed the hungry, you give water to the thirsty, you shelter the stranger. You clothe the naked and visit the abandoned. You have welcomed Me and My talmidim every time we've come to Jerusalem, and you've never asked for anything in return. You've listened to My teachings and embraced them."

Martha squirmed as He spoke. Those in Bethany weren't used to praise for their works. Jerusalem treated Bethany as a servant to be ignored, caring for those whom the city refused to even look upon.

"I've told My talmidim this, and now I tell you. You've been a refuge for Me, and I thank My Abba for you. But soon, everything that is written by the prophets about the Son of Man will be fulfilled. He will suffer many things from the elders and chief priests and scribes. He will be betrayed and handed over to the Gentiles. They will mock Him, insult Him, and spit on Him. They will flog Him and kill Him. But on the third day, He will rise again."

Silence filled the sukkah, stealing the air. Martha's stomach rebelled. The thought of anyone—let alone this Man they believed to be the promised Redeemer—being mocked, spit on, flogged, and killed... It was too much to bear.

She searched the faces of the talmidim. Though Yeshua had said He'd told them before, their faces registered shock and sorrow.

"But this is the festival of joy, and Adonai commands us to rejoice, so we'll talk about this more at another time. We must give thanks to Adonai for His abundant gifts and for all that He has done." His somber face lit up. "For now, let us go to My Abba's house for the ceremony of lights." He rose and headed for the gate, His talmidim following Him like obedient children.

Asher offered his hand and helped Martha to stand. "Are you coming?"

She shook her head and patted her very rounded belly. "I don't want to climb those stairs and then stand in that crowd all night. I'll see you all when you get back."

"All right. Let me help you gather up these dishes."

"Todah. I can't see my feet even when I'm not carrying a basket." She looked down at her body. "I feel like a giant olive. Or a grape. I could roll easier than I can walk."

He leaned near and kissed her cheek. "I think you're beautiful." He placed his hand on hers. "And I can't wait to meet this child." He kissed her again before gathering the dishes and food and taking them to the basket of sand for cleaning before meeting the others in the courtyard.

Mary passed out the citrons and lulavs—the palm, myrtle, and date fronds bound together that were waved in the courts to thank Adonai for His abundant harvest gifts.

Yeshua, His talmidim, Abba, Lazarus, and of course, Mary, marched up the path, fragrant lulavs in the right hand and the bright yellow fruit in the left. Mary's sweet, strong voice rose above the others as they sang the Hallel.

Martha closed her eyes and drank in the words of praise.

> *"With boughs in hand, join in the festal procession up to the horns of the altar.*
>
> *You are my God, and I will praise You; You are my God, and I will exalt You.*
>
> *Give thanks to the Lord, for He is good; His love endures forever."*

The mizmor faded as the worshipers left the village behind them, and she remembered Yeshua's dire words. What were they to do with such a horrifying prediction?

What would He tell them to do?

He would tell them to trust.

Her favorite Scripture returned to her mind.

I am like an olive tree flourishing in the house of God; I trust in God's unfailing love for ever and ever.

Trust. That was the answer. The only thing she could do.

It would not be easy.

CHAPTER TWENTY-SIX

"Whoever believes in me, as Scripture has said, rivers of living water will flow from within them."
—John 7:38 (NIV)

Tishri 21

As the shofar blew three times, Mary scurried up the steps to the balcony the priests had erected around the court for Sukkot. She stopped a few steps down so she could remain on the front row, albeit on her toes.

Levites stood on the fifteen semicircular stairs that divided the women's court from that of the Israelites. Their voices filled the temple with the songs of the Hallel as the mixture of the water and wine drained from the bowls into silver tubes that deposited the mixture in the Kidron Valley.

Priests holding willow branches marched once around the great altar, reciting for all to hear, "Adonai, save us! Adonai, grant us success!"

The singing and chanting faded away and a great silence fell upon the temple.

Mary closed her eyes and raised her face to the sky. The wind kissed her cheeks and whispered in her ear, and she remembered the words Yeshua had spoken to Nicodemus.

"The wind blows wherever it pleases. You hear its sound, but you cannot tell where it comes from or where it is going. So it is with everyone born of the Spirit."

"Let anyone who is thirsty come to Me and drink."

Her eyes popped open. Yeshua? She'd know that clear, strong voice anywhere. She stretched as tall as she could, searching the crowd for the Rabbi and His talmidim. There! In front of the Levites, He stood with arms outstretched, offering an embrace to all who heard. His students formed a ring around Him, facing outward, as if protecting Him from any who might try to harm Him.

She shoved her way across the front of the balcony, closer to the Nicanor Gate, ignoring the scoffs and reproofs thrown her way.

"Whoever believes in Me, as Scripture has said, rivers of living water will flow from within them."

Rivers of living water? What did that mean?

Whispers surrounded her, and the criticism was no longer directed at her.

"He's a prophet."

"He is the Mashiach."

"Isn't this Yeshua of Nazareth? How can the Mashiach come from Galilee?"

"He can't. We know the Scriptures say the Mashiach will come from David's descendants."

Mary knew the Scriptures also said He would come from Bethlehem, where David lived when he was a shepherd. If women were allowed to study Torah, they would all know this.

After the water ceremony, Martha joined Mary and the others on Solomon's Portico to hear Yeshua teach. The Rabbi sat on the covered colonnade chatting with His talmidim and others who had gathered to hear the young Rabbi.

Several strides away, a group of Pharisees huddled together, their eyes locked on Yeshua and His followers. Caiaphas anchored the group, standing with his hands together, hidden under voluminous sleeves. He remained silent while the others whispered among themselves, their hatred and fear of Yeshua palpable even from this far away.

Movement behind her drew Martha's attention. Another group of Pharisees strode across the Court of the Gentiles. Her heart stopped. Were they coming to arrest Yeshua?

She moved toward Asher, slipping her arm through his and pulling him near. "Look!" She pointed at the tight ball of men hurtling toward them.

"Oh no," whispered Asher.

Adonai, protect Him.

The crowd parted, allowing the leaders to come closer to Yeshua. He rose to face them, but they made no move to harm Him. Instead, those in front moved to the side, and those behind shoved a woman, barefoot and unclothed, to the ground.

Martha covered her mouth to suppress a gasp and struggled to breathe. *Why? What could she possibly have done to deserve such treatment?*

Her eyes landed on the woman. She'd curled herself into as small a ball as possible, trying to make herself invisible to the prying eyes of a crowd full of arrogant, judging Pharisees and scribes. Her arms wrapped over her ears and head, as if she were trying to shut out the angry voices demanding her death. Bare feet, cut and bruised from being dragged along the stone streets, peeked out from under her. Unbound hair lay down her bare back and fell to the far side of her face, but Martha noticed her eyes, squeezed shut, blocking out the leering faces of those who had come just to mock the controversial miracle worker, and found themselves gawking at her instead.

Martha studied the men who had dragged this poor woman to Yeshua. What kind of men would do this to a woman, no matter her sin? Wasn't everyone entitled to the smallest sliver of dignity, simply because all men—and women—were created in the image of Adonai?

But no, these were men like Gershom, who avoided even talking to women, let alone touching them. In their world, women were inferior, unintelligent, a necessary evil to be hidden and controlled.

Their apparent leader stepped forward. "Rabbi, this woman was caught in the act of adultery. In the law, Moses commanded us to stone such a woman. Now what do *You* say?" They stared at Him, almost daring Him to answer them.

But He didn't. He bent and drew in the dust. With His finger! What was that supposed to do?

An older Pharisee stepped closer and demanded an answer. Yeshua remained still.

The men behind the Pharisee shook closed fists in the air, calling for Yeshua to respond.

Martha searched their faces, contorted with rage and indignation. Then she saw their hands. Her stomach coiled into a hard knot, and bile crept up her throat.

Each raised fist clutched a stone. She quickly scanned the robed and tasseled men, searching for even one who had not already judged and condemned this woman.

She found none.

On the other side of the walkway, James and John, the Sons of Thunder, stood ready to defend their Rabbi. On the balls of their sandaled feet, hands clenched into fists, their eyes focused on the same rocks.

But was it the Rabbi the men intended to stone, or the woman?

A physical pain engulfed Martha as she watched the woman huddled on the tiled floor of the stoa.

Martha well knew the agony the judgment of men could bring. She'd been the victim of one man's unreasonable but private judgment. How much worse was the public judgment of twenty or more?

She tried to understand why this woman had been brought to Yeshua. Although the Romans reserved for themselves the right to execute criminals, the Jewish leaders had been able to stone people on occasion. But they did it outside the city, and they allowed the people to do it so they could claim the mob had been out of their control. So why bring her here?

"Martha!" Mary's harsh whisper reached her ears, and she grasped Martha's arm. "What do we do?"

Yeshua rose. "All right. Let whoever of you has never sinned be the first to throw a stone." He sat again, His finger moving along the dusty tile.

What do we do? What *could* she do? Surrounded by their leaders, was there anything that could make this any better?

Around her the men mumbled and whispered.

What do we do? An idea formed. It wasn't much, but it was all she could think of. While Martha knew the suffering one man could bring, she'd also been the recipient of one man's grace. The love and care of just one person could be a balm that covered the judgment of many.

Could Martha be that for this woman?

While they were distracted, Martha moved to the woman on the ground, shrugging her cloak from her shoulders as she did so. She bent over the woman and placed her garment over her bare back and feet. The woman moved her arms from over her head, her fingers grasping at the cloth, then tucked her arms under her chest, pulling the cloak inward.

Martha's heart shattered. Was there more she could do?

Not much, not in front of these men.

Beside her, a stone hit the tile. Her head jerked, searching for the source of the sound only to see another, and another fall.

One by one, the oldest first, the men dropped their weapons and slipped away.

Soon, only the gawkers were left.

Yeshua twisted and placed a gentle hand on the woman's cloaked back. "Rise," He whispered.

Martha tried to steer the others away, away from the woman and Yeshua. His words now would be for her alone, and they needed no others. Men, even some women, ignored her pleas, preferring to see what this Man would do now that the Pharisees had left.

Abba joined her, and Asher as well, their outstretched arms herding the people farther down the stoa, and just as quickly as the crowd gathered, it now dispersed. The talmidim stood several strides away from the pair, facing away from her, keeping any crowd from forming again.

Martha neared Asher again.

"That was beautiful," he whispered. "I can't imagine what that meant to her."

Martha nodded, the ache of the woman's disgrace still weighing on her. "I wonder what she'll do now?"

"What do you mean?" asked Asher.

"Surely she won't be welcome at home anymore." At the other end of the women's court, the Pharisees huddled, whispering, now and again glancing this way, their embarrassment fueling their anger.

But none was angrier than Caiaphas.

CHAPTER TWENTY-SEVEN

*When Jesus spoke again to the people, he said, "I am the
light of the world. Whoever follows me will never walk
in darkness, but will have the light of life."*
—John 8:12 (NIV)

Tishri 22

Mary hurried to the common room. "Martha, Yeshua is going to teach at the temple. May I join Him, or do you need help?"

Martha laughed. "Go. Enjoy."

Mary rushed to catch up to Yeshua and His students. All around her, sukkot were being torn down, the faded and drying limbs tossed aside on the mount. On the slopes outside the city walls, it was the same.

She hurried up the underground steps and exited onto the Court of the Gentiles, then followed the Rabbi into the Court of Women.

Levites were busy dismantling the colossal candelabras that stood taller than the women's balcony. Golden bowls, ladders, pitchers—all were carried away to be cleaned and stored until next year. Every night of the feast, holy flames threw light over all of Jerusalem while the Levite choir sang and the men danced.

A group of young boys approached a priest overseeing the operation. Their leader spoke.

"Teacher, can you explain to the children the meaning of the illumination ceremony?"

The Pharisee puffed out his chest. "Of course. I'd be delighted to share my learning with you." He cleared his throat as he surveyed the group. "Light has always been a part of our worship and a sign of Adonai. Remember the story of the burning bush? And the pillar of fire that guided us in the wilderness? And the Shekinah glory that rested upon the tabernacle? These lights draw our attention to Adonai and to His provision, and they call us to look forward to the coming of the Mashiach."

He continued speaking as if addressing the Sanhedrin instead of small boys, his voice deep and his arms moving in grand gestures. "As the great prophet Isaiah said, 'The people who walked in darkness have seen a great light; those who dwelt in a land of deep darkness, on them has light shone. You have multiplied the nation; you have increased its joy; they rejoice before you as with joy at the harvest, as they are glad when they divide the spoil.'"

"But when will the Mashiach come?" asked one of the oldest.

The Pharisee answered with a knowing smile. "Ah, no one knows. It may yet be a long time off."

"I am the light of the world." Mary whipped her head around to see Yeshua, standing on the steps of the Nicanor Gate, which separated the Women's Court from the Court of the Israelites. "Whoever follows Me will never walk in darkness, but will have the light of life."

The Pharisee's face turned crimson, and as he stormed toward the Rabbi, he was joined by several others.

Mary followed, trying to get close enough to hear the conversations already heating up among the teachers. "How can *You* claim to be the light?" His finger jabbed at the air between the teachers and Yeshua. "At the very least, You cannot appear as Your own witness. Testimony without witnesses is not valid."

Yeshua nodded as He moved halfway down the steps toward them. "Even if I testify on My own behalf, My testimony is valid, for I know where I came from and where I am going. But you have no idea where I come from or where I am going."

"What is this man talking about?" The teachers whispered among themselves. "He makes no sense. He's a lunatic."

"You judge by human standards," Yeshua continued. "I pass judgment on no one. Yet even if I did, My judgment would be correct in every respect because I am not alone. My Abba, who sent Me, is with Me. In your own law it is written that the testimony of two witnesses is true. I am One who testifies for Myself; My other witness is My Abba, who sent Me."

The Pharisees cackled, then looked around, hands spread. "And where is Your abba?"

Yeshua shook His head, and it seemed a great sadness darkened His face. "You do not know Me or My Abba. If you knew Me, you would know My Abba also."

Mary's heart broke for Him, but the Pharisees only scowled and muttered.

"We should stone Him here and now."

"No. Not here. Not now."

Mary recognized the calm but determined voice.

Caiaphas.

She moved to one side trying to catch a glimpse of the high priest, but he was surrounded by his attendants, their angry faces belying their attitudes about Yeshua.

She pulled her scarf farther forward and bowed her head before she moved closer to the whispering group.

"Why is He still here?" One of the oldest of the teachers spoke, his voice gravelly and angry. "I thought He had gone. He doesn't show up for a year and a half, and when He does He decides to *teach* the people, every day spouting more and more lies."

"What are we going to do?" asked another.

"I don't know," a third added. "But this has to stop, and it has to stop soon."

"We were humiliated yesterday, in that whole episode with that woman," said the first. "If this keeps up, if word gets out about how He has ignored us, defied us, we will have no authority left with the people."

"The people?" Caiaphas said. "I'm more worried about the Romans than the people. The people are like sheep. They can be led wherever we want them to go. But the Romans… They already choose the high priest each year, and they keep my vestments in Caesarea. I have to beg for them every feast like a child begging for sweets."

One of the men looked over one shoulder and then the other. He caught Mary's eye for only a moment.

Her heart rate sped up, and she turned her back to him and hurried away.

"Let's go to our chambers." A voice reached her from behind. "We don't know on whose ears our words will land or who we can trust."

CHAPTER TWENTY-EIGHT

He told them, "The harvest is plentiful, but the workers are few. Ask the Lord of the harvest, therefore, to send out workers into his harvest field. Go! I am sending you out like lambs among wolves."
—Luke 10:2–3 (NIV)

The sun splashed brilliant color against the western sky, and a cool breeze wafting through the sukkah cooled Martha's skin. The meal was almost finished, and the Rabbi and His students would leave in the morning.

Yeshua swallowed, and pushed His plate forward a bit. He leaned on His forearms and cleared His throat. "I have a plan some of you might like to be part of."

"What's that?" Lazarus stuffed a huge piece of bread into his mouth.

"Several months ago, I sent My talmidim to various towns in Galilee. They were to share My message, to spread the news that salvation has come to Israel."

"Why did You need to send *them*? Isn't that Your message?" asked Abba.

"As I told them, the harvest is ready, but there are not enough laborers. Thirteen is far better than one."

Abba reached for a pitcher and refilled his cup then reached for Yeshua's. "Then is this Your plan? To do so again?" He passed the pitcher to Lazarus.

"My plan is much bigger this time. I wish to send out many more—six times more, in fact. I will again send them in pairs. My talmidim had been with Me for quite some time when I sent them, and were ready to go, but I'll need to spend some time with my new followers first."

"And how would we be part of this?" asked Zar.

"I thought you might like to be one of them."

Lazarus nearly choked on his bread.

Yeshua grinned. "You know My message better than any. Those in Bethany have joyfully received My teachings from the first."

"Where would they go?" Martha asked.

"Everywhere. Every town and village that can be reached."

"Even those in Samaria?" Mary asked.

Yeshua nodded. "And the Decapolis."

Martha stopped midbite. Surely He didn't mean that. "You would send them to the *Gentiles*? With the message of Israel's salvation?" That didn't even make sense.

"My Abba desires that none should perish. Mary, what did I say that first day you saw Me, in the temple courts?"

"You said Your Abba's house was to be a house of prayer for all nations."

He smiled. "You remember well. *All* nations. My Abba desires that all people shall be offered salvation."

Martha couldn't stop the fear that began to choke her heart. "How long would Lazarus be gone?"

"I think this assignment will be completed before the Feast of Dedication. The harvest is over and the rainy season is likely two months off, so I think now is the perfect time to go."

It wasn't the harvest that worried her, or the rain. It was the Samaritans. The Gentiles. The Romans.

The bandits…

"Martha."

Wild animals…

"Martha!"

She blinked, having been shocked out of her fear. "Yes, Rabbi?"

"Whoever goes will return safely. This I promise you." He held her gaze, a soft smile on His lips.

She nodded, forcing a weak smile.

I trust in God's unfailing love for ever and ever.

Maybe if she repeated it often enough, she'd believe it.

Tishri 23

Mary hurried after Lazarus as he marched toward the vineyard. "Zar! Zar, wait!"

He turned slightly and looked at her over his shoulder. "Well, hurry!" He grinned but did not slow.

She ran to catch up to him. "So are you going?"

"What? Where?"

"With Yeshua. Are you going?" She fell into step beside him.

"I'm thinking about it." He turned into a row and began inspecting the vines, now devoid of fruit and flowers.

What did he mean, *thinking about it?* "What's to think about? Why wouldn't you want to go? Hearing the words of God spoken from His lips day after day. Witnessing the healings, the miracles, everything we saw in Gennesaret, and not just seeing but being part of it! And not just for one day but for who knows how long?"

"Being gone from home, sleeping on the ground, never knowing where the next meal is coming from, or what is—"

She resisted stomping her feet. "Aarrrgh! It's not fair. *You* can go, and no one would say a word. Wouldn't even be unusual. Just another Jewish young man following another rabbi."

His hands stilled and he turned to face her. "Is that what you think He is? Just another rabbi?"

"Of course not. But if you don't either, why aren't you *aching* to go?"

She could see her words hit their target, but he remained silent. "Anyway, that's how most people would see it. Perfectly normal. You can go with no problem, and you don't even want to!" She balled her hands into fists and shook them. "Oh, why wasn't I born a boy?"

"Because Adonai didn't want it to be that way."

Mary whirled around to see Yeshua standing behind her, soft eyes drilling into hers.

"Wh-what?"

"Did you think it was random?"

"What was random?"

He stepped nearer. "Adonai created you to be exactly as you are. He created you for this time, for this place."

Her frustration built. "Then why give me a burning desire to know His word and then forbid me to study it?"

"Not all the laws handed down by the priests are of Adonai. He wants all His children to know Him."

What did that mean? Should she be allowed to study Torah?

"I'll be back in a week, the day after Shabbat. If you want to join Me, be ready then, at dawn." He headed back out of the vineyard.

Mary fought her jealousy. She should be happy for Zar.

After only two steps, Yeshua turned around. "That goes for both of you."

Her heart soared as if it had taken flight. "I can go? Truly?"

"Of course. There are several women who travel in Galilee with me, so I see no reason you can't join them if your family approves. If you're with Lazarus, they'd have no reason to worry. And I can keep you close, here in Judea." He raised His hand. "Shalom."

"Oh, Zar, you have to go! You have to go so I can go." She clasped her hands in front of her chest. She would beg if she had to.

He chuckled. "We'll talk to Abba tonight."

Tishri 28

Martha looked behind Yeshua as He entered the yard alone. "You said Your talmidim won't be joining You?"

"No. I've sent them home for a bit. They'll join Me later."

"I assume You'll be leaving as soon as my siblings come out." Martha handed Him a bag full of loaves of bread and cheese. "It's not much, but it should get you to Jericho."

"Todah rabah." He accepted the offering. "And yes. I need to spend time with those that are joining Me, teaching and instructing them before I send them on their own, and we have a limited amount of time."

"Before the rains come?" asked Abba.

"That too."

"You promise she'll be safe?" Martha's voice lowered.

Yeshua smiled. "She will be safe."

"There are not many women like her." Abba turned to see Lazarus and Mary enter the courtyard.

"Indeed, there are not many men like her," Yeshua said, "who treasure the sacred texts and have hidden them in their hearts."

Martha stepped toward Mary and handed her a smaller bag. "This is just for you," she whispered.

Mary peered inside. "Raisin cakes! Todah!"

"Are you sure you want to do this?"

Even before the words left her mouth, Martha knew the answer.

"I'm sure." Mary's voice wavered just a bit. Was she having second thoughts?

"You'll be a wonderful part of this group. You know the Scriptures, and you know Him, better than almost any but His own talmidim."

"I do, don't I?" She flashed a sly smile. "But I'll still miss you. And you'd better not have this baby before I return."

"I'll do my best, but you know I have no control over that." She chuckled.

"I know." She looked over Martha's shoulder. "Rabbi, when do You plan for us to return?"

"We'll be back by Kislev's new moon."

Mary turned back to her achot. "Is that soon enough? I can stay."

"Don't be silly. There's no way I can tell you when the baby will come, and I wouldn't want you to miss this even for my baby. You'll have plenty of time to spend with us later. This is the only chance you have to do this." *I think.*

"I love you, achoti." Mary pulled Martha into a fierce embrace. "And I'll miss you."

"I love you too." Martha fought her tears. No need for Mary to see how hard this was for her. She would face enough hard times soon.

"Come on. Time to go." Lazarus patted Mary's back.

"Come here." Martha hugged her brother. "You'd better take care of her."

"I will," he whispered.

The pair followed the Rabbi out of the village toward the road to Jericho.

Adonai, keep them safe.

The fact that Lazarus would be with her offered comfort. He would die to protect her. And Yeshua had promised that not one of those who followed Him on this assignment would be lost.

Mary was born for this. She knew the Torah, she knew the mizmorim, she even knew the prophets.

And she was fearless.

Unlike Martha.

She could barely remember life before Mary. Mary had been daughter, sister, friend, and partner in their work here in Bethany. How could Martha ever manage without her?

CHAPTER TWENTY-NINE

"But when you enter a town and are not welcomed, go into its streets and say, 'Even the dust of your town we wipe from our feet as a warning to you.'"
—Luke 10:10–11 (NIV)

Cheshvan 2

Mary sat as close to Yeshua as she could, drinking in every word. For four days, since they reached the banks of the Jordan just beyond Jericho, He had been teaching them about the kingdom of Adonai.

Now the time she had been waiting for—and dreading—had come.

"There is a great harvest waiting," Yeshua said, "but there are not nearly enough workers to bring it in. We must pray that Adonai will send more laborers to help you. But I must warn you: I am sending you out like lambs among wolves."

Mary shuddered. She'd seen a lamb once who had been devoured by a wild animal. Bits of wool and bone lay scattered near a pool of dried blood. But Yeshua had promised she would return safely, and she needed to hold on to that promise.

"When you enter a town and are welcomed, stay in whatever home offers you shelter and remain in that home for as long as you are in that village. Eat whatever is given you."

Simple enough so far.

"When you enter, say, 'Peace to this house,'" Yeshua continued. "If peace is welcomed there, your peace will rest on them; if not, it will return to you. Wherever you are, heal the sick who are there and always tell them, 'The kingdom of God has come near to you.'

"Don't take anything with you. Not food or coins or extra sandals or even an extra cloak. Move quickly from town to town and village to village, and don't waste time chatting with other travelers on the roads."

"That doesn't sound so bad," she whispered.

Lazarus nodded his agreement.

Yeshua's face darkened just a shade. "But if any place will not welcome you or listen to you, leave that place and shake the dust off your feet as a testimony against them. You must be as shrewd as serpents and as innocent as doves. Always be on your guard, for there may be men who will try to hand you over to the priests and have you punished. So when you are persecuted in one town, flee to the next town."

Mary tensed. Persecuted? Punished? Had she made a mistake by coming?

"Even as you flee, don't fear those who aim to kill the body but are unable to touch the soul."

Mary's breath came a little faster.

Yeshua rose. "Look, if you sold a few sparrows, how much money would you get? Not much. And yet My Abba knows every time even one of these birds falls to the ground." His face brightened as a wide smile appeared. "And you are worth so much more than a whole flock of sparrows!

"Today you will go out, in pairs, ahead of Me to every town and place where I will go. Although you will not be able to visit them all, go to as many as you can in the time we have left." He stretched His hands out over the group. "I now give you authority over all demons and the power to cure diseases. And remember: Everywhere you go, you are to announce that the kingdom of God is near."

The crowd rose and moved in pairs toward Yeshua for their assignments.

Mary slipped her arm through Lazarus's as they waited. She scanned the crowd. So far she'd seen maybe ten women in the group, and most seemed to be with their husbands.

"Ah, My favorite people. Two of them, anyway." Yeshua chuckled.

"Where do you want us to go?" asked Zar.

"I'm sending you to all the villages near Jericho. There are perhaps fifty within walking distance, all up and down the Jordan. Stay within a day's walk of the river."

Mary tried to hide her disappointment. She'd been hoping for something more exciting, somewhere in Samaria maybe. But He'd promised they'd be safe, so He was obviously keeping them close.

"This is a difficult area," He said. "Jericho loves that this is where Israel first entered the land. Indeed, all of Judea feels superior because they are of the House of David. But that pride makes their hearts harder than any in Galilee. My Abba detests pride, because when pride comes, then comes disgrace. So I'm entrusting you with this ancient and precious area."

Mary, too, had almost let pride get in her way and keep her from realizing how much He trusted her.

Forgive me, Adonai.

Cheshvan 9

Even though the days grew shorter and the nights stretched longer, there was always plenty of work to do in Bethany. And with Mary gone, the work that fell to Martha was even more than usual.

One of Mary's tasks was to collect and clean the bowls from the bet each day so they'd be ready for the evening's meal. It had taken Martha a week to remember to bring them home with her each morning, and the sun had reached its peak today before she'd had the chance to clean them. She dipped the last bowl in the bucket of sand in the corner of the courtyard and scrubbed off the remains of stew. She rinsed it in water and dried it, then placed it atop the stack.

Her feet were swollen. She stood and arched her aching back. The residents of the bet had received their morning bread, fresh from the oven, and tonight's stew already simmered.

Perhaps she should rest a bit before finishing and serving the evening meal. She rubbed her ever-expanding belly as she bent over, picked up the stack, and took them inside.

"Martha, Martha! I'm ready for my lesson!"

She turned at the sound of Selah's voice. "Your lesson?"

Her head bobbed. "You promised to help me make bread with leaven. Don't you remember?"

Ah yes. Rest would have to wait a while. "Of course. Come on." She trudged to the table and pulled the large jar of flour and the smaller containers of salt and leaven closer. "All right. Up on the stool."

Selah pushed the stool closer to the table and climbed on it. "Now what? You said it's different from the flatbread."

"Not completely different. You'll still mix the flour and water together. Do you remember how to do that?"

"I think so." She scooped out the ingredients and mixed them well. "Now what?"

"Now we add the leaven and knead it into this." Martha added a bit of the bubbly, leftover dough.

"It smells kind of funny!" Selah laughed.

"It does." Martha laughed with her.

"Martha!" A pair of young girls burst inside. "They need more wool at Avigail's house."

Why were they telling her? "I, um, I don't even know where it's kept."

The girl shrugged. "Mary usually makes sure they have enough."

Another Mary job that was now hers.

"I know where it is." Selah continued kneading.

Martha waited. "Well, can you tell me?" She tried to keep her frustration from showing.

"They store it in a room at the poorhouse." Selah spoke without looking up.

Martha sighed. "I'll be back." Several strides away, she turned back. "When you're done kneading, put it back in the bowl and wait until I return."

"Yes, Martha."

She trudged down the road to the bet. Apparently, there was to be no rest for her today.

Rest in God alone, my soul, for my hope comes from Him.

Mary cringed as the priest stood before her and Lazarus and ripped his robe. "Utter blasphemy!" He raised his hands and face to heaven. "Adonai, save us from Your wrath!"

His helpers grabbed both Mary and Lazarus by the shoulders of their cloaks and dragged them to the gate of the village. Lazarus's long legs gave him an advantage, but Mary's feet hardly touched the ground. The men gave them a hard shove onto the road.

She stumbled as she tried to avoid falling, but she slammed against the dirt road, landing on her hands and knees. She managed to get herself upright and looked for the man who threw her to the ground, but he conveniently hid himself behind the priest.

Lazarus stood tall and faced the leader, then lifted one foot and shook it. "We don't want even the dust of your town, so we shake it from our feet as a warning to you." His voice was strong and even, without a trace of the anger and resentment that filled her heart. "You may not realize it yet, but you have never been nearer the kingdom of God than today, and you rejected it."

"Leave, blasphemers!" The priests and his helpers turned and marched back into town.

Mary inspected her palms. Fresh cuts from the rocks in the road joined the tens of others already there. The sting on her knees told her new cuts were there as well, but she couldn't very well pull up her tunic standing here.

"Oh, Zar, how many times will this happen? In less than two weeks, we've been kicked out of six different villages. We've been welcomed in only one."

"Yes but in that one, we taught every day for three days. Every person in that village heard about the kingdom of Adonai. And remember, Yeshua did say this was a particularly difficult area."

"I know. But I'm getting very tired of sleeping in a different place every night."

He wrapped his arm around her waist and led her away from the village. "We should consider it a blessing that we've only slept on the ground once. We've at least managed to arrive somewhere just in time for a meal and a bed before offending everyone." He chuckled.

She huffed. "I don't find this as amusing as you do."

"I know, achoti. And I'm sorry. But we need to get on our way to the next village if we don't want to sleep outside again."

"Do you know how far away the next one is?"

"No, but He said none were farther apart than a day away."

She resisted telling him how sore her feet were. Or her knees and palms.

Or how much she was beginning to regret her decision to come at all.

Martha sat on the edge of their bed and let her head fall back onto the mattress.

Asher chuckled. "Hard day?"

She sighed. "I had no idea how much Mary did around here. Not only do I feel bad I didn't know that, I'm exhausted because it's all falling to me."

"Like what?"

"She keeps the spinners supplied with wool, she helps the women at the poorhouse gather reeds for the mats, and I found out today she's been teaching them to count money and whatever they need to know to sell in the market so they can learn to support themselves and leave the bet. How much to charge and things like that."

"I'm sure that can wait until she returns." He sat next to her.

"Of course it can, but did you know she helps at Abigail's house? Every time she delivers wool, she has to help them get started again. So that little task took much longer than I expected, and when I returned, Selah had gotten impatient and cooked the bread before it rose. It was completely ruined. And she let the stew burn, so I had to start all over."

"So that's why it tasted different."

She lifted her head long enough to glare at him.

"Ahuvati." He twisted and leaned on one arm to face her. "I'm absolutely sure that Elisheba or Adah or any of the other women would be happy to share Mary's jobs with you. In fact, Yoash was asking me about it at the olive press today."

She sat up. "They'll have enough to do when the baby comes."

Asher placed his hand on her belly. "You've taken over for a new imma many times. Have you ever resented it, even for a moment?"

"Of course not. Children are a gift from Adonai. I rejoice with them."

"Then why don't you allow them to rejoice with you?"

"I will. Just as soon as this baby comes."

He chuckled. "One day, Martha. One day you'll learn."

"Learn what?"

"Not to try so hard."

CHAPTER THIRTY

I praise you because I am fearfully and wonderfully made;
your works are wonderful,
I know that full well.
—Psalm 139:14 (NIV)

Cheshvan 17

She was supposed to be here.

Martha groaned as she gripped the table with both hands, her knuckles turning white, until the pain subsided.

Leave it to Mary to be gone exactly when Martha needed her. As always, she was being selfish, thinking only about what was happening right now and not about the future.

Or anyone else.

Waves of pain again cascaded through her body. She clenched the worktable as if holding on could take away the agony. The contractions were coming faster, closer together, but there was still a good bit of time between.

Just enough time to summon the midwife.

Mary froze as a group of three blocked their way.

"You were with the Rabbi!" One man stepped closer, his finger pointing at them.

"What?" asked Lazarus.

"That Rabbi, the one who performs miracles. You were with Him. I saw you there."

Mary held up her hands, palms out, and backed away. "No, I'm sorry, but—"

"You were with Him," said another of the group, leaning on a crutch. "We saw you! In Jericho."

Lazarus took a step forward, partially shielding Mary from their view. "Yes, we are students of Rabbi Yeshua, and yes, He has healed many."

"Zar!" Mary whispered harshly. "He said not to talk to anyone on the road."

"I believe He said not to *waste* time chatting." Lazarus spoke over his shoulder. "These people are looking for Him."

"Yes, we are!" said a third, the tallest of the men. "We heard He was near Jericho, so we're on our way there. Is He still there?" His face begged Lazarus to tell them He hadn't yet left.

"I don't really know where He is. But He has sent students out to share His teachings. Perhaps we can share with you?"

"Yes, please. Come to our home!" The one with the crutch spoke.

Please, not one we've already been thrown out of...

"Where?" asked Lazarus.

"Not far. Maybe half a morning's walk back that way." The tallest pointed a thumb over his shoulder.

"We walk slowly, though," said the one with the crutch.

Mary gestured to his right foot, twisted inward. "Is this why you were seeking Yeshua?"

He nodded.

"You two came with him?" she asked.

"Of course. If he is healed, we all rejoice," the tallest said.

"That's a very generous attitude," she said.

"We're brothers." The first one shrugged.

"Not to mention if he can work, it's less for us to do." The tallest laughed, and the injured one smacked his arm.

"May I ask what you wanted Him to do for you?" Mary asked.

The tallest stepped forward. "I'm Noah. This is Natan, and this is Nahum. When he was a child, he fell through our roof. It never healed correctly, it didn't grow as the other did, and now he can barely walk."

Nahum sighed. "We thought that since Jericho is so close, we could maybe make it there to see Him. But I guess we're too late."

"Would you like us to pray for you? To be healed?"

Nahum's eyes grew as wide as figs. "Can you? Did He teach you that?"

"He did give us the power to heal. Would you like to be healed?"

"Yes, of course!" All three bobbed their heads, their eyes bright and faces expectant.

"First," said Zar, "you must understand that we are not the ones who heal or not. It is Adonai's decision alone. All we can do is ask."

"We understand," said Noah.

Mary neared Nahum, and she and Lazarus laid hands on him.

"Adonai," Mary began. "We ask in the name of Yeshua that You heal this man. He wishes only to care for his family, so we ask You to strengthen his leg, and straighten his foot."

She stepped back. Nahum bent over and stared at his misshapen limb.

His foot jerked. The leg slowly lengthened, then straightened.

Nahum gasped as his foot gradually untwisted until the toes pointed straight out.

He laughed, although his eyes brimmed with tears. "Oh, it's so...so straight!"

"Can you put weight on it?" Lazarus asked.

"I—I don't know." He held the crutch away from his body and Lazarus took it. Nahum gingerly placed his foot flat on the ground then leaned forward until all his weight rested on it. He looked at his brothers, his breath coming fast.

"Do it! Take a step," Noah said.

Nahum lifted his left leg, balancing on his right. Then he moved his left foot in front of his right. "I did it! I walked!" Tears streamed down his face. "I walked!" He took several more steps as his brothers laughed and cried with him.

"Praise Adonai!" Noah shouted. He grabbed Nahum by the shoulders and pulled him close. "Achi, you are healed!"

Nahum slipped one arm around Natan and the other around Noah. He kicked his feet as though dancing, and his brothers joined him. Noah grabbed Lazarus, and the four were soon dancing and singing in the street.

Mary laughed, tears running down her cheeks. The humiliation, the pain, the discomfort, the waiting… Even if this was the only miracle she saw on the whole trip, it was worth it all.

Martha squeezed Elisheba's hands until it was over.

"Here. Have some wine. It has lots of honey." Elisheba lifted a cup to Martha's lips, and the drink trickled into her mouth.

"Good, good. That should give you some energy."

Martha lay her head back against Elisheba's shoulder. "You're doing so well. Much better than I did. Your babe will be here soon."

Martha appreciated Elisheba's attempts to comfort her, but it should be Mary's voice in her ears. They'd talked about being with each other for births since even before Daniel. But Mary had abandoned her for the excitement of traipsing all over Judea.

All the pain and frustration that had built up over the weeks broke free in a great sob. "I want Mary! Why isn't she here?"

"Martha, I need you to concentrate. One more great push and your baby will be delivered. Now breathe deep for me." Adah's firm voice drew her back to the task at hand, but before Martha could take a breath, another contraction slammed through her. She grabbed Elisheba's knees and pushed and screamed through the pain.

"The head is out!" Adah spoke over Martha's cries. "Just one more and he will be delivered."

"He?"

"I always say *he*. Give me one more strong push, and we'll see."

She sucked in a deep breath and pushed with all her might as the baby slipped from within her.

"And here she is...."

She? A daughter? Joy and wonder shoved all pain aside. "Can I hold her?"

"Just a moment. Elisheba, oil and salt."

She felt Elisheba reach to one side, and then her hand appeared from behind her to give Adah a bottle and a lidded jar along with some cloths.

Adah poured oil onto a cloth and gently drew it over the babe's skin. Then she rubbed salt into the oil. The babe drew in a shuddering breath.

Martha craned her neck to see what Adah was doing at her feet. "Is that her?"

Adah smiled. "Yes. This is your daughter. And she is perfect."

"May I hold her now?"

"Of course." Adah rose on her knees and laid the babe in Martha's arms.

Martha gazed at her perfect, tiny form, her pursed lips, her dark eyes blinking in the unwelcome light.

Adah helped Martha place the infant's mouth at her breast. The babe shook her head a few times, whimpering.

"What's wrong? Why can't she do it?"

"She can. Give her a moment."

Finally she settled in and began to suckle.

The odd sensation brought a gasp from Martha.

"Let her drink a little while you deliver the afterbirth."

One more contraction delivered the placenta. The baby seemed confused for a moment as Martha tensed, but she soon returned to suckling.

Exhaustion hit Martha like a felled tree. She fought to stay awake, afraid to take her eyes off the baby. "Does Asher know?"

"He will very soon. Now, if you let Elisheba hold her for just a moment, we'll help you change your tunic and the straw, and then you can sleep."

Martha reluctantly handed over the infant. Elisheba wrapped her in strips of fresh linen while Adah washed Martha and changed her tunic, then helped her to move to a fresh pile of straw covered by a clean blanket.

"Lie down." Adah grabbed a pillow from the bed and placed it under Martha's head, and Elisheba laid the baby in Martha's arms.

"Now I know you know this, but I remind all my immas, since birth can scramble your thoughts." She laughed. "You are contagiously unclean for two weeks. Anyone or anything you touch will also be unclean. You'll remain in here, and Asher can sleep in one of the guest rooms. Elisheba and I will be taking care of you and bring you food. Your family will also be taken care of, so take advantage and rest as much as you can.

Sleep when she sleeps. After the two weeks, you'll have sixty-six days of being unclean the way most of us are so much of the time anyway. Clear?"

"Yes," Martha mumbled.

Right now, two weeks alone with her baby, unable to work, sounded wonderful.

CHAPTER THIRTY-ONE

As Jesus and his disciples were on their way, he came to a village where a woman named Martha opened her home to him. She had a sister called Mary, who sat at the Lord's feet listening to what he said.
—Luke 10:38–39 (NIV)

Kislev 2

The evening air chilled Mary's skin as she climbed the Jericho road toward Bethany. The sun was behind the mount, taking its warmth with it but not all of its light. If they hurried, they'd reach the village just before sunset.

The last five weeks had been more than she could ever have hoped for, and countless memories crowded in her mind, vying for attention. Most of the names had been lost, but she would cherish the faces forever.

Although they were thrown out of more towns and villages than they were welcomed in, what happened in those villages was beyond anything she could ever have dreamed.

"Can you believe what we've seen, Zar?" Her voice was quiet.

"Hardly. Most of it is truly amazing."

"Do you think anyone will believe us?"

He drew in a long breath. "I think so, only because they know Yeshua. And they've seen what He can do. What He has done."

"What was your favorite event?"

"That's a good question. I think the brothers, that first healing right there on the road. They were all so happy that if I didn't know, it would be hard to tell which one was healed."

She laughed. "And your dancing. That was the best part."

He chuckled. "What about you?"

They turned off the road down toward Bethany. "The little girl in the last town we stayed in. She was so weak she could barely open her eyes. Her breathing was so noisy. Then to see her running and playing with her brothers as if she'd never been sick a day in her life…"

The house came into view, and Mary raced ahead. She burst inside, with Lazarus right behind her, but it was empty. Where was Abba? Martha?

The harvest was over. There were no crops to attend to. Work for the bet cholim and the poorhouse should be done for the day.

She looked around the common room. No pot sat on the oven. No stew simmered. That was so unlike Martha, but perhaps she was in a huge hurry this morning. Or the baby in her womb was causing her to move more slowly than usual.

"I'll check the olive press." Lazarus left her in the common room.

Mary wasn't a terrific cook, but she could begin the evening meal. The stew was always so much better when it had all day to cook, but if she brought the mixture to a boil they could still enjoy it tonight.

She counted out five handfuls of lentils into a pot, then reached for an amphora of water from next to the shelves and returned to the table.

"What are you doing?"

Mary spun on her heels to see Martha, a babe on one hip, a fist on the other.

"Martha!" Mary rushed toward her. "You had your baby!"

Martha stiffened. "Yes. Now, what are you doing at my table?"

"I—I thought I'd get the stew started. It looks as though you didn't have time this morning."

"Because Yoash's abba died last night. We were with the family all night, preparing the body. We just buried him. I did make stew—lots of it, but it's all at their house." She brushed past Mary and grabbed a basket, then piled cups and bowls and serving spoons into it. "I only came to get these for the meal. We're going to sit with them." She scanned the house. "Where's Zar?" Panic flashed across her face. "Did he not return with you?"

Mary hurried toward Martha, placing her hands on her arms. "Yes, yes, of course he did. He went to the olive press. We thought Abba might be there."

"Abba's with Yoash and his brothers." Martha refused to meet her gaze.

"Achoti, I know we're late, but it really wasn't up to me. The new moon arose on Shabbat, so we couldn't travel."

Martha fixed her gaze on Mary.

In the fading light, it was hard to tell what she was thinking. Was she sad over the death, angry at Mary for being late, or just tired and hungry?

"What can I do to help?"

Martha's face seemed to soften. A little. "Why don't you bring that basket? And make sure Zar knows where we are."

"Of course."

Martha crossed the road, and Mary was again left standing alone in the dark. Not quite the homecoming she'd expected.

And she didn't even get a chance to meet the baby or tell Martha that Yeshua and His talmidim would be there tomorrow night.

This dinner had to be perfect. It was the first meal Martha would cook for Mary and Zar since their return yesterday. She'd hoped for a simple meal, time together with Mary. She hadn't been kind last night.

Instead, Yeshua would be here, as well as the twelve. As always, she wanted to give them her best.

She stirred the first of two enormous pots of stew set upon the open ovens under the tree. She brought a spoonful of broth to her mouth and sipped. Deciding it needed salt and cumin, she let go of the spoon and removed the lid from two small jars sitting next to the ovens. A large pinch of each went into the bowl. She stirred again and tasted.

Perfect.

She repeated the process with the other bowl, using a little less salt and a little more cumin.

"Can I help?"

Mary's voice distracted her.

"The meal is nearly ready, but it's my day to take the stew to the bet."

"Wasn't last night your night?"

Martha shot her a lopsided grin. "It was your day."

Mary's jaw fell. "You did my day and your day? All this time?"

"Of course. Who else would do it?"

Mary shrugged. "I don't know. I thought some of the others would help you, or maybe you'd divide up the days again without me."

"Others did offer, but they have their own days and their own tasks for the bet. And they ended up covering for both of us for two weeks after Neriah was born."

"I'm so sorry, achot." She winced. "I guess I should apologize to everyone."

Martha rose and neared here. "Don't be ridiculous. I was happy to do it and so were they. I'm just so glad you're back. I love working with you to care for the others. I really missed you." She pulled Mary into a hug.

"I missed you too." Mary pulled back. "There must be something I can do to help. I can take the cups and bowls up. I can take the pistachios and the figs up too, if you want. And some wine."

"That would be helpful. Oh, did you remember to collect and wash the bowls from the bet? It's your first day back, so it would be easy to forget."

"I did." She grinned as she gestured to the shelves. "Well, I collected them. I'll wash them as soon as I come back down."

"They'll be so much harder to wash now!"

"It won't be that bad. Don't worry."

"All right. I'll go feed Neriah, so hopefully she'll sleep through most of the meal."

"I'll be back then." Mary stacked several filled bowls and nestled them in the crook of her arm, grabbing an amphora with the other.

Martha headed for her chamber. She sat on the bed and scooted to the head to rest against the wall. She loved this time with Neriah. Surely Adonai designed it so mothers had to feed their babies so often so they could withdraw from the world, spending the time only with such tiny, perfect creations.

Neriah gazed at Martha as she drank greedily. She studied her imma as if she might disappear at any moment, as if she were trying to memorize every feature.

Little wonder. Martha had already learned every look, every sound, every move of Neriah and what it meant. And though she was too young to really smile yet, Martha knew Neriah loved her.

Too soon, Neriah was satisfied. She rested her cheek on Martha's breast and slipped off to sleep. If only Martha could stay here a while, away from the others, the work, the demands.

But duty beckoned. Martha stood, settled the babe in the sling on her back and headed for the common room.

She glanced through the open roof at the quickly darkening sky. She'd need to hurry. She grabbed the pot, wrapped in cloths to avoid burning her skin. She turned to grab the stacks of clean bowls. The dishes had not been touched.

Mary.

How was she supposed to feed everyone without bowls?

Martha grabbed them and stomped to the basket of sand. She squatted before the tree and grabbed handfuls of sand, scrubbing vigorously to dislodge bits of lentil and onion that had been hardening for a full day. She poured water over them one by one, dried them and stacked them, then carried them along with a pot of stew to the bet.

The sun was below the horizon by the time she returned and carried the stew up the stairs with Neriah on her back. "I'm so sorry I'm late. But I have hot stew for you all." She set the pot down and reached for bowls.

"You stew is worth waiting for, Martha. Don't worry about it," Yeshua said.

Mary sat near James and John, laughing and talking.

Martha filled bowl after bowl.

"Of course I'd love to go out again!" Mary said.

What little control Martha had left snapped. She grabbed the almost empty pot and hurried back down.

Abba hurried to follow her. "Is everything all right? I looked for you, but I couldn't find you."

"Blame Mary for that." She dropped the stewpot on the table.

"What?"

"For two months I have done *everything*. Everything at home and both my and her jobs for the bet. And I gave birth, and I'm feeding Neriah day and night."

Abba shrugged. "And I did Zar's. We knew that when they left."

"And I was happy to do it. But when she came back, I expected she would take up her tasks again. I went to take the night's meal to the bet, and there were no clean dishes! She had all day to do it, so I had to do it, with a crying baby on my back."

Mary appeared in the doorway. "Oh, Martha, I'm sorry. I just forgot."

She did look regretful, but the damage was done.

Yeshua approached. "Is everything all right here?"

"She's left me to do it all by myself! Don't You care? She should be helping me instead of reliving her adventures! And now she wants to leave me again! Tell her she is needed here!"

"What are you talking about?" Abba asked.

Yeshua came closer and Mary backed away. "Martha, Martha, you're worried and upset about so many things." He put his hands on her upper arms. "But really, you need to concern yourself about only one thing." He glanced at Mary for a moment. "Mary has chosen what's better, and I will not take it from her."

Martha's face heated.

"For now, though, let us eat." Yeshua said. "All of us."

Later that night, Martha lay wide awake, staring at the ceiling.

"He had a point, you know, ahuvati," Asher whispered.

"I know." She slapped her hand over her eyes. "I can't believe I got so upset. I'm humiliated."

"You've been working too hard. You need to rest, for you and for Neriah."

"I can't rest. There's too much work."

"Don't you remember what He said?"

"I remember He said Mary had chosen better." Surely her bitterness was apparent, but she couldn't help it.

"That was part of it." Asher's voice was firm. "He also said you need to concern yourself about only one thing. If you believe He is the Mashiach, you need to pay attention while He is here. Taking care of people is a good thing. You've heard Him say so. But not at the expense of learning from Him."

"I know," she whispered.

"Now, you really need to get some rest."

She closed her eyes as Asher softly recited the blessing. "Blessed are You, Adonai our God, King of the universe, who brings sleep to my eyes, slumber to my eyelids."

Adonai, grant me the wisdom to choose the better part.

CHAPTER THIRTY-TWO

*Now a man named Lazarus was sick. He was from Bethany,
the village of Mary and her sister Martha.*
—John 11:1 (NIV)

Shevat 8

Eighty days had passed, and the day for offering the prescribed sacrifice at the temple was at hand. Martha didn't go to the temple as often as Mary, but not being allowed to enter His Holy courts for almost three months had taught her how much she desired to worship Him as part of the nation of Israel.

With Neriah in her arms, Martha followed Asher up the stairs onto the Court of the Gentiles, then turned to face the Royal Stoa behind them. Beyond the double rows of columns soaring high above their heads, vendors lined the wall. Bleats, chirps, and moans filled the air, along with the smell of sweat and dung. No wonder Yeshua chased them from the temple three years ago.

In the center of the stoa, oxen, the most expensive of the sacrifices, were sold. To one side were sheep and to the other goats. Beside the sheep at the east end, cages of turtledoves were stacked eight and nine high, while the slightly larger pigeons were sold at the western end. All were guaranteed to be free of defects and blemishes and ready to be offered to Adonai.

After handing Neriah to Asher, Martha reached into the sash around her waist, withdrew two small coins, and exchanged them for two doves.

"They're beautiful." She held the cage up and inspected the small birds with blue-grey heads, pale pink chests, and four black and white stripes below their cheeks. "What now?"

"We find a priest," Asher answered. He led her to the steps that bordered the Court of Women and they ascended, then found a waiting priest.

"Tell him," Asher whispered.

"I—I need to make a sacrifice."

The priest looked behind them. "And where is the lamb?"

"I have only two doves."

"Oh."

Was that the face of disappointment or disapproval?

He picked up the small cage at her feet and left.

"Where's he going?" She stood on her toes to try to follow his path.

"He's going to the altar, but we cannot follow. Only priests can get that close. We just wait here."

After what seemed like far longer than necessary to sacrifice two tiny birds, the priest returned. "Your sacrifice is complete. You are now pure and may join your people in worship."

A sense of relief Martha had not expected washed over her. She'd only missed Hanukkah and most of Sukkot, and even though that was because she was too uncomfortable and not unclean, the fact that she could once again fully participate in worship for all of Pesach brought joy to her heart.

"Let's go home." Asher kissed her temple.

After the crowds and noises and smells, the chilled breeze whispering through the olive trees on the mount was more than welcome.

The village lined the road, awaiting their return. Shouts of praise to Adonai intermingled with their names and the name of baby Neriah as their neighbors came forward in ones, twos, and families to offer a blessing for the new life.

They finally reached the courtyard. Abba and her siblings had prepared a great meal to celebrate Neriah.

"We have a gift for you. Well, it's for Neriah, but you'll like it too. We hope." Lazarus led her inside to the corner by the door. A willow basket hung from an acacia frame, close enough to the fire to warm her on cold mornings while Martha made endless loaves of bread. Both ends were attached to short upright posts, allowing the basket to sway gently.

Martha knelt and ran her fingers over the basket.

"Mary made the basket, and I made the frame," Lazarus said.

Mary knelt beside her. "I made sure there's not a single piece of willow exposed that might scratch her."

"It's absolutely beautiful, Mary." Martha stretched to hug her. "Thank you, achoti. I can't imagine how many hours this took you."

"What else was I supposed to do after harvest? You do spend an awful lot of time with her, you know." Mary smirked. "One day you'll have to let me hold her."

"How about right now?" Martha held Neriah out and placed her in Mary's waiting arms and watched her heart melt.

"Oh, I understand now." Mary drew her fingers over Neriah's cheeks. "You might not get her back."

"I think I will when it's time to feed her."

Mary laughed. "Zar was wounded in this whole episode, you know."

Martha's jaw dropped. "What? Where? Let me see!"

He held out his thumb, a short but deep slice across the pad. "It's nothing. I caught it on an acacia thorn."

"Did you put honey on it?"

"No, but I washed it. It'll be fine. Forget about it. This is your day. Let's eat!" He pulled his hand free and headed for the table.

Martha pulled the basket closer to the table between herself and Mary, who placed the babe in the basket and gently touched it to set it swinging.

Abba cleared his throat. "Before we offer the blessing, I want to remind us of all the blessings Adonai has given us in the past two years. Not only has He healed me and restored me to the community, He has given us Asher, and now Neriah. He has allowed us to shelter the Mashiach, to bear witness to many more signs and wonders, and to hear His teachings from His own lips. What more could we ask for?"

"Truly He is good," Mary said.

"This reminds me of a mizmor of David," Abba said. "'But I will sing of Your strength; I will sing aloud of Your steadfast love in the morning.'"

Mary joined him. "For You have been to me a fortress and a refuge in the day of my distress. O my Strength, I will sing praises to You, for You, O God, are my fortress, the God who shows me steadfast love."

"We must always remember, no matter what comes, He is and will always be our fortress." Abba sat.

Neriah whimpered, and Martha picked her up. She silenced instantly. Her trust in her imma was complete and unconditional. Was Martha's that strong?

Thank You, Adonai. Like this babe, help me to trust in Your unfailing love for ever and ever, no matter what comes.

The waxing moon shone through the open roof of the common room, bathing everything in silvery light.

Mary smiled. "What a beautiful end to an important day."

Martha picked up Neriah from her swing. "I think it's time for Neriah to go to bed. Me too, as she'll awaken me at least once."

"You love it though, don't you?" Mary grinned.

"I do. You know me too well." She turned to Asher. "Can you hold her a moment while I clean up a bit? I don't want this mess here in the morning, or I won't get the bread made on time for the bet."

"Of course." He held out his arms, and she placed the babe in them. "Come here, motek. Let's look at the stars." He wandered away while Martha began collecting serving dishes.

"Do you feel all right, achi? You're quite pale." Mary placed her hand on Zar's cheek and gasped. "And hot!" She held his face in both hands.

"I'm perfectly fine, Mary." His voice was ragged, and his words ran into one another.

"Martha!" she repeated.

"What?" Martha asked.

"Zar is ill. Come see."

"No, I'm *not*."

"I'm sure he's just tired," Martha said as she passed them. "Let him go to bed."

"No, Martha! Come!"

Martha returned, but not nearly fast enough. Why wasn't she more concerned? Couldn't she see how ill he was?

Martha stood on the other side of their ach, and Mary lifted an oil lamp to shine on his face.

"See?"

Martha studied Zar's glazed eyes and deep pink cheeks.

"He probably just got chilled the other day in the rain. Why were you out in it, anyway?" Martha put her fists on her hips as if chastising a child.

"I needed nails," he muttered. "For the swing."

"See? He'll be fine after a good night's sleep." Martha jerked a thumb toward his door. "Go. Sleep. We'll see you in the morning."

He nodded lazily.

Martha returned to cleaning the dishes, and Mary grabbed cups, but their work was interrupted by a great crash.

Mary caught Martha's gaze. Her eyes were wide and for a moment, both were frozen. They ran to the door, but Abba reached it first. He shoved it open, slamming it against the wall. "Lazarus!"

Asher rushed inside the house as Mary grabbed a lamp and shoved her way past Abba. She held it high and gasped at the scene it illuminated.

Lazarus lay on his back on the floor beside the bed, arms and legs sprawled every which way and a shattered oil lamp next to him. His breath was fast and labored.

Abba turned to Asher. "Asher, help me get Lazarus onto the bed."

Asher handed Neriah to Martha and rushed in.

Abba knelt to slip his arms under Zar's chest, and Asher placed his under Zar's knees.

"One, two, three." They rose on Abba's count and placed him gently on the bed. "I guess we'll just let him sleep." Abba ushered everyone out.

Mary turned to ask him something, but he stayed inside and shut the door behind him. What was he doing?

She gently opened it just enough to see inside.

Abba knelt by the bed, Zar's hand between both of his. The lamp shone from behind him, outlining his face. His lips moved in prayer.

"I pray with the prophet Jeremiah. Heal him, Adonai, and he shall be healed; save him, and he shall be saved, for You are our praise."

She pulled the door softly closed.

Adonai, hear our prayers.

Shevat 11

Mary blotted the sweat from Zar's face and neck. "He's not getting any better."

Martha nodded. "I can't believe he's gotten so much worse so quickly."

It was hard to believe only three days ago he was laughing and eating, vibrant and joyful.

How could such a tiny cut take over his entire body?

"He's so hot. He sweats through his tunic in half a morning." Mary set the cloth aside and lifted his hand. The cut was even angrier, redder, than yesterday. His hand was so hot and swollen she could barely bend his fingers at any of the joints.

A soft knock on the doorframe interrupted her thoughts. "How is he? Did he get any rest?" Asher stood in the doorway, Neriah asleep in his arms.

Martha shook her head. "He was either burning up or shivering. He seemed to be in quite a bit of pain. He went in and out of consciousness and was saying strange things."

Even Abba, at his worst, didn't suffer so.

A thought struck Mary. "Maybe we should try to find the Rabbi. He healed Abba."

"I'm not sure this is the same thing," Martha said. "Zar's much worse. He's barely breathing. Abba was never in danger of dying. Besides, we don't even know where He is."

Asher stepped farther into the room. "Didn't He say He was going to the other side of the Jordan—where the Baptizer used to preach?"

"Besides, you know He can't really hide." Mary rose up on her knees. "Remember your sister's house? The crowds were there almost before He was. All we'd have to do is ask where the miracle worker is."

Asher nodded. "That's true." He turned to look over his shoulder. "Your abba is coming. Why don't we ask him what he thinks?"

Abba entered the room, and Mary explained her idea.

He shrugged. "Even if we knew exactly where He was and could go straight to Him, it's a day to Jericho and another day back, and that's not counting how far beyond the city He may be or the time spent finding Him."

Mary jumped to her feet. "I can find Him. Let me go."

Abba aimed a hard look her way. "You're not going."

She spread her hands to her sides. "Why can—"

He pointed a finger at her. "I'm *not* losing another child!"

She recoiled. "Zar isn't lost yet!" How could he say that?

Abba raised his hands in a gesture of surrender. "I know. I'm sorry. That's not what I meant. But we *are* in grave danger of losing him, and I won't allow you to be in the same position."

Mary had never seen him look so fierce. Love and fear, desperation and authority mingled on his face.

"Mary." His voice dropped to nearly a whisper. "I want you here, with me, *with him*, safe and close."

"It's not a bad idea. Couldn't it be worth trying?" Martha's soft voice seemed to soften Abba's resolve. "What's the worst that could happen? He can't come. Or He can't heal him. We'd be no worse off than we are now."

"I guess it's worth a try." He jutted out his chin. "But Mary's not going."

"Someone needs to go." Mary folded her arms over her chest.

"I'll go."

All heads whipped around to Asher.

"You will?"

"Of course. I'll do anything to help. He's my ach too."

Martha rose and stepped toward him. "Thank you." She wrapped her arms around his neck and buried her face in his chest.

He pulled her closer. "I love you," he whispered and kissed her temple. He raised his face to the others. "If I leave now, I can make it to Jericho by nightfall. I'll stay with Orpah and Levi, and hopefully I'll find the Rabbi in the morning. Bethabara isn't that far from Jericho."

Abba frowned, his head shaking slightly. "I don't like you going much more than I like the idea of her going." He tipped his head toward Mary.

Martha pulled back from Asher and faced Abba. "Asher's traveled from Galilee to Jerusalem every year. He knows how to be safe."

"Still, you shouldn't go alone. It's too dangerous."

"I'll see if Yoash can go," Asher said. "Hannah's from there, isn't she? If Orpah and Levi haven't heard where Yeshua is, Yoash might have an idea of where to look."

Abba breathed in slowly through his nose. He stared a long moment at Asher then gave one sharp nod.

"Thank you, Abba!" Mary grabbed his face and kissed his cheek.

"Why don't you get ready to go, Asher, and I'll go talk to Yoash." Abba placed his hand on Asher's back and steered him from the room.

"I'll get you some food." Martha followed.

Mary lowered herself to the floor again. Would there be enough time?

Yesterday Zar's breathing had been raspy and shallow. This morning he struggled for each breath. She laid her head on his chest, placing her ear over his heart. The thundering heart rate of two days ago was gone. Weak beats came slowly and spaced far apart.

She recalled the words Abba had spoken at dinner.

"For You have been to me a fortress and a refuge in the day of my distress."

She needed Adonai to be her fortress.

Zar needed Him to be his healer.

Asher would need Him to be his protector.

Adonai, hear our prayers.

CHAPTER THIRTY-THREE

> L*ORD*, *be gracious to us;*
> *we long for you.*
> *Be our strength every morning,*
> *our salvation in time of distress.*
> —Isaiah 33:2 (NIV)

Martha lit an oil lamp and placed it on the niche above Zar's bed.

Mary paced, chewing her thumbnail. "There's no hope now. Even if He arrived here right now, it would be too late."

"I don't think that's true, achoti. We know He's raised others from the dead."

Mary halted, her fists clenched at her chest. "He's not coming. He doesn't care enough to come."

"You don't believe that."

"I don't know what to believe anymore."

Martha shrugged. "I trust Him. I have to."

"I don't know if I can."

"After all you've seen?"

"Maybe this is just too much, even for Him." She stormed from the room.

The best things in Martha's life had been preceded by something bad, even horrible. Asher only came to her after she lost Daniel. They experienced Yeshua's power after Abba developed tsara'at. How did they know Yeshua couldn't bring something good from this?

Shevat 12

Mary awoke from a fitful sleep. How long had she slept? The gray sky told her the sun wasn't quite up yet. Her knees ached, and she rose from Zar's bedside to sit beside him. His eyes had sunken into his pale face, and his breaths came even farther apart.

She began counting between them. Nine, ten, eleven… Was this the last one? She laid her head on his chest. Thank Adonai, a heartbeat.

Then a long moment of silence. Another. More silence.

Then nothing.

He was gone.

A scream ripped through the air, and Martha jolted awake. She reached for Asher, but his side of the bed was empty. Cold. She sat up.

Then she remembered. Asher had left yesterday to find the Rabbi because Zar…

Who was crying? Was someone hurt?

"No!"

Oh no. Mary…

Martha scooped up Neriah, jumped from bed, and hurried to the chamber Zar shared with Abba, who reached the door and jerked it open just before she got there.

Mary sat on the bed with Zar, her head on his chest. She looked up, staring at them with empty eyes. "I…I fell asleep. When I awakened…"

Martha moved to the bed and laid the back of her hand on his forehead.

He was cool.

She knelt beside him and took his hand. She tried to interlace her fingers with his, but his stiff fingers refused to move.

The silence roared. Weak light slithered through the leaves of the olive tree. The grief settled upon them like a wet woolen blanket.

It was over.

The emptiness threatened to consume her. How was she even still alive? Why was she still breathing?

Mary stared ahead, unseeing. How long had it been? The sun was only a quarter of the way to its apex—perhaps two hours had passed since… She couldn't say the words even in her head.

She pulled her cloak tighter around her body. The stones of the courtyard wall were cold and hard against her thighs.

She could get one of the cushions they sat on at the table, but the very thought of getting up, finding one, and bringing it back, let alone actually doing it, was beyond exhausting.

Abba stepped outside. His eyes were red-rimmed and swollen.

Mary envied him. If she could cry, she might feel better, but no tears had come since that final moment.

"He is ready. I'll let everyone else know." He left the courtyard.

"Are you ready?" asked Martha.

"Of course not. How can I be ready?" She squeezed her eyes shut. "I'm sorry. Forgive me."

Martha slipped her arm around her shoulder and rested her head on Mary's. "Nothing to forgive."

Abba returned with Yoash's brothers. They disappeared, then a few moments later stepped back into the courtyard carrying the bier, the body now washed and wrapped in linen. Zar's prayer shawl had been wrapped around his shoulders, one corner fringe cut off to show he was no longer responsible for obeying the commandments.

The men raised the bier to their shoulders and slowly marched from the courtyard to the tombs below Bethany.

Mary rose and took a piece of her tunic between one finger and her thumb, doing the same with her other hand close to it. She yanked, leaving a small tear. "Blessed are You, Adonai our God, Ruler of the Universe, the Judge of Truth."

Then she followed the procession.

Wordless.

Joyless.

Faithless.

Martha's heart panged at the sight of Asher's face when he returned. Realization was replaced by disbelief, which was swept away by sorrow. She weaved her way through a courtyard full of priests and Pharisees to meet him.

"I'm too late?"

She nodded. "Early this morning."

"Then he was already…by the time I reached the Rabbi."

"I suppose so."

Mary joined them. "You didn't bring Him with you?"

Asher shrugged. "He told me to go ahead but that He'd be here."

"When, exactly?" Mary demanded.

"I don't know. He didn't say any more."

"Come. Eat something." Martha grabbed his hand and pulled him toward the table.

Mary sat in the courtyard under an inky black sky, her back against the wall. The Jerusalem guests had all gone home for the night, but they'd be back almost before the sun was up. No one in Bethany wanted them here, but Lazarus and Abba were honored among them for their service each month watching for the new moon. Or perhaps they just enjoyed being seen to mourn so loudly and publicly.

The new moon would appear at the end of the month. Someone else would have to run to the temple in the dark next time.

How was it the moon—and sun—continued to rise and fall on time? Zar was dead.

And Yeshua didn't care.

Martha lowered herself to sit next to Mary, an oil lamp in hand.

"Why didn't He come?"

"What?" Martha turned to face her, the fire twisting her face into strange shapes.

"Yeshua! Who else? He should have come!"

"I'm sure He had a reas—"

"What possible reason could He have for letting Zar die?" Her voice was louder than she intended.

"We couldn't think of any reason He would have to miss Pesach last year, but He had a very good one. Perhaps there are things we don't know about."

"Even with the Pharisees after Him, He could have come here, healed Zar, and slipped away before they even knew He was here. He got away from them so many other times. Why not now?"

No matter what Martha said, there could be no reason good enough.

"He could still come. He's raised others from the dead."

"All of them were immediately after death. Before burial, even. Zar is behind that stone. It's too late."

She'd spent so much time listening to Him, following Him, learning from Him, doing everything He'd asked. And she'd only asked one thing in return.

But He'd refused to give it to her.

CHAPTER THIRTY-FOUR

On his arrival, Jesus found that Lazarus had already been in the tomb for four days. Now Bethany was less than two miles from Jerusalem, and many Jews had come to Martha and Mary to comfort them in the loss of their brother. When Martha heard that Jesus was coming, she went out to meet him, but Mary stayed at home.
—John 11:17–20 (NIV)

Shevat 15

Asher burst into the house.

"He's here! Martha, He's finally here!"

She turned to see her husband, his eyes bright, radiating excitement.

Now? He comes *now*? After she had finally reconciled herself to the fact that He wasn't coming at all, that He didn't plan to heal her ach…that they maybe weren't as important to Him as they had believed.

"You should at least go talk to Him, ahuvati."

Asher was right. She owed it to the Man who had spent so many days and nights in their home, who claimed them as His Bethany family, to allow Him to offer some kind of explanation.

She slipped out the door of their chamber to avoid the Jewish leaders and headed for the well.

What would she say when she saw Him? What would she do? Should she beg? Demand an explanation?

She stopped short at the sight of Yeshua and His talmidim strolling toward her as if this were any other visit.

As if He hadn't just let Zar die.

He stopped several strides away from her. Too far away to talk.

She straightened her shoulders and neared Him, but when she finally faced Him, she froze, bereft of word and thought.

He took the last step and embraced her. "Martha," He whispered.

She collapsed against Him, drawing from His strength, His peace. After several long moments, she pulled away, blinking back tears. "Why didn't You come?" She stepped away from Him, mirroring the distance she felt. "If You'd been here, he wouldn't have died."

She clapped her hand over her mouth. That wasn't what she wanted to say, and certainly not how she wanted to say it. If He was sent of God, she had no right to accuse Him of anything. She'd spent four days chastising Mary for such words, and here they came pouring from her. "But I know that *even now*, Adonai will give You whatever You ask." She spoke between great sobs—of guilt? Anguish? Bewilderment? She wasn't sure.

Yeshua placed His hand on her arms. "Your ach will rise again."

That much was true. Like the Pharisees, she waited for the resurrection of all souls. "I know he will rise again in the resurrection at the last day."

Yeshua fixed a gentle but unwavering gaze on her. "*I am* the resurrection and the life. Everyone who believes in Me will live, even if they die; and those who live by believing in Me will never die." He stepped closer. "Do you believe this?"

Zar believed, and he still died. And how could anyone live even if they die? His words made no sense, as though they'd all been tossed in a stewpot, stirred up and poured out.

But somehow, she did believe, even though she didn't understand it all. She'd seen and heard too much to throw it all away. Her trust overshadowed her doubt and confusion.

"Yes, I do."

But what exactly did she believe? She pondered His baffling words and sorted out the pieces she should cling to. "I believe that You are Mashiach, the Son of God, the Promised One we've been waiting for."

His soft smile warmed her broken heart.

"And Mary?"

And Mary. What would He say to her if He knew her sorrow had swallowed up her faith? "Come. I'll take You."

"I'd rather you bring her out."

Of course. Even from here she could see the Pharisees and priests crowding the courtyard, competing with each other to show their love and respect and profound mourning for Zar.

She raced back to the house, leaving Yeshua and His students at the well. She halted at the edge of the courtyard. How to do this without provoking a confrontation between Yeshua and the Pharisees? She scanned the crowd. Where was Mary?

There, closest to the house.

Martha picked her way between the men and their wives until she reached Mary. She bent to whisper into her ear. "Come inside a moment."

"Why?" Mary pouted and looked away.

"Now, please."

Mary turned toward her, frowning at Martha's use of the tone she hadn't used in years. She rose and followed her into the common room.

"The Rabbi is here, and He is asking for you."

"He's here?" Mary moved to the door and glanced beyond the courtyard. "It's too late. You know as well as I do that the soul hovers near the body for three days. On the fourth it leaves, and there is no hope."

"The sages say that. The sacred texts do not. And why would the Son of God be bound by such thoughts, anyway?"

"Where is He?" Mary snapped.

"Near the well."

Mary bolted from the house and marched up the road. The priests and Pharisees followed.

So many things she wanted to say to Him bounced around in her mind. She—they—deserved an explanation.

When she reached Him, however, despair choked out all her words. She fell at His feet, her throat burning, her face in her hands, her forehead on the dusty path. Her shoulders jerked with silent sobs that threatened to break her body in two.

A gentle hand rested on her head. "Mary."

She caught her breath and raised her face to meet His eyes. "If You had been here, my brother would not have died."

He looked over her shoulder and frowned for only a moment.

She turned to see what He saw.

The Pharisees stood off to one side, some arms crossed, clearly disapproving. Others seemed expectant. Still others confused.

His eyes held pain. Sorrow? Despair?

Or disappointment?

Martha made her way through the crowd and stood beside Mary. He turned His gaze back to her. "Where have you laid him?"

"Come and see, Rabbi," Mary replied.

He held His hand out to help her rise.

"Southeast of the village," Martha said.

They followed Him as He strode to the tomb, His gait full of purpose.

What did He intend to do there?

He reached the caves that lined the side of the Mount of Olives below Bethany.

Mary grabbed Martha's hand while they waited. Yeshua turned as if to survey the scene: Mary and Martha, behind them Asher and Abba, then the residents of Bethany and pious Jews farther back.

He dropped His head into His hands for a long moment.

"See how He loved him!" Mary didn't recognize the voice as a resident. Probably one of the leaders.

"Could not He who opened the eyes of the blind man have kept this man from dying?" Another Pharisee spoke, his voice laced with disdain and sarcasm.

Yeshua wiped away tears, then raised His head and marched toward the tomb. He turned toward the family. "Take away the stone."

Take away the stone?

Martha believed with all her heart He could have healed Zar. And perhaps He could even bring Zar back to life if He chose. But couldn't it be done less…messily? Couldn't He simply command Zar to appear here before them, like He commanded the sores on Abba's skin to disappear? Or like He miraculously brought forth fish for five thousand?

She neared Him, coming close enough to whisper. She had no desire to embarrass Him in front of the Pharisees. "But Rabbi, he's been dead for four days. By this time there will be a terrible stench."

He faced her squarely. "Did I not tell you that if you believe, you will see the glory of God?"

She pondered His words. Could she believe? Could she believe even this, that He could raise her ach, who was so unquestionably dead?

"I believe." She pronounced her words evenly, firmly.

"Then have the stone taken away."

"Yes, Rabbi." She turned and moved back to the family. "Asher, Yoash. Take away the stone."

Asher left first. Yoash raised a brow, but he neither complained nor argued, and then raced to catch up. Together they placed their hands against the stone and pushed. And pushed.

The stone refused to budge.

She looked to Yeshua, but His gaze was fixed on the tomb. He was God of creation. Couldn't He command the stone to move itself?

Her heart beat fast. Surely this wasn't the end. Surely Yeshua could not be frustrated by a rock, no matter how big.

Abba bolted, joining Asher and Yoash, adding an abba's love and determination to theirs, shoving until the stone moved, leaving a space big enough for a man to enter—or leave.

Chests heaving, they returned. Asher's face told her she was right about the smell.

Yeshua raised His hand and looked up. "Abba, I thank You that You have heard Me." His voice was loud enough for all of Bethany to hear. "I know that You always hear Me, but I say this for the benefit of the people standing here, that they may believe that You sent Me."

He lowered His hands and head, His attention only on the space between the stone and the tomb. "Lazarus, come out!"

Martha's heart pounded so loudly she feared everyone could hear it. She'd risked everything to believe in something so preposterous, so unimaginable... If Zar did not return to them, then what? What would the Pharisees do to Yeshua? To them? To Bethany?

Something caught her eye. Was that movement behind the stone? A flash of white?

Her breath came quicker. She slipped her arm through Asher's, and his other hand grasped hers.

Zar stumbled out from the cave. Behind her Abba choked on a sob. "My son!" He whispered.

Zar could only move a hand's breadth at a time as hands and feet were still tightly wrapped with strips of linen. A wider cloth was wrapped more loosely about his head.

"Take off the grave clothes and let him go," ordered Yeshua.

Abba raced to his son. He unwrapped the cloth from Zar's head, time moving slower than Martha would ever have thought possible.

Hair appeared. An ear. An eye.

A choked gasp of relief escaped her, and a trembling hand flew to her mouth.

Abba threw his arms around Zar's bound shoulders, his body shuddering with great sobs of absolute joy.

Asher dropped her hand and sprinted to the pair. Starting at Zar's neck, he ripped strips of cloth from the brother of his heart. As soon as Zar's arms were free, he embraced his abba.

Martha's legs gave way, and she dropped to her knees in worship and wonder, words of praise flowing from her lips.

"Praise God in His holy place!

Praise Him in the heavenly dome of His power!

Praise Him for His mighty deeds!
Praise Him for His surpassing greatness!
Let everything that breathes praise Adonai!"

Mary stared at the scene unfolding before her. Was it really Zar? Could it be? Was this even possible?

But what was the alternative?

Zar neared them, his arm around Abba. Abba was satisfied, judging by the smile on his face. Beside her, Martha silently prayed.

Zar removed his arm from Abba's shoulder and approached Mary, arms outstretched. "Achoti."

Mary's feet refused to move. This could not be her ach.

"It's me, Mary."

"How can I believe that?" Her voice was small. Everything in her longed for it, ached for it to be true, but he had died in her arms. She heard his heart slow to a crawl, heard its final beat.

But could the sound that had showed her beyond doubt he was gone also prove he was alive?

"Let me hear your heart," she whispered.

He came to her and enveloped her in a tight hug.

She listened for that precious sound, the only one that would convince her this was her Zar.

It took a long moment, but then she heard it.

His heartbeat, as strong as ever.

"Achi!" Tears now poured from her as the full realization of what had happened hit her.

If Yeshua had come earlier, healed Lazarus at the first sign of illness, it would have been seen as natural healing. No one would have believed it was a work of Adonai.

If he'd arrived the day after Zar died, or the next, or even the next, there would still be doubt. The Pharisees would proclaim from the walls of the temple his soul had merely returned to his body. Rare but not a miracle, and certainly not the work of Adonai.

But on the fourth day…

He'd given them all an indisputable sign that He was in fact, the Mashiach. The Promised One. The Son of God.

She'd thought all she wanted was her brother, alive and healthy.

He'd given her so much more.

Martha rose. How could she have not thanked Him by now? But Yeshua was no longer standing near her. She spun, searching the crowd for her Redeemer.

Asher came to stand beside her. "He left. He said to let you know He'd be back for Pesach."

"What? Why? We didn't even have time to thank Him."

He smiled. "Oh, I think He is fully aware of your gratitude. You should see your face. Besides, look."

Martha searched the crowds rushing toward them. Some of the leaders seemed overjoyed. Some were even praising Yeshua, announcing their belief He was indeed the Mashiach.

Others stormed furiously away, sputtering, practically spitting.

"Oh no."

Asher nodded. "It's not going to be pretty."

However anyone described what just happened, or what they thought of it, today had caused everyone to choose a side.

The war couldn't be far off.

CHAPTER THIRTY-FIVE

Six days before the Passover, Jesus came to Bethany, where Lazarus lived, whom Jesus had raised from the dead.
—John 12:1 (NIV)

Nisan 8

Panic crawled up Martha's throat. "What do you mean He's here now? Why now? Pesach is six days away!"

Asher shrugged. "I have no idea. All I know is that I just saw Him and His talmidim on the road."

"But I don't have anything ready! I have nothing but stew and bread, and not nearly enough for thirteen extra men!"

Asher placed his hands on her arms. "Martha, ahuvati. Did you learn nothing from last time?"

The Rabbi's words rang in her ears. *"Martha, Martha, you are worried about a great many things…"* "You're right." She blew out a sharp breath. "You're right." She scanned her kitchen. "I'll get some more stew on, and I'll make flatbread."

"Can I help? I can't do much, but…"

"Maybe get some water boiling while I make some dough? And then find Mary."

He nodded as Martha reached for the jar of lentils. This stew wouldn't be nearly as good as the pot now simmering over the fire, but it would have to do.

It wasn't the varied and sumptuous spread she would've wished, but somehow Martha had managed to get enough food on the table. And Yeshua was just as grateful.

The common room was crowded, but this meal was nothing like the others she'd served them. Even when they came for Hanukkah, everyone in Bethany had known and had come to greet the Rabbi who had done so much for their village.

This time, the meal was simple, quiet, and the warnings He had given them at Sukkot—and again at Hanukkah—were on everyone's mind.

Beside her, Mary squirmed.

Martha leaned near. "What is the matter? Can't you sit still?"

Mary rose and left the room.

Martha handed Neriah to Asher and followed Mary to the pomegranate tree in the courtyard. "Mary, what's wrong? I've never known you to miss a single word He spoke."

"I keep hearing His words from before. You know, about dying."

"I know. But He's been saying that for months. Or longer. Why is it different this time?"

"Because I think it'll be soon. Very soon."

"I'm sure you're right."

Mary tilted her head. "If they hand Him to the Romans, will anyone even be there with Him? Will He be alone?"

"I'm sure the twelve will be with Him."

"Who will bury Him? Who will be there to anoint His body?"

"I don't know, achoti." She spoke softly.

Mary huffed. "I wish I hadn't broken Imma's alabaster jar."

"What?" Even Mary didn't usually change directions this fast. "And you didn't. You broke mine. Yours is in my chamber."

She shook her head. "That's yours. I gave it to you." She dug the heels of her hands into her eyes.

"What does it matter now, anyway?"

"If…" Her voice broke. "If I had mine, I'd anoint Him now."

That explained it. "You would?"

She nodded. "I can't bear to think of him dying alone, then thrown in a pit dug by Romans to be food for wild animals. It's the ultimate indignity! The law commands even criminals to be buried."

"Why do you think that's what will happen?"

"He's not from here. He has no family to ask for His body. The Pharisees will want Him humiliated, disgraced."

Martha poured her a cup of spiced wine and added a spoonful of honey. "Drink this. I'll be back."

Mary's childish behavior had probably annoyed Martha. Everyone knew how the Romans did things, and their absolute disregard for any life other than that of their citizens. Why complain about it? It did no good.

Mary swallowed the wine. The honey tasted good but did little to soothe her grief.

Martha appeared before her, the alabaster jar in her hands. "Do it."

"What?"

"Anoint Him, if you feel you should."

"Martha, no! I can't. It's yours."

She shook her head. "I don't need it, you know that. Take it. Do what you must."

"Martha, are you sure?"

"I've never been more sure." She held the bottle out.

Mary ignored the bottle and wrapped her arms around Martha.

"We've known this would happen ever since He gave Zar back to us," Martha whispered in her ear.

"Then why does it still hurt so much?" Mary sniffled.

Martha stepped back and placed her hand on Mary's face. "Because we love Him. And He loves us."

Mary nodded and swiped the tears from her cheeks.

"Take it." Martha pressed the jar and a towel into Mary's hands. "Come on." She placed her hand on her back and steered her back to their guests.

Mary crept toward the Rabbi and stood at his feet. Zar sat to his right, and Abba to his left. She scanned the faces of the men, laughing, chattering, joking. To be fair, this was a celebration of Zar's life and gratitude for the Rabbi, but at the same time, the thought of Yeshua's death weighed on her like a millstone, and she couldn't crawl out from under it.

She knelt at His feet and snapped the neck of the bottle. The woody, earthy scent of nard escaped, filling the air. Yeshua alone turned toward her, His eyes radiating love. She tipped the bottle, allowing the thick pale yellow oil to dribble onto His bare feet.

Her throat burned as she caressed His feet and massaged the liquid into His skin. Her heart agonized for what was to come.

The tears she hadn't cried for Zar's death gushed from her eyes, dropping onto the pure perfume and forming tiny, perfect beads.

"The Son of Man must suffer many things and be rejected by the elders and chief priests and scribes. He will be betrayed and handed over to the Gentiles. They will mock Him, insult Him and spit on Him. They will flog Him and kill Him."

All Roman forms of death were especially brutal, and the more savage it was, the more popular it seemed to be. That her Redeemer should face such unspeakable pain—

Silence jerked her from her thoughts. What had happened to all the noise?

She looked up to see Judas leaning over the table to leer down upon her. "This is outrageous! Why wasn't this perfume sold and the money given to the poor? That has to be worth a year's pay!"

If only she could disappear! What a foolish move! She shifted her gaze to Martha, who nodded. "It's all right," she mouthed.

Mary wanted nothing more than to get out of there, but she couldn't very well leave His feet dripping in oil. He'd slip and fall as soon as skin hit leather.

She reached for the towel, but it wasn't there! She looked back toward the courtyard and saw it on the ground where it must've slipped from her grasp. She pulled her scarf from her head and swiped at the oil, but it was too flimsy and became soaked almost instantly.

Now what? She should have known she'd turn this into a total disaster. She bowed her head in shame and her hair fell over her shoulder.

Why not? Grabbing a fist full, she began drying his feet.

Someone's hand landed softly on her head. "Leave her alone." Yeshua's voice was gentle as always, but firm. "She's done a beautiful thing. The poor you will always have with you." He gestured to the poorhouse down the street. "Should you desire, you can help them any time you want. But what she did could only have been done tonight. She has prepared Me for My burial, and I promise you, what she has done here will never be forgotten."

CHAPTER THIRTY-SIX

*So the chief priests made plans to kill Lazarus as well,
for on account of him many of the Jews were going
over to Jesus and believing in him.*
—John 12:10–11 (NIV)

Nisan 14

Frantic, insistent thumping wormed its way into Martha's dream. She struggled through a sleepy haze and blinked awake.

Asher rose on his elbows, his brows furrowed. "Is that someone at the door? Who would be calling at this hour?"

Martha shoved the hair from her face as she glanced out the shuttered windows above the bed. No light appeared around the edges. Was it the middle of the night?

Beside her, Neriah cried, her face scrunched up in confusion and fear. "I just fed her."

"She's frightened." Asher picked up the infant and kissed her head, then handed her to Martha. "I'll see who's at the door." He left their room, closing the door softly behind him.

Martha rolled over and pulled her daughter against her chest. "Shhh, motek. Imma's got you. You're all right." She rubbed her tummy, and the cries subsided. Martha's eyes closed, and she slipped once again toward sleep.

Asher poked his head in the door. "You'd better come out here."

She opened one eye. "Why?" Abba, Asher, and Zar could handle whatever was happening out there.

"Nicodemus is here. He wants to talk to all of us."

She sat up. "In the middle of the night?"

"It's almost dawn."

This could only be bad news. What could have happened to drag Nico all the way out here at this hour?

Martha rose from her bed and threw on a cloak. As well as they knew Nico, she couldn't appear before a Pharisee in only a tunic.

She picked up Neriah and followed Asher from their room, ignoring the chill of the stone against her bare feet. She stepped into the common area, moving to stand between Mary and Asher. Abba and Zar stood on the other side of Nico, who stood in the center of the room, his face etched with agony.

"I have some very bad news," the Pharisee said, "and some good advice which I hope you'll take."

Abba nodded. "Tell us."

"Very early this morning, Yeshua ben Yosef was arrested."

All the air left Martha's lungs. Neriah must have felt her stiffen, as the babe squirmed and whimpered until Martha gently rubbed her back.

"Arrested? Why?" Mary's voice was barely audible.

"There were a number of charges," said Nico. "They were mostly ridiculous ones, such as subverting the nation and opposing Roman taxes. The main one was His claiming to be the Mashiach."

"But He *is* the Mashiach!" Abba stated.

"Of course He is, but they don't believe that. And His entry into the city from the east on the same day as the prefect's parade from the west was, I think, the final insult. The crowds for Pilate were noticeably smaller. The priests are worried Rome will take action if they don't."

"What did they do? Where is He?" demanded Mary. She bounced on the balls of her feet, evidently ready to go to Him instantly. But what did she think she could accomplish?

"I can only tell you what I've heard, but this comes from people I trust. Yeshua was tried by the high priest, Caiaphas, and his father-in-law, Annas—"

"Annas is not even in office!" Abba's voice was strained. Martha could count on one hand the number of times she'd ever heard him speak angrily. "What makes him think he, as a private individual, can question anyone? And at night?"

"There is a whole list of reasons this is all illegal," Nico said. "But it *is* happening, and it *cannot* be stopped except by Adonai alone. At any rate, they found Him guilty of blasphemy and sent Him to Pilate. They asked the praetor to have Him condemned to death."

Zar scoffed. "For blasphemy? Pilate won't care about that."

"They changed the charge to treason."

"Treason?" Martha's voice squeaked. This was becoming worse by the moment. "How is what He did treasonous?"

"They said He claimed to be king, in opposition to the emperor."

Martha struggled to understand. "But..."

"When Pilate learned that Yeshua was a Galilean," Nico continued, "under the jurisdiction of Herod Antipas, and realized Herod was in Jerusalem because of Pesach, he tried to get out of the whole mess and sent Him to the Hasmonean palace. Herod questioned Him for some time, but Yeshua refused to answer. This seemed to infuriate Herod, who apparently had hoped to see Yeshua perform some sign or wonder. The chief priests and scribes who started it all stood by, loudly and viciously accusing Him. Herod allowed his soldiers to mock Him and put a purple robe on Him, but then sent Him back to Pilate."

"Let's back up a moment. How did this happen? Couldn't you convince them to stop this, as you did last time?" Abba's voice was soft.

Nico held out his hands as if to slow them down. "Now, you need to remember I witnessed none of this. The meetings were called in the middle of the night and not all the members were informed. Neither Joseph the Arimathean nor I were invited—He believes Yeshua is the Mashiach as well. There are a few others. Younger men, none with the status or influence of Joseph or me." He grunted. "Gershom was invited, I hear. All of which tells me the end of the meeting was decided before it began."

Gershom. Bile crept up Mary's stomach at the mere mention of the man's name.

Nico must have noticed. He turned to her. "Gershom is a follower, not a leader, Mary. Don't waste your anger on him. Anyway, when Yeshua showed up, a friend who serves in Herod's court sent a message to me. I went to Joseph and woke him, but by the time we got there, He'd been sent back to Pilate. Joseph went on ahead to the praetorium, but we decided I should come here to warn you."

"What will happen now?"

Nico's face darkened. "Make no mistake, they will not give up until Yeshua is on a cross outside the city walls. It has to be done today, before sundown, before Pesach begins. They've planned it all quite carefully."

"Wait," Martha said. "What do you mean, warn us?"

"You are all in the gravest danger." He turned to face Zar. "When Yeshua brought you back to life, they decided you needed to die. They did nothing as long as He stayed away, but after today—"

"*I* need to die?"

Mary heard panic in Zar's voice for the first time in her life.

"You are living, walking proof of His power and of the truth of His claims. They don't want you around. It would be far easier to dismiss what happened to you as a myth if you weren't here." He caught Abba's gaze. "You are one of the handful of lepers He healed. Gershom insists you violated the

Law, and Yeshua's healing of you not only directly contradicts that, it can be claimed that He cares nothing for our laws." Martha felt his eyes on her. "You declared, in front of many of the members of the Sanhedrin, that you believed He could bring Lazarus back from the dead." He chuckled dryly. "Which He then did." He turned to Mary. "You anointed Him, and Yeshua endorsed your actions as preparing Him for His death—"

"Wait," Mary said. "None of you were even here. How do you know that?"

"Oh yes. I forgot. Judas betrayed Yeshua to the Sanhedrin. They paid him for the information."

"He was in the temple every day this week. Why should they pay to find Him?" asked Zar.

"They wanted to do it when there was no one else around. They feared the reaction of the people."

"And what is the advice you have for us?" Abba asked.

Nico sucked in a deep breath. "Leave Bethany."

Mary's head throbbed, her body felt like lead. Had she heard what she thought she'd heard? "What?"

"You need to leave Bethany. Now. Pack only what you need."

"And where are we to go?" asked Lazarus.

"Anywhere but here. The farther away the better."

"Galilee? I have family there." Asher looked to Martha.

"Galilee would be perfect," said Nico.

"How long do we have to stay there?" asked Mary.

Nico shrugged and offered a sad smile. "Most likely for good."

Leave Bethany? Forever? Leave everyone, everything she'd ever known?

Beside her, Martha's face paled, the same thoughts obviously invading her head as had entered Mary's.

What was Martha supposed to do if she was not in Bethany? Martha had never known a time when she wasn't serving. The only time she'd been out of Bethany was when she was in Gennesaret with Asher and his family, and then she'd felt out of sorts most of the time.

What would she do there?

And who would she be if not Martha, the hostess, the one who took care of everyone else?

Neriah would never know the life she had come to love. And Mary? What about her? She had no interest in marrying, and in Bethany that wasn't a problem. Would she be accepted in Gennesaret? Would she be able to continue studying the scriptures? What would Joel say?

And Asher. He'd left Galilee for a reason. Did he really want to go back there, or was he doing this for her? And for Neriah?

"Martha, Martha, you are anxious and worried about so many things…"

When would she learn to trust? Every time she thought she'd learned to master her doubt and fear, they slithered up to harass her again.

"Do we need anything else?" Asher held up the bags.

"Maybe a blanket for Neriah. I'll get it. You go see what we do next."

He nodded and slipped from the room.

She moved to the chest Asher had so lovingly carved for her and knelt before it. She traced the olive branches, her finger circling each fat, round fruit.

I am like an olive tree flourishing in the house of God; I trust in God's unfailing love for ever and ever.

Daniel. Abba's illness. Even Zar's death. Each time, Adonai had used unspeakable darkness to bring about brilliant light.

Could He do it again? With His Son on a cross?

Of course He could.

I trust in God's unfailing love for ever and ever.

Mary shoved her hairbrush in a bag.

If Nico was right, Yeshua would soon be dead. Hung on a cross like a criminal, like a traitor.

Was it all over?

It couldn't be.

He had warned them about this. *"…the Son of Man must be delivered into the hands of sinful men, and be crucified…"*

But there was more. Mary struggled to remember Yeshua's exact words.

"…and the third day rise again."

She halted, one foot in midair. Rise again...the way Zar had? Would Yeshua live again after death, as her ach had?

Rise again.

She reached into the chest at the foot of her bed and retrieved her two tunics.

His words had never been false before. Misunderstood, yes, but never untrue. Was there any other way to interpret his words? *"And on the third day, rise again."*

She could think of none.

Her heart lightened. When Zar died and Yeshua did not come, she'd lost all her faith in Him. Even when He came to them, she couldn't believe there was anything He could do. She shuddered as she remembered the horrible things she'd allowed herself to think about Him.

She picked up her bag and knocked softly on the door to Martha and Asher's chamber.

Her achot opened it.

"I'll take your things and Neriah's."

Martha frowned. "You have your own to carry."

"And you have a *person* to carry." She neared the bed and sat beside her niece, rubbing her finger over a fat cheek. "You won't remember any of this, will you?" But was that good or bad? Right now, she wouldn't give up a single moment of knowing Him for the entire world.

Martha sat on the other side of the babe. "I'll take mine. You can carry Neriah's." She handed Mary the smaller of their bags. "And todah."

Martha scooped up the baby, and they regathered in the common room where Nico waited for them. The scent of nard still lingered, reminding Mary of that beautiful, awesome night, the last night when things were still almost normal, when Yeshua the Mashiach was a guest in their home. Yet even then, the scent of death was in the air.

Nico tipped his head toward the courtyard. "Let's go."

They stepped outside and Mary stopped short. Eight huge men waited outside the gate, each with a long dagger strapped to his hip.

Asher jerked his thumb toward them. "Who are they?" He may have asked about their identity, but it was clear he was questioning their trustworthiness.

"They're temple guards," said Nico.

Levites. The tribe entrusted with the sanctity of the temple. Mary moved toward Nico. "Wouldn't they be more interested in silencing us than protecting us?" she whispered.

Nico's face hardened. "The job of the Levites is to guard the worship of Adonai. What *those men* are doing is not worship." His jaw softened, and a hint of a grin appeared. "Besides, these men believe Yeshua is the Mashiach. Stay with them, and you'll be safe. They'll take you anywhere you want to go, even Galilee. I vow this with my life."

She nodded.

Nico extended his arm, and the family moved to the courtyard gate and followed the Levites to the edge of town. Four marched in front of them, and four followed.

A sliver of sun dared to peer over the edge of the earth, giving just enough light to walk safely to the Jericho road.

"And on the third day, rise again."

Mary smiled. Life as she had always known it was being upended. She might never again worship in the temple courts, hear the Levites sing the Hallel, or smell the holy incense.

But none of that mattered.

Because Yeshua would live again.

Letter from
THE AUTHOR

Dear Reader,

Are you a Martha or a Mary?

Most of us have either thought of ourselves as or been told we are one or the other.

But as I researched Mary and Martha, I learned they were not always viewed as polar opposites of each other. Over the centuries, they've been used as support for any number of lessons or causes by church leaders: law and grace, action or contemplation, temporal versus eternal, practicality and spirituality.

In our day, Martha is often the "bad example." She's missed the point and concentrates too much on "doing" and not enough on "being." But that attitude ignores several crucial points.

- Martha also sat at Jesus's feet. "And she had a sister called Mary, who was also seated at the Lord's feet, and was listening to His word" (Luke 10:39, NASB).
- Jesus often praised—indeed commanded—service. His parable about the Good Samaritan, His statement that "Anyone who wants to be first must be the very last, and the servant of all" (Mark 9:35, NIV), and His command "in the same way,

let your light shine before others, that they may see your good works and glorify your Father in heaven" (Matthew 5:16, NIV) all speak to a life of ministry.

- The word used for Martha's activities, *diakonia*, means "ministry," "service," "relief," or "support." It is the same verb used to describe the actions of Matthias (Judas's replacement), the apostles, and Paul and Barnabas, and we know these men were not serving food!
- After Lazarus died, Martha marched out to meet Jesus. She boldly proclaimed her faith in Jesus as the Messiah (John 11:27), while Mary had evidently fallen apart and was at home crying.

But Jesus loved them both.

I've always been considered a Martha. I've even been called a "human doing." Martha's actions are not bad, but any kind of service to others belongs to this age—it will one day be gone. Her service will "be taken away" (Luke 10:42, NIV) when Jesus comes again. But what Mary was doing will not only continue but increase as we worship at the feet of Jesus for all eternity. As Augustine told his listeners, "We are where Martha was; we hope for what Mary was. Let us do well what Martha did so that we can have fully what Mary had."

Scripture tells us nothing about Mary, Martha, and Lazarus after that famous dinner in Bethany. They are not mentioned as being at the cross or the tomb, nor are they listed as among the leaders of the early church, so many scholars believe they fled Judea due to the threat to Lazarus's life. Whatever happened to them, we know they spent their time in Bethany caring for, serving, and loving Jesus. Both are good examples, and I pray this story can affirm both the Marthas and the Marys of the world.

Signed,
Carole Towriss

A SCHOLAR'S VIEW OF BETHANY

Way back in the dark ages of the 1970's, I made my first visit to Bethany to see if I could locate the home of Mary and Martha, as well as the tomb of Lazarus. I had no idea what I would find. My guide led me to the entrance to the tomb and asked me if I remembered what Jesus said. I answered, "'Lazarus, come out!'"

"Yes," the guide said. "And if Jesus had cried only, 'Come out,' all the dead everywhere would have risen."

That was my introduction to Bethany.

The little village is around the side of the mountain and on the back side of the Mount of Olives, standing on the well-traveled road down to Jerusalem. Often designated as a "Sabbath-day's walk" from Jerusalem, in our time the distance is nothing. However, 2,000 years ago, one would have left the ancient walled city of Jerusalem and had to walk down the steep slope to the Kidron Valley. At one time, a drainage pipe ran down the slope, emptying blood from the temple sacrifices into the stream at the bottom. Then one would walk up the other side of the mountain to come to Bethany, which the Arabic people now call Al-Ayzariyyah, or "the place of Lazarus." While only two actual miles from Jerusalem, you can bet that would not be an easy journey in the first century.

The actual meaning of the name Bethany has been debated by some. It's generally considered to mean "House of Dates or Figs," though a few scholars have searched for a non-Hebrew root. The great scholar Jerome called the village "House of Affliction." In a Syriac translation, it could mean "House of Misery" or "Poor House," the idea being that Bethany might have been a place where the sick or patients with contagious diseases stayed. I'd suggest we stay with "House of Dates," as it was a Jewish village and the name is an ancient designation.

Today Bethany is controlled by the Israeli military rather than the Palestinian Authority, although it is on the West Bank. Not counting East Jerusalem, Bethany has become one of the largest cities in the Palestinian area.

Scripture reports many significant events happening in Bethany. Nearing the end of his ministry, Jesus came there six days before the Passover. The Palm Sunday entry into Jerusalem began in Bethany. Jesus stayed there during the time we call Holy Week. He dined in the house of Simon the Leper where His feet were anointed by Mary. Perhaps as significant as any other event, Jesus was there again just before His Ascension into heaven.

The hallmark of Bethany is the tomb of Lazarus. One enters the tomb by descending twenty-four steps cut out of rock, which takes the pilgrim down to a square chamber that appears to have been a place of meditation and prayer. Then another set of steps descends to the actual place of the tomb. The area was strengthened by the Crusaders, who covered the original wall with masonry. The small chamber appears to originally have had three funerary niches that were also mostly covered up by the Crusaders. Tradition places Lazarus's tomb to the right of the entrance. It is believed that Jesus was standing in the chamber above Lazarus's grave when He called him forth. Standing in that same chamber gives visitors pause and encourages them to reflect.

Scripture not only looks upon Bethany in the past, but with anticipation to the future. Zechariah 14:4 forecasts the Kingdom of God coming to the Mount of Olives, which is just over the hill from Bethany. Jesus will return as the King of Kings and the Lord of Lords, so although the village may have been small, it has never been insignificant.

Scripture further tells us that when Jesus came proclaiming the Kingdom of God, He was met by important women who provided for Him. We are told that Susanna cared for Him out of her own substance. In a time of limited provisions, such care was important. Her kindness makes us consider how hospitality was offered during New Testament times.

As we follow the ministry of Jesus, we discover how important hospitality was, not only in welcoming guests, but as a strategy for social engagement. Beyond following the polite expectations of the times, Jesus urged His disciples to practice the same with no expectation of recompense. The New Testament has a number of examples of hospitality being offered to Jesus—Mark 1:29, Luke 7:36, Matthew 8:14–15 and 13:36. The clue to recognizing the offer of hospitality is in the phrase "He went into their house."

During one of these invitations, Jesus gave clear instructions. He suggested that the homeowner should not only invite their relatives and special friends, because such guests would reciprocate with invitations of their own. Rather, if the affluent were to hold a banquet, they should invite the maimed, the poor, the lame, and the blind because those people do not have the ability to repay the invitation. This perspective appears to be Jesus's standard practice. His promise was that they would be repaid in the resurrection of the righteous. Jesus took the standard practices of the day and lifted them to a higher level.

This practice of hospitality carried over into the early church and was part of the values they practiced. Such kindness was a crucial part of what was expected of church leaders. Paul saw this provision as one of the defining marks of a Christian. In his letter to the Romans, he called on the church to "distribute to the needs of the saints..." (Romans 12:13). Some translators suggest this passage should be interpreted, "Welcome into your homes as guests those who are traveling." The idea is that Christians should not only respond to a traveler, but to search carefully for them even out in the streets.

Suetonius reported that Emperor Claudius expelled Jews from Rome because of regular disturbances instigated by one "Chrestus." Luke, writing earlier, appears to confirm that Claudius expelled Jews from Rome, although he omits the cause (Acts 18:2). Claudius was concerned that these Jews received hospitality. Suetonius's brief report, though somewhat more complete than Luke's, raises a number of questions but mainly confirms what occurred.

There were at least two expulsions of Jews from Rome before the reign of the Roman emperor Claudius. In 139 BC, the Jews were expelled after being accused of missionary efforts. Then in AD 19, Tiberius once again expelled Jews from the city for similar reasons. The lapse of the Edict of Claudius seems to have opened the door for a large number of Jewish Christians and leaders to return to Rome, which meant there was a great need for housing and food. Hospitality would have been crucial for these believers.

There are not many references to the word "hospitality" in the New Testament because the literal expression in Greek is "stranger-love." The original language expresses an even more imperative expression of Christian love. Concern is shown not only for friends but also for people one doesn't know. Biblical hospitality is a welcoming love for all.

Fiction Author
CAROLE TOWRISS

Carole is a Californian living on the East Coast. When she isn't writing, researching, or editing her latest book, you can find her (and her cat) watching British television, googling obscure facts, or talking to one of her four kids.

Nonfiction Author
ROBERT L. WISE, PH.D
MA Biblical Studies

The Rev. Robert L. Wise, Ph.D., is the author of thirty-five books and numerous articles published in English, Spanish, Dutch, Chinese, Japanese, and German. On the internet he weekly publishes *Miracles Never Cease* and monthly presents live interviews on YouTube with people who have experienced divine interventions.

Read on for a sneak peek of another exciting story in the Extraordinary Women of the Bible series!

THE BEGINNING OF WISDOM: BILQIS'S STORY

BY ROBIN LEE HATCHER

"Royal One! Jerusalem is near."

A shiver of excitement ran through Bilqis, and she brushed aside the curtain that shaded her as she rode the camel.

Jerusalem. At last. After more than two months of travel, long nights spent swaying in time with the camel's laborious gait, her destination was at hand.

In the dim light before dawn, she saw the servant boy bow before her. When he looked up, he grinned, showing a missing front tooth. "Riders have been spotted."

Messengers from King Solomon, no doubt. A caravan of this size did not go unnoticed. The Israelites would have been watching for its arrival for many days. Perhaps awaiting it for two weeks or more. But did they know that it was the caravan of Bilqis, the queen of Sheba? And if so, had King Solomon tried to learn as much about her as she had about him before she'd set off on this journey?

"You'll need much wisdom to rule, my daughter. Seek it where you can find it."

Oh, how she missed her father. She closed her eyes, picturing him in her mind. King Dawud had been her country's greatest ruler. Peace had blessed the nation of Sheba for all but the earliest years of his reign.

"My queen."

She opened her eyes to look at Kaseem, the high priest of the temple of Shams, as he came to stand beside the camel. One of the advisers from her council, Kaseem had been like a second father to Bilqis. Her memories were few when he hadn't been somewhere nearby. He had led worship at the temple of Shams. He had counseled with her father on a wide variety of subjects. He had snuck sweet delights to Bilqis when her nurse wasn't looking. He had been a comfort to her mother when the king died, and he had been a support to Bilqis when she was uncertain in her role as queen.

"Your guard believes we should make camp here," Kaseem said, "then continue into Jerusalem tomorrow or the next day. There is plenty of water and food for the camels."

She nodded to Kaseem. "The boy says riders have been seen, coming from the city."

"Yes. It may be that King Solomon will want to arrange a particular time for your entrance into Jerusalem."

A handler appeared at the camel's head, and while Bilqis gripped the saddle, the large animal folded in upon itself, going down to its knees. A short while later, Bilqis stood on solid ground. She gave herself a moment to get used to the stillness of earth beneath her feet.

"We will camp here," she confirmed. "You will meet the emissaries from the king."

Kaseem put his right hand over his heart and bowed at the waist as he took a long step backward. "As you wish, my queen." Then he turned and strode away, the hem of his deep blue robe skimming the dusty ground.

The encampment soon became a hive of activity. Tents were raised, the queen's large pavilion going up first. The many camels were freed of their burdens and taken to water. Cook fires were built, and food began to be prepared.

Ignoring the busyness that happened every time they stopped traveling, Bilqis settled onto the cushions Fatina, one of her attendants, had placed in the shade of the pavilion. As she washed her hands, she wished she could bathe her entire body, but that would have to wait. Her stomach growled softly, and as if in answer, Fatina set a bowl of dried fruit in front of her.

"We are here, Fatina. At last."

"Yes, Royal One."

Bilqis lifted a date from the bowl. "There were times I thought the journey would never end." She popped the date into her mouth.

"I too."

"Remember when the traders first brought news of King Solomon? They told the court of his great wisdom and of his great wealth. And of the greatness of his God. Now I shall see if it is all true. I shall see it with my own eyes."

Fatina nodded but didn't speak.

Bilqis's memories were filled with Fatina, even more so than of Kaseem. The slave girl had become her companion when both of them were four years old. In those early years, Fatina had been more friend than slave. As they grew up, their roles had changed significantly, but they remained close. Bilqis couldn't imagine her days without Fatina nearby. She was always present, waiting to serve, willing to listen whenever the queen wanted to talk. As she was now.

"Do you suppose King Solomon is handsome?" Bilqis took another date from the bowl.

"He must be to have so many wives."

Bilqis shook her head. Israel might be different because their God was supposedly different from the gods of other nations. But the marriages of kings and queens could not be all that different from one nation to another. Royal weddings had to do with alliances, with borders and treaties, with contracts for peace, with power and advantages. That was one reason Bilqis still resisted any talk of a marriage for her. She would rather rule alone than marry unwisely.

A smile crossed her lips as she remembered her parents, seated beside each other in the throne room. True, their marriage had secured a border, but it had also been a union of devotion. Bilqis had no intention of settling for less.

"I'm told Jerusalem can be seen from the top of that hill." Fatina pointed. "Would you like to walk up there to see it for yourself?"

Bilqis considered the question then shook her head. "No. I will wait. I want to see it for the first time as I ride into the city. Does that seem strange?"

Fatina shook her head. "No, my lady. You would like to savor the moment. Yes?"

She laughed softly. "Yes."

After eating the meal that had been prepared for her, Bilqis washed her hands again and then went to the bed in her pavilion. After two months of traveling mostly at night to avoid the intense heat of the day, she wondered how long it would take to learn to sleep when it was dark.

That was the last thought that drifted through her mind before sleep overtook her.

When Bilqis next opened her eyes, the light inside the pavilion was growing dim, indicating the waning of the day. She thought to rise, to begin preparing for another night of travel. Then she remembered they were within reach of her destination. Jerusalem was near. Perhaps tomorrow she would see the splendor of both the palace and the temple.

She closed her eyes again with a sigh. For a time, she thought of nothing but how glad she was not to spend night after night atop a camel. Not until the return journey to Sheba began. When would that be? She supposed much depended upon King Solomon.

Solomon. What would he be like? Was he as wise as the stories made him out to be? She recalled the first time she'd heard his name and of the wisdom he displayed when administering justice.

Traders had told of two harlots who went before King Solomon. The women lived in the same house, and both gave birth to sons. One of the babies died in the night, and his mother switched her dead infant for the living one. Later, standing before the king, they each claimed the living child as their own. King Solomon called for a sword and commanded the baby be divided in two, with each woman receiving half. But the true mother stopped him, saying to give the child to the other woman. And the king said, "Give the first woman the living child, and by no means kill him. She is his mother."

Remembering it now, Bilqis felt the same stirring in her chest as when she'd first heard the story. In the years that had followed, more stories of Israel's king reached the land of Sheba with every returning caravan and every trading ship that came to port.

Soon she would meet this renowned man. Soon she would see the temple he'd built to his God. Seven years it had taken to be completed. And his palace had taken another thirteen years to build. What must those buildings be like? Jerusalem itself was not a huge city. Perhaps two thousand souls. Much smaller than the city of Ma'rib. Could the palace be more elegant than her own? She couldn't imagine it.

"Royal One?" Fatina's voice was barely above a whisper.

"I am awake."

"Would you like something to eat?" Her slave stepped forward. "Or would you like to bathe? There is a stream nearby."

"A bath, please."

Her luxurious bathing room in the palace in Ma'rib seemed a fantasy to her after weeks of traversing the desert. Hastily washing from a pitcher was not the same as soaking in perfumed water and having her skin rubbed with scented oils before clothing herself in a soft robe. But it was better than being covered in dust and sweat.

Bilqis and Fatina walked to the stream in companionable silence. While Bilqis had slept, a small tent had been erected near the bank of the stream. Hidden from view by trees and brush, as well as the shelter, and with a few more female servants standing in strategic spots to keep out possible intruders, Bilqis could take her time washing.

Two months of travel dust—or so it seemed to her—was swept away by the cool water. She scrubbed her skin and washed her long black hair and thought once again of the bathing room in her palace. Homesickness welled inside, warring with anticipation for what she might see and hear in the coming days.

With a deep sigh, she left the stream and stood inside the small tent as Fatina dried her skin, then helped her dress in a clean robe. Afterward Bilqis sat on a stool while Fatina combed her hair. She closed her eyes, enjoying the sensation. When she was a girl, her mother had often sat nearby as a servant combed Bilqis's hair in the quiet of the evening.

"You will be the queen one day, my daughter. May the gods give your father a long life. But you must listen to all he has to teach you so

you will be ready when the time comes. Sheba needs a strong and wise leader in you, just as it has in your father."

The time for her to be queen had come much sooner than either Bilqis or her mother had expected. Certainly much sooner than they'd wanted. Eight years on the throne did not make her miss her father any less.

Twilight blanketed the camp as Bilqis and Fatina made their way to the queen's pavilion. Fires dotted the landscape, and the murmur of many conversations wove through the city of tents and lean-tos. Camels hummed and grunted, sounds she had grown used to. So much so she hardly noticed it anymore.

"My queen." Kaseem stood as the two women approached the pavilion. He gave a slight bow.

"Kaseem."

"King Solomon sent word via his emissaries. There is to be a banquet in your honor in two days, but you and your retinue are invited to use a suite of chambers in the palace tomorrow. The entire city is ready to welcome Queen Bilqis of Sheba, from shepherds on the hillsides to courtiers in the palace. Everyone has anticipated the arrival of your great caravan from the time word of it first came."

Bilqis settled onto her cushions, her heart racing. Tomorrow she would go into Jerusalem, the holy city of Israel. Tomorrow she would see the famed temple King Solomon built for his God and the palace he built for himself.

She looked at the priest. "And our tribute for the king?"

"King Solomon will know how generous you have been well before you pass through the city gates. He will know the honor you have paid him even before the two of you meet."

"I knew you would have it all in hand, Kaseem."

Tomorrow, Bilqis and her entourage would enter Jerusalem. It would be unlike anything the city had seen before, no doubt, for her caravan was very great. It would have been a fraction of its size were it not for the tribute Bilqis had brought from Sheba. It had taken over fifty camels to carry the nine thousand pounds of gold meant for King Solomon's treasury. Far more camels had been needed to bear the abundant gift of spices—Arabian balm, cassia, myrrh, and frankincense—and the variety of precious stones—topaz, agates, diamonds, rubies, amethysts, sapphires, emeralds, jasper, onyx, and more. And, of course, even more camels had carried the many people—her counselors, guards, servants—and all the supplies required for a journey of over fifteen hundred miles, a journey that had passed through harsh and dangerous terrain.

A troubled expression crossed the priest's face.

"What is it, Kaseem?"

"I feel I must caution you one more time."

Bilqis knew what he would say but motioned for him to speak.

"King Solomon has married many royal women to protect and enrich his nation. He must be very…appealing."

She laughed softly. "My old friend, I have not traveled all of this distance to find myself a husband. And what good would such a union do either of us? I could not rule Sheba from Israel. He could not rule Israel from Sheba. No matter how... *appealing*"—she gave the man a tolerant smile—"King Solomon may be, I have come for another purpose."

"To test his wisdom," the priest said. Then he, too, smiled. "And perhaps to obtain a trade agreement between our nations?"

Her laughter was stronger this time. "Perhaps."

Kaseem bowed again before leaving her, disappearing into the gathering night.

"My lord Kaseem is not happy with you," Fatina said, appearing with a platter of food.

Bilqis looked at her servant. "He was smiling when he left."

Fatina shrugged.

"What aren't you saying?"

"You do not listen to him the way you once did. You do not immediately do as he thinks you should."

Bilqis was about to protest, but pressed her lips together before she could speak. What her servant said was true. As Bilqis had become more secure, more confident, in her role as queen, she hadn't sent for the priest as often as she had in the first few years of her reign. But that was to be expected. She had many advisors. Kaseem's role was primarily as a priest of Shams, was it not?

Something unsettled stirred in her chest. A sensation that had been growing stronger over the past year. She shook her head, trying to focus instead on what her slave had said.

Kaseem had been against this journey. Vocally against. Passionately against. He had thought it unwise for her to leave her mother in charge of the kingdom. If the queen had questions for King Solomon, he had said, she should send her own emissaries to get answers. Such a journey was fraught with danger. Wild animals and poisonous snakes, bandits and sandstorms. Anything could go wrong. The queen didn't have an heir. If something happened to her, the peace in Sheba could fracture. Who would reign in her stead?

But Bilqis had not let him dissuade her, and in the end, he had asked only one thing. That he be allowed to join her. She'd granted the request without reservation.

But was he still unhappy with her decision to come to Israel? Did he truly think she should immediately do as he asked? No. He was a priest to the goddess Shams. Bilqis was the queen, the supreme ruler of her nation. He wouldn't expect her obedience to his wishes. Fatina must be wrong.

A Note from
THE EDITORS

We hope you enjoyed another exciting volume in the Extraordinary Women of the Bible series, published by Guideposts. For over seventy-five years, Guideposts, a nonprofit organization, has been driven by a vision of a world filled with hope. We aspire to be the voice of a trusted friend, a friend who makes you feel more hopeful and connected.

By making a purchase from Guideposts, you join our community in touching millions of lives, inspiring them to believe that all things are possible through faith, hope, and prayer. Your continued support allows us to provide uplifting resources to those in need. Whether through our communities, websites, apps, or publications, we inspire our audiences, bring them together, and comfort, uplift, entertain, and guide them. Visit us at guideposts.org to learn more.

We would love to hear from you. Write us at Guideposts, P.O. Box 5815, Harlan, Iowa 51593 or call us at (800) 932-2145. Did you love *The Ones Jesus Loved: Mary and Martha's Story*? Leave a review for this product on guideposts.org/shop. Your feedback helps others in our community find relevant products.

Find inspiration, find faith, find Guideposts.

Shop our best sellers and favorites at
guideposts.org/shop

Or scan the QR code to go directly
to our Shop

While you are waiting for the next fascinating story in the Extraordinary Women of the Bible series, check out our other Guideposts biblical fiction series!

ORDINARY WOMEN OF THE BIBLE

From generation to generation and every walk of life, God seeks out women to do His will. Scripture offers us but fleeting, tantalizing glimpses into the lives of a number of everyday women in Bible times—many of whom are not even named in its pages. In each volume of Guideposts' Ordinary Women of the Bible series, you'll meet one of these unsung, ordinary women face to face, and see how God used her to change the course of history.

A Mother's Sacrifice: Jochebed's Story
The Healer's Touch: Tikva's Story
The Ark Builder's Wife: Zarah's Story
An Unlikely Witness: Joanna's Story
The Last Drop of Oil: Adaliah's Story
A Perilous Journey: Phoebe's Story
Pursued by a King: Abigail's Story
An Eternal Love: Tabitha's Story
Rich Beyond Measure: Zlata's Story

The Life Giver: Shiphra's Story
No Stone Cast: Eliyanah's Story
Her Source of Strength: Raya's Story
Missionary of Hope: Priscilla's Story
Befitting Royalty: Lydia's Story
The Prophet's Songbird: Atarah's Story
Daughter of Light: Charilene's Story
The Reluctant Rival: Leah's Story
The Elder Sister: Miriam's Story
Where He Leads Me: Zipporah's Story
The Dream Weaver's Bride: Asenath's Story
Alone at the Well: Photine's Story
Raised for a Purpose: Talia's Story
Mother of Kings: Zemirah's Story
The Dearly Beloved: Apphia's Story

Find more inspiring stories in these best-loved Guideposts fiction series!

Mysteries of Lancaster County
Follow the Classen sisters as they unravel clues and uncover hidden secrets in Mysteries of Lancaster County. As you get to know these women and their friends, you'll see how God brings each of them together for a fresh start in life.

Secrets of Wayfarers Inn
Retired schoolteachers find themselves owners of an old warehouse-turned-inn that is filled with hidden passages, buried secrets, and stunning surprises that will set them on a course to puzzling mysteries from the Underground Railroad.

Tearoom Mysteries Series
Mix one stately Victorian home, a charming lakeside town in Maine, and two adventurous cousins with a passion for tea and hospitality. Add a large scoop of intriguing mystery, and sprinkle generously with faith, family, and friends, and you have the recipe for *Tearoom Mysteries*.

Ordinary Women of the Bible
Richly imagined stories—based on facts from the Bible—have all the plot twists and suspense of a great mystery, while bringing you fascinating insights on what it was like to be a woman living in the ancient world.

To learn more about these books, visit Guideposts.org/Shop